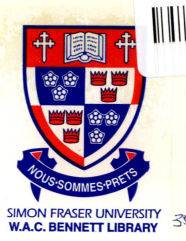
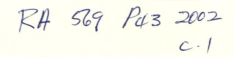

Life Exposed

FORMATION *Series*

Series Editor
PAUL RABINOW

A list of titles in the series appears at the back of the book

Life Exposed

Biological Citizens after Chernobyl

Adriana Petryna

PRINCETON UNIVERSITY PRESS
PRINCETON AND OXFORD

Copyright © 2002 by Princeton University Press
Published by Princeton University Press,
41 William Street, Princeton, New Jersey 08540

In the United Kingdom: Princeton University Press, 3 Market Place
Woodstock, Oxfordshire OX20 1SY

Library of Congress Cataloging-in-Publication Data
Petryna, Adriana, 1966–
Life exposed: biological citizens after Chernobyl /
Adriana Petryna
    p. cm.— (In-formation)
Includes bibliographical references and index.
ISBN 0-691-09018-1 (alk. paper) — ISBN 0-691-09019-X (pbk.)
1. Chernobyl Nuclear Accident, Chornobyl', Ukraine, 1986—Health
aspects. 2. Chernobyl Nuclear Accident, Chornobyl', Ukraine, 1986—
Environmental aspects. 3. Radioactive pollution—Ukraine—
Environmental apsects. I. Title. II. In-formation series

RA569.P43   2002
363.17'99'094777—dc21   2002016948
British Library Cataloging-in-Publication Data is available

This book has been composed in Sabon

Printed on acid-free paper. ∞

www.pupress.princeton.edu

Printed in the United States of America

10   9   8   7   6   5   4   3   2   1

For João and Andre

Contents

CONTENTS

Figures and Tables

Acknowledgments

I would like to first thank those who shared their thoughts and lives with me under very tough circumstances. Allowing me in as a participant-observer, they opened an unprecedented space for seeing and reflecting on difficult contemporary dilemmas that this book is about. Physicians, lawmakers, and civil servants among others were consistently generous with their time. I thank the late Heorhii Hotovshyts, the founding minister of the (then) Ministry of Chernobyl, without whose institutional support and direction I could not have carried out this work. I thank members of the Parliamentary Commissions on Chernobyl and on Human Rights, Ivan Los, Angelina Nyagu, as well as the late Valentyna Ferents and Professor Kindzelskyi, among the many scientists and administrators whose reflections helped clarify key issues. I am deeply grateful to the individuals and families who extended their hospitality to me while I was in Ukraine. I learned much from them. My work could not have been accomplished without several distinguished teachers. Paul Rabinow offered generous guidance and the tools for actualizing this work. Nancy Scheper-Hughes provided critical insight and direction from the beginning. Other teachers to whom I am grateful for engagement throughout the years at Berkeley include Dell Upton, Stefania Pandolfo, Lawrence Cohen, Yuri Slezkine, and Anthony Dubovsky. I thank Rayna Rapp and Mark von Hagen whose careful review, comments, and criticisms of the manuscript were essential to its final rewriting. A number of individuals offered clarity on things technical and ethical, including Ronald Jensen, James Ellis, Tom Sullivan, Frank Von Hippel, Burt Singer, Naomar de Almeida-Filho, Valerii Tereshchenko, Guilherme Streb, Maria Pilinskaya, Zhanna

Minchenko, Aloke Chatterjee, Leon Trilling, Volodymyr Husatenko, Natalia Baranovska, Mark Petryna, Marilyn Pogensee, and Andrew Bazarko. I thank the intellectual community of Harvard University's Department of Social Medicine. I am particularly thankful to Arthur Kleinman, with whom I had the privilege of working, and Joan Kleinman. I am also very grateful to Byron Good and Mary-Jo Good. Michael Fischer and colleagues at MIT's Program in Science, Technology, and Society, among them Joseph Dumit, Hannah Landecker, Chris Kelty, Kaushik Sunder Rajan, and Aslihan Sanal brought meaningful insights to this work. Other friends and colleagues from whom I have benefited greatly are Greg Castillo, Natasha Schull, Corinne Hayden, Marianne DeLaet, Joseph Masco, Mariana Ferreira, Ricardo Ventura Santos, Clara Han, Kathy Mooney, David Eaton, and Michele Rivkin-Fish. I am especially grateful to Bruce Grant and Cathy Wanner who read the entire manuscript and offered important comments and criticisms. For their support, I thank colleagues in Anthropology and the Graduate Faculty of Political and Social Science at the New School and at Lang College and its undergraduate program in Science, Technology, and Society. I also thank colleagues at the University of California, Irvine, who engaged this work. Students in my graduate and undergraduate anthropology of science and medical anthropology seminars, including Maurizio Albahari, Amanda Moore, Simanti Dasgupta, and Sarah Orndorff provided helpful readings. This book and parts of it have traveled with me for some time to conferences, as lectures, and to workshops. I thank the organizers and participants of several events that helped to sharpen the ideas here, particularly the Conference on the Discourses of Genocide at the University of California, San Diego; the Workshop on Travel, Fact, Media at the Wissenschaftskolleg, Berlin; the Seminar on the Anthropology of Science and Medicine at the California Institute of Technology; the Notestein Seminar of the Office of Population Research, Princeton University; and the Science Studies and Anthropology Workshop at the University of Chicago.

Several institutions have supported my endeavors, from graduate training, to field research, the writing of the dissertation, and the writing of this book. They include the Joint Committee on the Soviet Union and Its Successor States of the Social Science Research Council (SSRC), Graduate Training Fellowship; the MacArthur Interdisciplinary Group, Breadth Fellowship; International Researches and Exchanges Board (IREX), Individual Advanced Research Opportunities; Fulbright-Hays Doctoral Dissertation Research Abroad Program (DDRA); Social Science Research Council, Eurasia Program Dissertation Fellowship; and the John D. and Catherine T. MacArthur Program on Global Security and Sustainability Research and Writing Grant.

I would also like to thank my editor, Mary Murrell, for her clarity and generosity in guiding this book to completion. Others at the Press who have been sources of lively engagement and support include Fred Appel and Paul Olchvary. Special thanks goes to Lauren Lepow for her thoughtful editing and suggestions. Two chapters in this book include parts of essays that have been previously published in *Cultural Anthropology*, "Sarcophagus: Chernobyl in Historical Light," 10, no. 2 (May 1995): 196–221; and *Social Identities*, "A Technical Error: Measures of Life after Chernobyl," 4, no. 1 (1998): 73–92.

I am especially grateful to Tania Petryna for her kind logistical support; to Noemia Biehl for her sustained help that ensured final revisions could get done; as well as Michael Petryna, Luba Veverka and family; Ruben and Margarida Kirschner, Fausto and Eliade Biehl, Marina and Edilson Ferraes; Natalia, Oleh, Oksana, and Danylo and families. I also thank Susann Wilkinson, the late Mary Lou Fitzgerald, Torben Eskerod, João Gilberto Noll, and Bob and Lorna Kimball, for clarity into things happening in the field. Most of all, I thank João Biehl. His ethics, acument, and care were fundamental to the writing of this book. With our son Andre, our life together is what I cherish the most.

Note on Transliteration

Interviews for this book were conducted in Ukrainian, Russian, or English. As scholars of this region know, language is one aspect of social tension in the former Soviet Union. While the legal status of the Ukrainian language was improved in the first years of transition from Soviet rule, Russian continued to be used among the majority of speakers I interviewed, particularly among scientists and physicians. I have tried to respect the language of choice among my informants, providing standard Ukrainian transliteration except for material from Russian-language interviews or published materials.

I employed the Library of Congress system of transliteration, except when another spelling has become commonly accepted in English (e.g., "Chernobyl" instead of "Chornobyl'," "Guskova" instead of "Gus'kova"). Place names in Ukraine have been transliterated from Ukrainian (Kyiv rather than Kiev) according to rules established by the Ukrainian Legal Terminology Commission. I rely on pseudonyms for the majority of people interviewed in this book. However, names that appear in scientific and legal print are in some cases actual.

Life Exposed

Chapter 1
Life Politics after Chernobyl

Time Lapse

On April 26, 1986, Unit Four of the Chernobyl nuclear reactor exploded in Ukraine, damaging human immunities and the genetic structure of cells, contaminating soils and waterways. The main reason for the accident is by now well known. Soviet engineers wanted to test how long generators of Unit Four could operate without steam supply in the case of a power failure.[1] During the test, operators sharply reduced power and blocked steam to the reactor's generators and disabled many of its safety systems. A huge power surge followed, and at 1:23 A.M. the unit exploded once and then again. Large-scale pressure gradients carried the radioactive plume to as high as eight kilometers by some estimates. The graphite core burned for days. Helicopter pilots dropped over five thousand tons of boron carbide, dolomite, sand, clay, and lead in an attempt to suffocate the flames of the reactor's burning core. These interventions are now known to have compounded risk and uncertainty. With suffocation, the temperature of the nuclear core increased. This in turn caused radioactive substances to ascend more rapidly, forming a radioactive cloud that spread over Belarus, Ukraine, Russia, Western Europe, and other areas of the Northern Hemisphere.[2]

Eighteen days elapsed before Mikhail Gorbachev, then general secretary, appeared on Soviet television and acknowledged the nuclear release to the populace.[3] Within that period, tens of thousands of people were either knowingly or unknowingly exposed to radioactive iodine-131, absorbed rapidly in the thyroid and resulting, among other things, in a

1

sudden and massive onset of thyroid cancers in children and adults as soon as four years later.[4] Such onsets could have been curtailed had the government distributed nonradioactive iodine pills within the first week of the disaster.[5] Contradicting assessments generated by English and American meteorological groups, Soviet administrators downplayed the extent of the plume and characterized Chernobyl as a controlled biomedical crisis. Soviet medical efforts focused on a group of 237 victims selected at the disaster site by Dr. Angelina Guskova; they were airlifted to the acute radiation sickness ward of the Institute of Biophysics in Moscow. Of those, 134 were diagnosed with acute radiation syndrome. Official reports set the death toll at thirty-one workers (IAEA 1991, WHO 1996). Behind such seemingly definite numbers lies a web of scientific, moral, and political uncertainties.

The fact is that over the years, 600,000 or more soldiers, firemen, and other workers, men and women, continued to be exposed to radiation.[6] Many were dispatched to the disaster site to carry out cleanup work ranging from bulldozing contaminated topsoil and disposing it as waste to working in one-minute intervals on the roof of an adjacent unit and shoveling radioactive debris into the mouth of the ruined one. Some of these so-called volunteers referred to themselves as "bio-robots," a term which suggests that the one-minute rule was not well enforced. Others were relatively well paid to construct the so-called Sarcophagus (*Sarkofag*, now simply called the Shelter), a structure enclosing the ruined fourth unit of the reactor and containing 216 tons of uranium and plutonium. Currently, fifteen thousand people work at the now decommissioned power plant or are paid to provide technical assistance in the Zone of Exclusion. The Zone is an area thirty kilometers in diameter circumscribing the disaster site. Access to the Zone is restricted to the plant's maintenance workers, engineers, health professionals, and researchers.

In 1992, during my first field trip to Ukraine, I met one of the maintenance workers who was on a two-week break from work in the Zone. He lived in a housing complex in Kyiv, Ukraine's capital, located about eighty miles south of the disaster site. Filled with anger, he said, "Now I'm a 'sufferer.' " He used the word "sufferer" in reference to a legal category introduced the previous year by a newly independent Ukrainian state for persons affected by the Chernobyl disaster. "I get five dollars a month compensation. What can I buy for that?"[7] He said he had no other option but to continue working in the Zone. Because of his work history, no firm outside the Zone would hire him. "This is from radiation," he said. He lifted his pant-leg and stuck his cigarette through skin that had puckered up to form a ring above his ankle. It was the result, he said, of direct contact with a radiation source, and what clinicians would call a "local skin burn." "This happened in the Zone . . . We're people no one

understands, in hospitals, in clinics." He characterize.
the "living dead." "Our memory is gone. You forget
walk like corpses."

In spite of the country's publicized efforts to improve safe.
in the Zone, a director of the Shelter complex told me in an .
"there are no norms of radiation safety here." The country's Min.
Health sets annual allowable norms of dose exposures, but, accordi.
the director, these norms are not strictly adhered to. That is because .i
Ukraine's current period of sharp economic decline, employment in the
Zone is considered premium. Referring to the plant workers, he told me,
"Taking this risk is their individual problem. No one else is responsible
for it." When I asked him to compare his country's enforcement of
worker safety norms with those of Western Europe, he told me quite
somberly, "No one has ever defined the price of a dose exposure here. No
one has ever defined the value of a person here."[8] In a situation where
economic forces drive people to become preoccupied with physical survival, the effects of leaving the value of a person undefined are far-reach-
ing. In such a world, physical risks, abuses, and uncertainties escalate.
The labor of the bio-robot appears ever more acceptable, desirable, and
even normal.

■   ■   ■

In an effort to map environmental contamination, to measure individual
and populationwide exposures, and to arbitrate claims of illness, government and scientific interventions have recast the Chernobyl aftermath as
a complex political and health experience with its own bureaucratic and
legal contours. The initial—contested—scientific and medical assessments of the disaster's extent and biological impact, the choice to delay
public announcement, and the economic incentives to work in the Zone
have uniquely shaped Chernobyl as a *tekhnohenna katastrofa* (a technogenic catastrophe), in the words of many of my informants, including
people fighting for disability status, local physicians, and scientists. This
term suggests that not only excessive exposures to radiation but policy
interventions themselves have caused new biological uncertainties. Rational-technical responses have exacerbated the biological and social
problems they tried to resolve, even generated new ones. This process, in
turn, contributes to further uncertainty concerning a resolution to the
crisis, an increase in illness claims, and social suffering among affected
individuals and groups.[9]

Chernobyl was an "anthropological shock" for Western Europe,
bringing the efficacy of everyday knowledge to a state of collapse and
underscoring how much the conditions for secure living in what have

3

been termed risk societies lie in the hands of experts of all kinds (Beck 1987). This collapse also took place, but in a different form, in the other Europe. Chernobyl was closely associated with the collapse of the Soviet system as a whole. In this process Chernobyl, or risk itself, became an important resource to be tinkered with. Though this technological disaster has generated a strange world, difficult to comprehend, in its aftermath a postsocialist state, social mobilization, and local knowledge and experiences of health have been constituted anew. This book explores the ways people have learned to engage with Chernobyl-related bureaucracies and medical and scientific procedures as a matter of everyday survival—and, particularly, with how biology, scientific knowledge, and suffering have become cultural resources through which citizens stake their claims for social equity in a harsh market transition. Access to such resources is refracted through the fault lines of gender, class, and social status, to be sure. More broadly, these interactions illustrate how in the modern state, spheres of scientific production and politics are engaged in a constant process of exchange and mutual stabilization.

This book is based on eighteen months of field research in Ukraine, Russia, and in the United States between 1992 and 1997, with an additional one-month follow-up visit to Ukraine in 2000. It is a historical and ethnographic account of the rational-technical administrations of the Chernobyl aftermath (both in the Soviet and post-Soviet periods) and of these administrations' economic, social, and biological impact on the populations affected, displaced, or sickened by the disaster.[10] My particular focus is on Ukraine, a country that inherited the nuclear power plant—along with a politically and scientifically unresolved Chernobyl crisis—when it declared independence from the Soviet Union. Approximately 8.9 percent of Ukraine's territory is considered contaminated. Most of the Exclusion Zone is located in Ukraine (see figure 3). During the period of my field research, the country witnessed the rapid growth of a population claiming radiation exposure that made them eligible for some form of social protection. Social protections include cash subsidies, family allowances, free medical care and education, and pension benefits for sufferers and the disabled. This new population, legally designated as *poterpili* (sufferers) number 3.5 million and constitutes a full 5 percent of the Ukrainian population.[11]

On average, Ukraine expends about 5 percent of its budget on costs related to the Chernobyl aftermath, including the cleanup and technical maintenance of the ruined reactor. In 1995, over 65 percent of that outlay was spent on social compensations for sufferers and on maintaining a massive legal-medical, scientific, and welfare apparatus. Neighboring Belarus, by contrast, spends considerably less than Ukraine does on the social welfare of its sufferers and has limited the number of Chernobyl claimants.[12] Twenty-three percent of this country's territory is considered contaminated, almost three times the percentage of contaminated Ukrainian land. The Belarussian government has tended to suppress or ignore scientific research; it downplays the extent of the disaster and fails to provide enough funds for the medical surveillance of nearly two million people who live in contaminated areas.[13]

Unlike Belarus, Ukraine has used the legacy of Chernobyl as a means of signaling its domestic and international legitimacy and staking territorial claims. It developed a politics of national autonomy through the Chernobyl crisis, devaluing Soviet responses to the disaster as irresponsible. The state established new social welfare and scientific institutions dedicated to a Chernobyl population and began to provide sufferers and the disabled relatively generous cash entitlements drawn from a statewide Chernobyl tax. Moreover, the new government defined new and ambitious safety measures for Zone workers. This meant stabilizing the deteriorating Shelter, following norms of workers' safety, mitigating future contamination, and closing the last remaining working units of the Chernobyl plant. The implementation of this new program had also become a key asset in Ukraine's foreign policy. In response to these efforts, Western European countries and the United States continue to promise Ukraine further technical assistance, loans, and potential trading partnerships. Such exchanges have legitimated a new political-economic arena in which profit, political influence, and corruption loom in the already powerful and tax-evading energy sector.

Ukraine's response to the Chernobyl legacy is unique in that it combines humanism with strategies of governance and state building, market strategies with forms of economic and political corruption. Such interrelated processes have generated new kinds of formal and informal social networks and economies that have allowed some segments of the population to survive on and benefit from politically guaranteed subsidies.[14] I worked in clinical and laboratory settings and in the now sizable social welfare apparatus dedicated to those affected by Chernobyl—in its state agencies, and in the offices of nongovernmental interest groups in Kyiv. Together, these sites make up a subsystem of the state's public health and welfare infrastructure where increasingly poor citizens—former and current Chernobyl plant workers and populations resettled from contaminated zones—mobilize around their claims of radiation-induced injuries.

I term this social practice that has emerged in Ukraine a "biological citizenship" (1999). In Ukraine, where an emergent democracy is yoked to a harsh market transition, the damaged biology of a population has become the grounds for social membership and the basis for staking citizenship claims. By examining how state-operated research and clinical institutions and nongovernmental organizations of "the disabled"

5

(*invalidy*) mediate individual and collective claims to biological damage, I show how rights and entitlements are contested, normed, and propagated. I also delineate the ways prior Soviet managements and scientific interventions into the lives of affected populations have patterned these dynamics. One can describe biological citizenship as a massive demand for but selective access to a form of social welfare based on medical, scientific, and legal criteria that both acknowledge biological injury and compensate for it. Such demands are also being formulated in the context of fundamental losses—losses of primary securities such as employment and state protections against inflation and a general corrosion of legal-political categories. Struggles over scarce medical goods and over the criteria that constitute a legitimate claim to citizenship are part of postsocialism's uncharted terrain. A stark order of social and economic exclusion now coexists with a generalized discourse of human rights.

The concept of biological citizenship sheds light on a fundamental practice of polity building in postsocialism. Recent ethnographies of postsocialist and market transitions have revealed the varying ways new nation-states find legitimacy in people's lives. These ethnographies have traced the way local narratives address the collapse of state socialism and the sudden conjuncture of capitalism, globalism, and new laws (Verdery 1996, Humphrey 1999, Wanner 1998, Ries 1997, Grant 1995). Contested forms of social inclusion and exclusion emerge through these processes. In the Ukrainian context, I consider the emergent form of biological citizenship from the following perspective: What is the value of life in that new political economy? How does scientific knowledge politically empower those seeking to set that value relatively high? What kinds of rationalities and biomedical practices are emerging with respect to novel social, economic, and somatic indeterminacies?

Existing ethnographic work shows that postsocialisms and conceptions of their future cannot be based on predictive models or treated as inevitably flowing toward free markets and democracy. Michael Burawoy and Katherine Verdery (1999) examine continuities between socialist and postsocialist societies as well as the evolving dependencies between state formations and global economics. Such dependencies, they note, "have radically shifted the rules of the game, the parameters of action within which actors pursue their daily routines and practices" (2). Ethnographic research methods remain fundamental for elucidating the dynamics of these processes at a local level, particularly where we are dealing with informal aspects of power relations and assessing the decisions people make based on limited choices available to them (Gledhill 2000:8).

Such "experience near" (Geertz 1983) studies of these transitioning political and economic worlds also reveal a fundamental reconfiguration of human conditions and conditions of citizenship. The traditional concept of citizenship casts citizens as bearers of natural and legal rights that are (and must be) protected as a matter of birthright. Such rights were indeed extended to all inhabitants of Ukraine, regardless of nationality, at the time of independence. Yet the issue of birthright as it relates to state legal protection remains vexed, particularly given the fact that persons born in some parts of Ukraine are arguably disadvantaged on the basis of intractable environmental and health threats. For these groups, the very idea of citizenship is now charged with the superadded burden of survival. Thus what is particular to Ukraine, what I will be illustrating throughout this work, is not just the forms given to a new democratic way of life (openness, freedom of expression, and the right to information) but the fact that a large and largely impoverished segment of the population has learned to negotiate the terms of its economic and social inclusion in the most rudimentary life-and-death terms. Moreover, these citizens' experiences expose the existence of patterns that ought to be traced in other postsocialist contexts: the role of science in legitimating democratic institutions; increasingly limited access to health care and welfare as the capitalist trends take over; and the uneasy correlation of human rights with biological self-preservation. This book guides the reader through some of the contested spaces and politics of population management in the Chernobyl aftermath, highlighting the patterns by which science has become a key resource in the management of risk and in democratic polity building, and showing how Ukrainians employ knowledge of biological injury as a means of negotiating public accountability, political power, and further state protections in the form of financial compensation and medical care.

■ ■ ■

In March 1996, in the early stages of a year of field research in Kyiv, I went to the city hospital's neonatal unit to talk with the neonatologists about what they saw happening among newborns. Were there any changes? Dr. Zoya, the head of the unit, bemoaned the fact that the hospital's hematology unit "gets all the humanitarian aid." She considered her labors to be unpaid charity work. "How did Chernobyl affect the birth and development of newborns?" I asked her. Before conversation started, Dr. Zoya assumed that I would want statistical data. She told me, "I will not be able to show you any statistics. You will have to go to the Health Ministry for that." Neither then nor later did I ever ask for statistical information, yet every subsequent hospital administrator with whom I spoke told me the same thing: statistical information was off-limits. The urgent desire to withhold statistics on the part of these administrators

7

(whose Chernobyl-related activities are directly controlled by state health administrators) only highlighted another point. Without statistics, the effects of the disaster had to be understood from other perspectives. What I understood was that bureaucratic windows on the Chernobyl reality were open to a certain kind of reality, inviting me to see its brute physical effects and nothing more.

Dr. Zoya then led me to the critical unit (*reanimatsiia*). Like any other guest, I was given a white overcoat to wear during the visit. In a corridor we passed a young affluent couple—the new Ukrainians, or "the new rich"—waiting for a nurse to finish swaddling their newborn infant. We entered the critical unit. Six newborns in German-donated Plexiglas incubators were visible. The transparent boxes were separated and arranged so as to give ample walking space for visitors. The physical state of the infants varied. As we walked, Dr. Zoya described their deformities. My notes say, "One born premature, another survived the death of his twin; another born with a dysfunctional esophagus; another with signs of prenatal asphyxiation. One born to a mother who at age nine was evacuated from the Chernobyl zones; her infant has half a lung. Another was born to a Chernobyl worker: there are six fingers on his left hand. He's missing a trachea. His gut lay on the outside of his body. His left outer ear is gnarled and deformed." It was as if something internal to the gestational process had been left unfinished by Chernobyl. Life was obstructed, and the forms of that obstruction lay bare.

A few weeks later, I spoke on the telephone with a U.S. embassy worker who told me she had personally arranged for Warren Christopher, then U.S. secretary of state, to visit that same critical unit (the goal of his trip was further reductions of Ukraine's nuclear arsenal). This embassy worker said she had "arranged every step," and that "the director of the hospital decided that all the displayed babies would have Chernobyl in their family histories." She said, "It always helps Ukraine when politicians see these Chernobyl children up close."

The display of these infants stressed Chernobyl's core issue: the destruction of human life. That issue was also at the core of a political economy and administrative apparatus that attempted to evoke public recognition of the disaster's pathological facts. These bodies bore Chernobyl histories. They were also vectors of Chernobyl destinies that touched both individual families and this society as a whole. In that space where the neonatologist led me, there was no—and there should not have been any—resistance to these new facts of life. The state used biological images such these not only to project to the world its image as victim but to justify its own sovereignty. Such images reminded viewers of the cause of physical suffering. Out of the mire and mess of the Soviet mismanagement of Chernobyl had come a dreadful accumulation of diverse malformations such as these. Now it is through such images that a society is struggling with the price of its health. And, meanwhile, citizens must rely on their disease, and the knowledge they accumulate about it, as the currency through which they negotiate social, economic, and political survival.

A Technogenic Catastrophe

The scale of the Chernobyl aftermath and its long-term health effects have been subjects of intense dispute and controversy. International scientific organizations insist that contamination from the Chernobyl reactor has been successfully contained, but argue the need for ongoing technical surveillance and for continual informational exchange (IAEA 1991, "Chernobyl's Legacy" 1996). The UN Scientific Committee on the Effects of Atomic Radiation, which relies on data from the International Atomic Energy Agency, has acknowledged the sudden increase in thyroid cancers among children living in affected territories. Along with international biomedical and social scientific literatures, these agencies have characterized most other disorders as products of "informational stress" (Sergeev 1988, WHO 1996), "somatization of fear" (Rumiantseva et al. 1996, Guskova 1995), or lack of proper "risk perception" (Drottz-Sjoberg 1995, Havenaar et al. 1996). Ukrainian scientists and clinicians acknowledge rampant stress among affected populations but have criticized international health assessments for ignoring the contribution radiation makes—even in low doses—to adverse physiological change (Pilinskaya 1999, Bondar et al. 1996).

Much of the disagreement between UN-related and local scientists centers on the significance of *proven* versus *expected* health outcomes. Based on studies conducted after Hiroshima and Nagasaki, an "excess" of 6,600 cancer deaths, including 470 leukemia cases, were expected. Other Japan-based studies on incidence and mortality of cancer indicate that the risk of disease varies according to cancer type. The highest risk is observed for leukemia, breast cancer, thyroid cancer, and lung cancer, as well as some cancers of the gastrointestinal tract. There is considerable disagreement between UN-affiliated scientists and their counterparts in Ukraine and Belarus regarding Chernobyl-related cancer rates. Leukemia estimates in particular vary widely. While UN agencies do not recognize rises in leukemia rates, Prysyazhnyuk et al. indicate the standardized incidence ratio (SIR) for leukemia to have increased significantly among the most heavily exposed cleanup workers in Ukraine (1999). A team of Belarussian physicians claims that leukemia rates are four times the Belarussian national average among the most heavily exposed cleanup workers

(Pearce 2000:12).[15] Gennady Lazjuk of the Institute for Hereditary Diseases in Minsk, along with collaborators in Japan and Europe, found that radiation exposure accounted for a 12 percent increase in birth defects in heavily contaminated areas in Belarus (Lazjuk et al. 2000). Notwithstanding the recognized increase in thyroid cancers in children, the International Atomic Energy Agency and the UN Scientific Committee on the Effects of Atomic Radiation have not acknowledged increases in cancers and congenital deformities, both of which have been anticipated on the basis of research on Hiroshima and Nagasaki bombing survivors (Pierce et al. 1996).

UN scientists and local experts also disagree over where research emphasis should be placed, or at what level biological changes should be detected. Human radiation effects vary according to whether they are deterministic or stochastic. Deterministic effects occur when levels of absorbed radiation doses are significant enough to kill cells that, if not adequately replaced, produce clinically observable pathologies. The severity of the effect is dependent on the radiation dose, with steep linear dose-effect relationships. This is opposed to stochastic effects, which, based on gene damage, confer a probability or chance that a harmful outcome will develop. In contrast with deterministic effects, stochastic effects are non-linear in terms of the kinds of harm they can produce, but are most commonly associated with cancer and leukemia induction. Unlike deterministic effects, they increase the probability rather than the severity of a given pathology (Gofman 1981:708). Recent collaborations among post-Soviet and Western scientists, some of whom are unaffiliated with international radiological committees and agencies, have yielded new data related to stochastic effects. Using techniques far more sophisticated than those available at the time of the Hiroshima and Nagasaki studies, researchers have shown increases in human germline alterations under conditions of chronic exposure to low-dose irradiation among children born in 1994 in Mogilev, Belarus, in comparison with a control population in Britain (Dubrova et al. 1996). Others have noted significant increases in the frequency of chromosomal aberrations and other genetic markers of radiation effects in children living in contaminated areas (Pilinskaya and Dibskyi 2000). Clearly, the science of the human health effects of Chernobyl is an evolving one. As new technologies and research funds become available, new fields of knowledge are established. But at the present moment, what we know of the precise figures of damage is far from complete.

What we can conclude with some certainty, however, is that the processes of making scientific knowledge are inextricable from the forms of power those processes legitimate and even provide solutions for.[16] How scientific knowledge is valued and the level at which it is said to hold significance can affect the planning of state interventions and medical surveillance, the size of populations considered to be at risk, and the courses of suffering and illnesses those populations experience. State interventions are predicated, in part, on policy makers' understandings of the relationship between radiation dose and bodily harm. The so-called linear hypothesis states that harm is proportional to dose indeed, that radiation is harmful at any dose.[17] Here it is not a question of whether harmful effects such as additional cancers exist but whether there are technologies available that are sufficiently powerful to make those effects statistically detectable, and whether governments desire to invest in or make use of those technologies. Hence, the issues raised by the linear hypothesis are of an ethical, political, and economic nature.

Policy makers have several intervention options at their disposal. The degree to which they accept or reject the linear hypothesis shapes the types of intervention they consider and eventually implement. At one end, those options can be described as "low-tech" and minimally interventionist. The rationale here is that because it is impossible to detect the small increases in cancer deaths predicted by the linear hypothesis, cancers—or, for that matter, many other diseases—should not be singled out as radiogenic. In the Chernobyl case, this rationale influenced the size of affected cohorts receiving intervention. Soviet officials claimed that except for the initial group of cleanup workers sent into the Zone, the radiation exposures populations received were insignificant to their health. Indeed, there are many experts who remain committed to the idea that the primary health effects of Chernobyl are of a mental or psychosocial nature. In line with this reasoning, Soviet interventions focused on information dissemination (as in, for example, the state's battle against "radiophobia") and on the introduction of therapeutic and surveillance regimes to address psychosomatic ailments, characterized as products of individual psychological weakness and self-induction. Psychosocial medical categories were applied to exclude the majority of claims.

An alternative course of action would involve a state's immediate full disclosure about what is and is not known about the complexity of health outcomes (including an acknowledgment of those health outcomes as being some combination of clinically observable, stochastic, and psycho-/logical effects). This kind of approach informed Ukraine's management of the aftermath and led, for example, to an improvement of the state's public health surveillance system. Lifting constraints on international collaboration and foreign aid, the state made a variety of research technologies, ranging from the epidemiological to the clinical and molecular biological, available to researchers assessing the disaster's health impact. A number of local scientists, in collaboration with molecular biologists and geneticists from Western Europe, the United States, and Japan, are still sorting out the genetic causes of radiation-induced cancers.

Both the Soviet and post-Soviet approaches entail social and political risks. If in the first case, Soviet managers can be accused of undermedicalizing or denying the health effects of the disaster altogether, Ukrainian managers can be accused of overmedicalizing their constituencies, and of creating a health system that fosters both rectification and abuse. My purpose, however, is not to allocate blame but to paint a clearer picture of the dynamic interplay between scientific and social orders, and how those orders come to define actual conditions of health: those aspects that protect or undermine it, and the moral and ethical discourses addressing its values and responsibilities. Following Veena Das's characterization of the aftermath of the Bhopal chemical disaster, I also aim to elucidate how "pain and suffering are experiences that are actively created and distributed" (1995:138) within scientific/social orders themselves.

The number, novelty, physical variability, and duration of the kinds of harmful particles that were released in the Chernobyl explosion make the open-endedness of the disaster's health effects hard to deny. This open-endedness necessitates further reflection on the ways the scientific research process itself contributes to the spread of pain and suffering by searching for easy answers and simple closures. In discerning the "true" causes of their subjects' suffering, researchers themselves have inadvertently reified categories of authentic and inauthentic suffering, thus marginalizing those who happen to fall into the latter category. So as not to contribute to this marginalizing, I avoided pigeonholing people affected by the disaster as suffering from either "hard" biologically induced symptoms or "soft" psychological ones—though their reasons for claiming the primacy of one etiology over another often entail moral and epistemological claims.

My decision to abstain from judgment is also supported on empirical grounds. Scientific understanding, along with policy decisions, popular pressures, and availability of technological resources, can shift the frames of what is considered evidence of the physical impact of the disaster. What becomes central to this analysis is the different social contexts in which scientific knowledge is placed and the ethical values it is used to support. Worlds of science, statistics, bureaucracy, suffering, power, and biological processes coevolve here in particular and unstable ways. How to discern their patterns as locally observable realities that affect people's daily lives and senses of moral and bodily integrity—or, put another way, how to do an ethnography of the relationships among biological, political, and social processes as those relationships evolve—is a major creative challenge of this work.

The concept of biopolitics provides a further key to making sense of the ways these processes are related and the way they shape the lives of individuals and populations. Biopower refers to controls over life, denoting "what brought life and its mechanisms into the realm of explicit calculations and made knowledge-power an agent of transformation of human life" (Foucault 1980a:143).[18] Such transformations are said to occur at two levels: that of the human body as the object of discipline and surveillance, and that of the population as the object of regulation, control, and welfare. Michel Foucault pointed to a particularly salient moment in the history of biopower in his analysis of eighteenth-century France (1980b). It was in this period, he argued, that the consolidation of centralized state administrative power went hand in hand with a new concern for the health and social welfare of populations. Health was recast in the service of the state; the capacities of individuals were to be maximized inasmuch as those individuals lived, labored, and reproduced within a given territory and ruling apparatus. Populations possessed biological characteristics that made them more predictable. Demographic statistics, calculations of life expectancy and levels of mortality, patterns of marriage and procreation, and the categorization of bodies as more or less useful with greater or lesser prospects of survival constituted new types of knowledge contributing to radically new experiences of control in modern life.

This model of government provides a useful counterpoint for understanding Soviet and post-Soviet responses to Chernobyl and their social and scientific arrangements. In both responses, state power is as concerned with making bodies and behaviors ever more predictable and knowable as it is with creating—both intentionally and inadvertently—spaces of nonknowledge and unpredictability. The biology of populations is held in question; the government of life is unmoored. Where Soviet officials generate medical statistics, they designate them state secrets. People become uncertain as to what medical categories they belong to, how sick or healthy they are. Given the array of scientific and medical uncertainties, old measures of suffering lose their meaning and validity. Into that void come new biological definitions, some by chance, others by design. Some individuals with certain symptoms are said to be sick, while others, with different symptoms, are said to be not sick. Statistics and the use of medical diagnostics become contested. As these governments grapple with creating zones of predictability and intelligibility where they can operate and increase welfare, citizens are faced with what seem like random instantiations of scientific measures, biomedical categories, and compensation criteria. According to international experts in the field of nuclear medicine, the death toll from Chernobyl is thirty-one. According to local experts, the figure is in the hundreds of thousands. Radiation safety norms demarcate contaminated from presumably safe territories, but are those norms too liberal or too conservative? The area of contaminated land shrinks, then expands, then shrinks again. As a result, some rural populations are resettled once, then again, only to return to the area

13

from which they resettled (see chapter 4). There is an absence of maps indicating the spread of contamination; then, in the Ukrainian period, an array of maps appear—unofficial maps, state maps, revisions of state maps. In short, daily life is characterized by overwhelming uncertainty and unknowability. It is in this social, scientific, and legal arena that defining and acquiring a biological citizenship takes on central interest.

■ ■ ■

Today, relations between the human body and populations are again being recast in the context of the life sciences revolution. The Chernobyl disaster happened at a time when there was considerable change in research priorities in the world of international science.[19] Knowledge of the genetic code and how to technically manipulate it is not only transforming public health practices but influencing national politics, global commerce, and medical ethics, as well as conceptions, experiences, and politics of health and disease. In conceptualizing new social groupings in the context of the Human Genome Initiative in the United States and in France, Paul Rabinow examines how genetic knowledge and techniques are bringing about a literal redefinition of self and social identity, what he calls "biosociality."[20] As genetics-based diagnostic tools refocus health care away from direct clinical intervention to risk factor analyses and prevention, patients are engaging in health-promoting behaviors that may help prevent future illness; thus they elude their genetic "fates."

The social and behavioral changes implicated here (from face-to-face medical encounters to databased assessments of individual risk factors) do not necessarily imply a new medical impersonalism. Far from it. They engender novel social groupings bound by the hopes, fears, fates, and politics that have been made available to sufferers on the basis of biological knowledge. Three points follow from this recasting of biopower and are relevant to this investigation of the Chernobyl aftermath. First, the linking of biology with identity is not new. What is new is how connections between biology and identity are being made. In contrast with older and discredited biologized categories such as race or ethnicity, which in the past reinforced political programs and continue to foster patterns of unequal medical access and social injustice around the world (Proctor 1988, Lewontin 1992, Farmer 1999), these "new" biological identities and the interest groups formed in their name now have the potential to drive political economies and forms of commerce, as in Iceland (Palsson and Rabinow 1999); to foster identity-based illness movements, as in the United States (Dumit 2000); to generate new affective disorders, as in Brazil (Biehl 2001); and to become central to contemporary forms of citizenship. Such transformations illustrate the extent to which explanations and claims of health and their failures are understood within the scientific, economic, and political domains in which they are coming to be addressed. A third point follows. In such domains, pain and suffering are experiences that are being rationalized and to some extent made into social instruments. This is not to say they are any less authentic, but that new determinations and values are being attached to them. Acts of suffering can carry stakes beyond themselves, organize social behaviors, and inform policy actions regarding welfare and insurance, health care delivery, and courses of scientific investigation and its funding.

Historians of science have commented on the irony of such dynamics of suffering in that "the process of pathogenesis [becomes] so complex that discussions of cause necessarily become a socially constructed domain" (Brandt 1997:67; also see Proctor 1995). Recent ethnographies of science have vividly portrayed how, more and more, biomedical technologies play a pivotal role in that social constructedness. Sonograms, PET scans, and genetically based diagnostics, by their imaging of biological facts, are inseparable from the objects they recognize and remake as disease (Martin 1994, Rapp 1999, Kleinman 1988). Research into the constructedness of pathologies expands well beyond biomedical circumstances to include diverse forms of violence that can significantly threaten health. Institutions sanctioned to respond to social problems—legal, welfare, and medical—organize distinct programs and policies that can result in distinct courses of health and disease (Das 1995, Kleinman and Petryna 2001).[21] The social making and expansion of populations at risk for disease is also determined by what Paul Farmer has identified as patterns of "structural violence." Lack of health care, limited treatment interventions, and persistent social inequalities that are intensified by structural adjustment programs have led to worldwide epidemics of preventable infectious diseases such as multidrug-resistant tuberculosis (Farmer 1999).

In the Ukrainian context, efforts to assess and remediate the Chernobyl aftermath have contributed to social indeterminacy and novel formations of power.[22] Widespread unaccounted-for radiation exposures, state interventions and failures to intervene, expanding clinical and bureaucratic regimes, and market economic changes came to bear on a rational-technical course of illness and suffering. Suffering—its experiences and interpretations—has been patterned and realized within the rational-technical dynamics that were meant to remediate Chernobyl over time. At the same time, these dynamics have laid the groundwork for a "counter-politics" (Gordon 1991:5) that currently involves 7 percent of Ukraine's population. Citizens have come to rely on available technologies, knowledge of symptoms, and legal procedures to gain political recognition and access to some form of welfare inclusion. Acutely aware of themselves as having

15

lesser prospects for work and health in the new market economy, they inventoried those elements in their lives (measures, numbers, symptoms) that could be connected to a broader state, scientific, and bureaucratic history of error, mismanagement, and risk. The tighter the connections that could be drawn, the greater the probability of securing economic and social entitlement—at least in the short term. This undertaking of "ill-ness-as-counter-politics" suggests that sufferers are aware of the way "politics shapes what they know and don't know" (Proctor 1995:7) about their illnesses, and that they are willing to exploit these politics to limit further assaults on their well-being which they see as resulting from a collapsing state health system and loss of adequate legal protections. Inconsistencies related to the interpretation of radiation-related biological injury, together with the social and political uncertainties generated by Soviet interventions and current political-economic change, make the enormity of the affected population in Ukraine and its claims to injury at once plausible, ironic, and catastrophic.

■ ■ ■

What follows is an account of my field sites, methods, and the challenges of developing an ethnographic sensibility in this environment. I began my work in 1992, and during the summers of 1993 and 1994 I returned to Kyiv to continue to interview and work among resettled families, mothers of exposed children, and radiation-exposed workers. I followed them to public events in the Kyiv area and sat in on their meetings with state administrators at the Parliamentary Commission on Human Rights, where they negotiated the broadening of Chernobyl-related social and health care mandates. My initial data collection was oriented around these key questions: (1) How does the Ukrainian government administer individuals and populations claiming to be affected by radiation exposure? (2) What scientific knowledge and administrative policies are applied in the categorization of risk groups and in the formulation of compensation laws? (3) What scientific knowledge and political strategies are deployed by groups pressing for compensation and social justice on the basis of their Chernobyl condition? I carried out interviews with members of the country's new Chernobyl Ministry, responsible among other things for attracting relief organizations and humanitarian aid; coordinating international efforts for financing and maintaining the Shelter unit; funding environmental monitoring and new building construction, such as homes for persons and families resettled from contaminated areas; coordinating the work of central and local state bodies and scientific and medical institutions; recommending policies for affected citizens; allocating finances for treatment and health care costs of affected populations; and distributing benefits and compensation. Heorhii Hotovshyts, the ministry's first head, afforded me access to state legislators, administrators, Zone administrators, and local civil servants. I was permitted to read memos and internal reports outlining the dynamics of social response to the disaster; rules of hygiene for living in the zones; reports on patterns of media coverage; policy recommendations and medical criteria that Ministry of Health officials used in compensation decision making; and reports on emerging social psychological problems and methodological recommendations for rapid assessments of psychological status. Investigating how Chernobyl-related social mandates legitimated Ukrainian state-building processes, I collected data on Chernobyl welfare budgets and related them to national priorities for health and social protection spending in Ukraine, and I gathered information on how and on what scientific bases laws of compensation for Chernobyl sufferers had been established and expanded since Ukraine's independence.

Along with my research at the level of state and civil society, I developed a brief social history of the scientific knowledge and technical experience that Soviet, American, and Ukrainian experts gained in the immediate and long-term management of Chernobyl. It became apparent that in order to do a fair analysis of the lived experience of Chernobyl, I had to do multisited work. That meant becoming scientifically literate—inquiring into the circulation and assimilation of scientific knowledge at national, international, and local levels, as well as exploring their tensions. I conducted interviews with key scientific and political players in both Kyiv and Moscow, comparing scientific norms of biological risk and safety in the Soviet and post-Soviet administrations of the aftermath. I also looked into expert claims at the International Atomic Energy Agency and at government laboratories in the United States. At Lawrence Berkeley Laboratory (whose scientific work is unrelated to Chernobyl issues), I learned some of the basic radiobiological techniques for assessing the biological impact of radiation at the cellular and DNA levels. But as one radiation scientist told me, the difference between this manipulable animal environment and populationwide exposures to low-dose radiation remains a "black box." Though causal links between high doses of radiation and human biological effects have been well-established, the same cannot be said for continuous human exposure to low doses. It is no surprise that health predictions made by international health experts have often contradicted people's lived experience. The calculus of cost and criteria of assessment of injury are, by definition, open-ended and contestable.

In the absence of agreed-upon standards, a new social and political arena opened in Ukraine. I learned in my long-term work with civil servants of the Chernobyl welfare apparatus that disputes over the scope of injury of this disaster, and over how to model it, continue to influence

17

policy, social mobilizations, and not least the very nature of the course of illnesses in the affected populations I worked with. From the field I could also observe that different scientific approaches (psychometric versus biological, laboratory versus field-based research), different funding priorities, and different senses of urgency concerning the unknown health effects of the disaster were not simply at odds with each other; nor were they simply waiting to be assessed for their suitability or unsuitability. Their confrontation and juxtaposition engendered a new environment— or, more precisely, a political economy of claims around radiation illness. Developing alongside the new scientific, biomedical, and legal institutions promoting "safe living" in Ukraine was another social phenomenon that caught my attention. It was the boom of civic organizations called *fondy* (funds) that administered international charity and the compensation claims of the Zone workers. Also, since these more than five hundred funds are tax-exempt, they have sparked a large informal economy based on imports of a variety of goods, including pharmaceuticals, cars, foodstuffs, and so on.

In this political economy of Chernobyl-related illnesses, it was common knowledge that a person categorized as "disabled" was far better compensated than a mere "sufferer." Persons completely outside the system of Chernobyl sufferers knew they had little chance of getting decent social protections from the state. In this economy, scientific knowledge became a crucial medium of everyday life. The effectiveness of relating one's dose exposures to radiation-related symptoms and experiences and work histories in the Zone determined the position one could occupy in the hierarchy of sufferers, and the extent to which one could wield capital that could further guarantee state protections. Broadly speaking, postsocialist Ukraine presented a unique constellation in which science, state building, and market developments were quite productively intertwined, generating new institutions and social arrangements through which citizenship and ethics were being transformed (see also Biehl 2001).

When I returned to Kyiv for a year's field research in 1996, my key field site became the Radiation Research Center.[23] In the Soviet period, the center served as the clinical research division of the All-Union Center of Radiation Medicine. The center's staff grew from ninety to over thirteen hundred by 1991. These numbers reflect its growth in status as an important social institution; they also illustrate how in the context of economic crisis, government bureaucracies expand rather than contract to provide their own forms of social protection. The center monitors patients with acute radiation sickness and conducts research on the clinical outcomes of human exposures to ionizing radiation. What is most important, it houses the national-level medical-labor committee (*Ekspertiza*), a group of scientists, clinicians, and administrators who are responsible for evaluating the health of Chernobyl Zone workers, resettled families, and inhabitants of contaminated areas. Their job is to evaluate a patient's level of disability (or loss of labor capacity) and to either verify or disavow the etiology of that disability in Chernobyl-related radiation exposure. Members authorize the Chernobyl connection or "tie" (*sviaz*)—a legal document attesting to the link between certain illnesses and radiation exposure. The tie entitles its bearer to social protections in the form of pensions, health care, and even education benefits for children. This package of benefits is, comparatively speaking, much better than average pensions and is therefore very desirable. As of 2000, the state paid an average twelve dollars per month for social insurance. The poverty line was approximately twenty-seven dollars a month. For persons disabled by the Chernobyl accident, for the same period, pension benefits averaged between fifty-four and ninety dollars per month, depending on degree of disability. A sufferer, a person who does not have disability status but has the status of having suffered from the Chernobyl accident, received twenty dollars per month, on average.

Through contacts with politically active groups of disabled Chernobyl Zone workers who frequented clinics, I obtained permission to conduct research in the clinical wing of the center (known as the Clinic). By 1996, the Clinic had become an epicenter of medical-scientific and legal wrangling. Exams, scientific resources, and specialized medical treatment became precious assets for patients who were fortunate enough to be there, helping them qualify for lifetime compensations. I was allowed to observe interactions among physicians, nurses, and patients; to attend decision-making meetings related to compensation claims; and to examine current research, particularly in the Clinic's Division of Nervous Pathologies. This choice of division was intentional on my part. Medical-labor committee members told me that the majority of all disability claims were channeled through neurological wards on account of a variety of nervous system disorders. Yet it was unclear whether these disorders stemmed from social stress owing to the country's dire economic situation or from Chernobyl radiation exposure, or from some combination of the two. In addition to talking with scientists, health workers, and administrators, I conducted extended interviews with sixty male and female patients (aged 35–55) and reviewed their medical records. I documented the course of their illnesses, diagnosis, and progress in obtaining disability status (*oformyty hrupu*, which means "to make the group"). I also worked with three of the Chernobyl funds, tracing the history of their membership and looking into their strategic relationships with the Clinic and the medical-labor committee. A final part of my work involved following the everyday activities of five of the Clinic's male patients and their wives and children.

I was interested in how these men's induction into this novel political economy of illness was influencing their identities as breadwinners and father figures, as well as affecting their mental health. I was particularly interested in these men's changing sense of *lichnost'*, a Soviet concept of personhood that was expressed in individual commitment to work and to the labor collective; and in how married couples were using radiation illness as a means of subsistence in the new economy.

The ways in which scientific and social knowledge circulated at public and private levels also framed aspects of the ethnographic encounter. How people expressed their grief, how the demands of institutional settings shaped their discourse and body language, and how they elicited the responses they needed from technocrats (and their choices of words or silences) all found their place in the political and scientific regime that defined everyday life. People's actions, politics, and sensibilities were encoded in and restricted by the professional and legal discourses of this rational-technical domain.

At the same time, codes are secrets, signals ensuring privacy; they are systematic abbreviations of human experience. In new technologically mediated contexts, social scientists have voiced concern that our capacities to think critically about moral values are being lost within the expedient languages of bioethics (Churchill 1999:259). What has been called a principlist approach to bioethics is said to work precisely because it is reductive and is widely adaptable to moral problems and dilemmas in a pluralistic society (Callahan 1999:283). One casualty of this standardization of bioethics is knowledge of how certain ethical norms propagate in actual and diverse settings, and of the particularities of local conditions and moral accounts as they may bear on or challenge universalized ethical framings (Kleinman 1999, Cohen 1999).

Such critiques of bioethics challenge ethnographers to restore language adequate to account for contexts where, in the terse words of the director of the Shelter complex, "the value of the human is yet to be determined." My concerns are not with the rhetorics and images that project the value of the human as universally given but with the mundane office spaces, clinics, wards, and homes where the chances for justice, benevolence, and nonmaleficence routinely disintegrate; where individual accounts of suffering, if they are to be heard at all, must transmogrify into numbers and codes fitting standard categories.[24]

Nation Building

Chernobyl was a watershed event marking communism's end, defining critical tensions in international relations, accelerating processes of

FIGURE 1. Map of Ukraine

glasnost, and giving glasnost exceptional relevance in Ukraine. The disaster generated consequences, many of which are yet to be grasped, and whose truths have been only partly revealed through estimates derived from experimental science. If, at the level of the modern state, spheres of scientific production and politics are in a constant process of exchange and mutual stabilization, then here stabilization proves to be a much more difficult task. That is because reality can subvert scientific claims to certainty and truth. As Ulrich Beck notes, in the flood of contradictory findings that is so characteristic of large-scale industrial disasters, scientific reason can break up into many sets of competing rationalities "with specific claims to errors, deceptions, and truths" (1992:167). Such uncertainty in scientific spheres can produce a social and political unraveling. In the Ukrainian context, the unraveling has taken the form of an expanding set of claims based on Chernobyl-related damages. Such claims reflect new experimental fabrics in which science, nation building, and market developments are interdependent, and where the biology of citizens becomes a contested part of a political process and a tool of government.

Ukraine is located between Poland to the west and Russia to the east, both of which (in addition to the Austro-Hungarian and Ottoman Empires) have laid claim to Ukrainian territories over the past three centuries

21

(figure 1). At the time of the disaster, Ukraine was the second largest of fourteen republics of the Soviet Union, with a population of approximately fifty million.[25] Once known as the breadbasket of the Soviet Union, the country is also a land of pogroms and wars. Many Ukrainians today regard the region as having been a brutal laboratory for Stalinist collectivization campaigns and the site of a state-induced famine of 1932–1933 in which, according to one estimate, six million people are said to have died.[26] Many immigrants know it as a place from which their Jewish ancestors, survivors of pogroms, fled in the late nineteenth and early twentieth centuries. During World War II, German and Soviet armies clashed in Ukraine's villages and cities, leaving behind ruins as well as new social spaces for the mobilization of public support for the socialist order, as evidenced by rapid and massive postwar reconstruction efforts. In the late sixties, Chernobyl was built as a kind of reactor theme park to show the world how advanced and well-organized Ukrainian socialist society and life had become.

Like other nascent post-Soviet states, Ukraine became sovereign and democratic without much prior experience. In the last century, Ukraine achieved sovereignty for a brief period in 1918, before Bolsheviks took over the capital.[27] One of the leaders of that failed attempt declared: "Truly, we were like the gods. . . . attempting to create a whole new world from nothing" (Vynnychenko 1920:258, quoted in Subtelny 1988:354). Interestingly, national identity in Ukraine is, in part, an effect of a Stalinist policy called *korenizatsiia* (rooting). *Korenizatsiia* created nationalities that were fundamental to a kind of ethnoterritorial administration of socialist republics (Slezkine 1994). The motto of this policy was "National in Form, Socialist in Content." Yet when the Ukrainians, Uzbeks, and Estonians among others emerged from their ethnoterritories, they did so at a time when prospects for building strong nation-states were faint. Ukraine was trapped in a paradox of having to constitute itself at the same time nation-states were increasingly becoming destabilized by globalizing forces. Although ethnically mixed, the country's metamorphosis from a Soviet republic to an independent nation occurred without armed conflict—Ukraine never became the ethnic tinderbox that some American observers predicted it would be. These predictions were based on assumptions about ethnicity as the decisive marker of national belonging and therefore of possible internal conflict or war. What these observers failed to recognize was that their imaginary ethnic types were not at all predisposed to war. Instead they were asserting values related to life, values that were expressed not in spite of but because of a Soviet experience.[28]

Neither do the processes leading to Ukraine's independence support a triumphal narrative in which a victimized Ukrainian nation subverts its colonizing master (Torbakov 2001:462). Soviet welfare legacies played an important role in shaping the way in which support for independence was won. At the time of independence, about 40 percent of all inhabitants of the Ukrainian republic were receiving one or more cash benefits. Legislators knew that in order to justify statehood and to win over citizens, they had to appeal to these inhabitants' materialist side. They had to promise enhancements to a Soviet-style welfare state, including health and welfare benefits, in addition to guaranteeing civic freedoms, human rights, and equal participation in political life—what are generally regarded as the principles of a "classical citizenship" (Schnapper 1997:201). Soviet welfare legacies, as well as the dire economic conditions in which Ukraine declared independence, created a context for division and competition among groups for social welfare.[29] Thus the struggle for claims rights went hand in hand with a more universally bestowed civic logic of citizenship (202).[30]

In 1991, the year Ukraine declared independence from the Soviet Union, leaders of this once socialist republic condemned the Soviet administration of the Chernobyl aftermath and began fostering their own political legitimacy. Nationalists, Communists, and Democrats alike entered into a novel (and short-lived) political alliance when they unanimously denounced the Soviet administration as an "act of genocide." The charge of genocide referenced a national symbol of Soviet oppression, the 1930s famine, often described as man-made.[31] Legislators claimed that not only had the Soviet state apparatus failed in its obligation to protect citizens' lives during Chernobyl but that in its denial of the event and its effort to restart the nuclear program, it had exacerbated patterns of morbidity by delaying intervention.

Legislators (many of whom had had roles in the Soviet administration as its dissidents, cleanup workers, and implementers) viewed their political alliance as an opportunity to quickly do away with central power. This was especially true of well-organized Ukrainian Communist elites who, after much of the initial symbolic power of anti-Soviet nationalist groups such as Rukh had waned, rose to central prominence.[32]

In this moment of nation building, one could observe how bioscientific knowledge became a crucial medium in state-building processes and in the establishment of new policies guaranteeing safe living, social equity, and human rights. Legislators assailed the Soviet standard for determining biological risk to populations. The Soviets had established a high 35 rem spread over an individual's lifetime (understood as a standard seventy-year span) as the threshold of allowable radiation dose intakes.[33] This threshold restricted the scope of resettlement actions. Ukrainian law lowered the threshold dose to 7 rem, comparable to what an average American would be exposed to in his or her lifetime. In effect this lowered measure for safe living increased the size of the labor forces going to the Zone (since workers' stints had to be shortened if they were to avoid exceeding the stricter dose standards). The change also expanded the territory considered contaminated. A significant new sector of the population would want to claim itself as part of a state-protected post-Soviet polity. One radiation protection specialist, who conducted retrospective dose assays on resettlers, recollected: "Long lines of resettlers extended from our laboratory doors. It wasn't enough that they were evacuated to 'clean' areas. People got entangled in the category of victim, by law. They had unpredictable futures and *they all wanted to know their dose.*"

The laws also made the "normal citizen" financially liable for the sufferer. A 12 percent tax was automatically deducted from the income of private businesses and state enterprises to fund Chernobyl laws on social protection. Such financial and moral obligations were meant to create a national bond—where otherwise there might not have been one—between sufferers and nonsufferers. Put another way, the Ukrainian laws attempted to "settle accounts" with the deleterious Soviet past, a retributive process first outlined by John Borneman in East-Central Europe (1997). The Ukrainian process was not about retribution per se, a process whereby people are rewarded or punished for past deeds; it was about compensation (*kompensatsiia*). Ukrainian administrators, many of whom had managed the Soviet containment of Chernobyl, were now authorizing payments on behalf of the state to those who claimed damages. These administrators did not thereby suffer any losses of employment or prestige, a key feature in retributive processes; in fact, many of them materially benefited from those processes by claiming material and physical damages themselves. The laws they implemented went beyond the goal of adding predictability to a democratizing process through retribution (ibid.). They inscribed Chernobyl as a key moral, economic, and political event in daily postsocialist Ukrainian life. They also fostered new appropriations (and misappropriations) of the law in the context of social and economic upheaval; compensation as a form of payment for past damage was reinterpreted as a form of market compensation.

With the lowered dose standard, more and more people became active participants in a system of compensation and social protections. State statistics registered sharp increases, starting in 1991, of Zone workers, resettled persons, and inhabitants of contaminated territories registering their disability, and in this new population's annual patterns of enrollment. Such social statistics became a kind of "moral science" (Hacking 1991) through which the government revealed the effects of prior mismanagement and guaranteed its own social legitimacy while keeping world attention on Chernobyl-related risk.

Injured workers, resettled families, physicians, scientists, lawmakers, and local civil servants were increasingly bound together through law. And together, they constituted a set of public interests in which state and civil society negotiated a new social contract based on a right to know and "safe living." Though the laws addressed a broad constituency, they were selectively applied, and "every one knew that." The fight for disability status became the source of new solidarities and tensions. As the market economy took over, access to state protections and benefits became restricted. Persons claiming injury and the arbiters of those claims became consumed in public dramas over who had right of access to a system of compensation and social protections.

The state's social welfare system expanded rather than contracted in order to accommodate the large influx of new Chernobyl sufferers. This rapid expansion defied Western prescriptions for a smooth transition to market economics—prescriptions that mandated a decrease in the social expenditures of the state. Sufferers became knowing participants in the logics of this transitional state expansion. These everyday events constituted a moral microcosm of the paradoxes of an emerging democracy founded on ethical principles of justice, benevolence, and human rights. If, on the one hand, these Chernobyl laws engendered new and demonstrably democratic forms of civic organizing and opportunities for nongovernmental action, on the other hand, they became one of the state's most notorious mechanisms of corruption, one through which *blat*, for example (a term denoting the informal practice by which access to state privileges and protections could be obtained with connections or material resources), could persist (Ledeneva 1998).

Experimental Systems

As the everyday experience of Ukraine's citizens—sufferers and non-sufferers alike—demonstrates, the Chernobyl aftermath is by no means a phenomenon confined to the past, interpretable as mere psychological trauma, or reducible in terms of scientific absolutes. Rather, it is a dynamic lens for understanding the role of science, economics, ethics, and politics in the arrangement of a postsocialist civil society. Fields as diverse as radiobiology, health physics, molecular biology, neurology, neuropsychiatry, and social psychology contribute to the aftermath's data-producing enterprise. These sciences define, quantify, psychologize, biologize, and geneticize; their isolated facts can thus obscure the aftermath's more general dimensions. From an anthropological standpoint, scientific facts become significant in terms of how, in their partiality, they become incorporated into an ongoing struggle for life, understood here as a complex

25

and often painful interplay between technical visions for managing the accident's effects and lived individual and social disturbances. The vitality of the aftermath's knowledge-production arises from the changing dynamic between the known and the unknown, and the complex ways that people become incorporated into it as subjects, objects, proxies, agents, and victims.

In scientific circles, Chernobyl has been valued as a kind of "experiment," allowing scientists to corroborate or refute biomedical data concerning the long-term health consequences of nuclear exposure ("Chernobyl's Legacy" 1996:653). In this analysis, I take the meaning of experiment in a wider sense, and examine how technical interventions aimed at containing the aftermath introduced new uncertainties in social and scientific arrangements. Hans-Jorg Rheinberger has observed that this kind of experiment is manipulative, "designed to give unknown answers to questions which themselves we are not yet able clearly to ask" (1995:110). Experimental systems are "machines for making the future" (Jacob 1988, cited in Rheinberger 1995:110). This definition provides an ethnographically rich alternative to the more traditional notion of experiments as "singular, well-defined instances embedded in the elaboration of a theory and performed in order to corroborate or to refute certain hypotheses" (109). Rather than achieving an isolated instance of certainty as the result of a rigidly controlled environment, experimental systems produce new and unanticipated resources in environments where little if anything is held constant.

In the Soviet setting, whole populations were understood as "new resources." "Our social psychology would be empty," wrote a leading Soviet social psychologist, "without the remarkable experiment of our people led by [the Party] in the reformation of the psychology and consciousness of the Soviet people." For these scientists, human nature itself was a newly liberated resource, open to tinkering with within an experimental paradigm. Thus, social psychologists sought to demonstrate the accumulation of "new facts and laws of socio-mental [*sotsial'no-psikhicheskii*] phenomena." Consciousness, epistemes, and mental phenomena were cogenerated within such a paradigm; they expressed themselves in the form of "socially conditioned reflections of reality" or "reflections of objective reality in the form of sensations, ideas, thoughts, feelings, voluntary actions, and the like" (Kuzmin, quoted in Slobin 1966:87).

That human nature could be engendered experimentally, that novel cognitive capacities could be constructed and accumulated over time, speaks to the profoundly interventionist character of science in everyday Soviet life. What has consistently come as a surprise to Western observers is the extent to which Soviet and post-Soviet individuals could describe the constructedness of their psychological capacities with such accuracy and without relegating them to the realm of an unknown or an unconscious (Inkeles and Bauer 1959:142).

The ability to unmask behavior as socially conditioned, the capacity to "disown" the psychological structures one inhabits, has been characterized as a by-product of Soviet pedagogical programs that focused almost exclusively on ensuring the dominance of the collective over the individual (Kharkhordin 1999). Mastery of these kinds of unmasking abilities is clearly evident in the way post-Soviet scientists related to some international scientific experts who framed Chernobyl as a largely psychosocial phenomenon; this framing was interpreted as telling an incomplete story and obscuring more complicated truths. In a speech commemorating the tenth anniversary of the Radiation Research Center in 1996, for example, I listened as the former Ukrainian minister of health at the time of the Chernobyl disaster toasted the progress of Chernobyl science. His audience included scientists and clinicians who worked tirelessly with leukemia, cardiac, and acute radiation sickness patients (among others) several floors above the meeting hall. With his glass raised, the slightly inebriated bureaucrat and scientist burst out, "Friends! Yesterday we were ignorant, today we are mental cases, and tomorrow, *who knows what science will bring!*"

These words resonated remarkably (and uncannily) with English philosopher Alfred North Whitehead's 1926 observation, "Heaven knows what seeming nonsense may not to-morrow be demonstrated truth" (Whitehead, cited in Arendt 1989:290). Whitehead's comment is a call for grounding scientific abstractions in their human consequences and realities. When such grounding is absent, persons, their behaviors, and their natures run the risk of conforming to illusory truths. And this loss of touch with reality was precisely what the former minister's mordant humor mocked. That he could draw humor from his own record of ethical neglect speaks to the essence of tragedy—to what Whitehead so aptly described as "the solemnity of the remorseless working of things" (1926:11).[34] In this moment, postsocialist scientists have before them the opportunity to transcend a personhood founded on a collective adherence to objective reality; to imagine and speak from different ethical locations; to deploy moral critiques of a science-as-human-progress paradigm.

Docta Ignorantia

Persons occupying "lower" orders of the social scale—the collective farmers, policemen, and industrial workers who became sufferers or persons claiming disability—deployed critiques of their own, albeit in much more subversive ways, as a means of asserting their human rights claims. They took up their roles—in many creative ways—as the "epistemic murk" of scientific progress (Taussig 1987). Where absolute truths prevailed, so did ignorance; where emphasis on the precision of facts ruled, so did imprecision. This is not to suggest these individuals were "anti-science." Rather, they became masters of the reality of what science did not know about them. Ignorance, understood as a form of self-assertion, is fundamental to scientific progress too.

A brief excursus into the processes by which modern forms of self-assertion could prevail over a period of self-abnegating absolutism may prove useful here. In *The Legitimacy of the Modern Age*, Hans Blumenberg devotes two chapters to the importance of ignorance in the story of progress in modernity. He takes his example from the formulations of a medieval speculative metaphysician, Nicholas of Cusa.[35] In his treatise, the *Docta Ignorantia*, the Cusan opposed the Scholastic belief in knowledge as "the end of a summation process of what is humanly knowable" and replaced it with a "novel cognitive procedure." Blumenberg interprets the Cusan's work as an attempt to provide "something like a mundane and human compensation for theological absolutism." The *Docta* reflects "skeptical resignation vis-à-vis the metaphysical pretensions of the age with an element of indefinite expectation of a knowledge that could no longer have the form it had had hitherto" (1983:492).

For Blumenberg, "ignorance" conveys a spectrum of meaning, from a "mere misfortune of the pretension to truth" to a "positivized negativity" (493). Ignorance does not represent a negative state of knowledge. Nor does it imply a simplistic lack of access to or unwillingness to recognize the truth. It refers to "a praxis, a method, a path to a certain sort of attitude" (490). The Cusan's example demonstrates how the modern idea of scientific progress will be the sum total of something like ignorance, knowledge, and imprecision as an important "intervening phase *between simpler truths and more complex ones*" (504; emphasis added).[36]

This last point marks a pertinent shift: from a scientific knowledge that is accessible to a privileged few, to one that acknowledges a lack of closure and thus provides more people with a stake in its epistemological rules (Kohler 2001). That this science can be the sum of knowledge, ignorance, and imprecision becomes part of the plasticity of the biosocial experience I illustrate here, and what enables many sufferers to get a foothold in this world. The indeterminacy of scientific knowledge about the illnesses people face and about the nature of atomic catastrophe emerges here as both a curse and a point of leverage.

The word ignorance expresses how the Ukrainians depicted here saw and continue to see themselves within (and, more recently, how they are capable of manipulating) a hierarchy of knowledge and power. The flip side of ignorance is what I saw as the savvy comprehension among affected individuals of the shifting stakes, experiments, and technologies in the international life sciences that implicated them in, or excluded them from, an experimental knowledge process. This "bios" of Chernobyl becomes an unexpected yet highly versatile cultural and political resource.

■ ■ ■

Ivan Nimenko learned how to navigate these new times. He was moving up the social-welfare ranks from sufferer to disabled person. While working in the state militia in the first weeks following the accident, he was ordered to evacuate the residents of Prypiat', a city of fifty thousand housing nuclear plant workers and their families, within thirty-six hours after the disaster. I met him in the Radiation Research Center. Once closed to foreigners, the center is a highly charged bureaucratic and clinical institution in which workers' occupational injury claims are made and stamped as authentic. Nimenko, like any prospective disabled person, sought the Chernobyl "tie." As he put it, "This is the document I need for my health." The "tie" would assert that his illnesses are not "general" but rather are attributable to Chernobyl.

Nimenko was admitted to the center's Division of Nervous Pathologies with a diagnosis that read "cerebral arteriosclerosis with arterial hypertension, osteochondrosis, gastritis, and hypochondriacal syndrome." Such a complex of diagnoses was not uncommon and suggested that he might be merely a "psychosocial" case, and therefore ineligible for the benefits he sought. He needed to eliminate that possibility and replace it with an unconditional radiation-based etiology. Fundamental to this task was a radiation dose assessment that he had fought hard to get. Nimenko knew that according to international nuclear industry standards, a worker can incur up to 25 rem over his entire lifetime. He had incurred at least 25 rem in just ten years. Through a brother-in-law, a laboratory director, Nimenko had managed to enter the system, to be assigned a coveted hospital bed, and to receive a medical examination. He could count on familial connections, old Soviet, primarily urban-based, informal exchange networks, and the system of *blat* to establish his legal status in the new state. He was successful.

Like many others, Nimenko maintained that he was historically unaccounted for in the Soviet administration of the disaster. Referring to the lax radiation monitoring of Chernobyl workers, he said, "Regarding our individual cases, they wrote nothing. If there was any distinctive mark written about us in the registers, it read 0.0 (*nul'-nul'*), whatever the unit of measurement was." In characterizing his dose exposure as *nul'-nul'*, Nimenko recognized himself as having gained no legal weight, no consequence or value, during his Chernobyl work. For Nimenko, this Soviet 0.0 symbolized false accountability. Even now, scientists involved in executing the Soviet state's disaster response maintain that only 237 people with known doses are legitimate acute accident victims, and that only 31 of those died from the disaster. These kinds of squared-off facts defined the scope of the disaster's consequences and foreclosed compensations to many like Nimenko, whose injuries might not become evident until later. Nimenko knew these numbers by heart.

A 1991 British television documentary shows the grueling labor Soviet administrators demanded of the workers sent to Chernobyl. The documentary describes a particular cleanup effort that took place in September 1986, four months after the initial explosion. Soviet administrators were intent on restarting Unit Three of the power plant, adjacent to the exploded unit. But debris from Unit Four covered the third unit's roof, delaying start-up. Initially robots were deployed to remove the roof's radioactive debris; radiation levels were so high that the electronics powering these robots failed. A month later young men, their bodies covered with primitive lead suits, rubber gloves, and thin cloth face masks, were conscripted to complete the job.

In one segment of the documentary, workers who are about to go up onto the roof are shown scenes from a video monitor posted on the roof of the third unit. "This is how your mates do the work," the work unit commander says. The workers are instructed to be on the roof for no more than one minute. They are told that within that time frame they must shovel radioactive debris and hurl it over the parapet into containers below. They are to repeat the process once more, and then run for their life.

At the end of the segment, a representative from a group of disabled persons is interviewed. He refers to these men as the original "bio-robots." The label suggests that Soviet administrators exploited workers' biology as a resource to contain the disaster. In the representative's own words, biological resources were "to be used and thrown out." According to one biochemist, many of these bio-robots were exposed to six to eight times the lethal dose of radiation, "They are alive," he said; "they know that they didn't die. But they don't know how they survived." This "ignorance" over how they survived does not stem from a lack of knowledge; it is a political consequence of decisions concerning how to approach what could and should be done to mitigate danger or disease (Proctor 1995:7). In the face of overwhelming danger, the state slated certain workers for bio-robotic death. Those who survived this political decision were abandoned to a gray zone of scientific and bureaucratic indeterminacy.

Approximately 50,000 of the 600,000 workers sent into the Zone over a ten-year period did work of this extreme nature. In the Ukrainian period of disaster administration, this experience was taken up as an emblem of the deadly effects of the Soviet response to the accident, and, more, it opened the possibility of a new politics which took that very injury as legal material. This process became part of the social history of an emerging postsocialist personhood. In his essay on the subject, Marcel Mauss states that personhood is "more than an organizational fact, more than a name or a right to assume a ritual mask. It is a basic fact of law" (1985:14). Indeed, the law of scientific indeterminacy introduced by the disaster's interventions allowed for new legal personhoods founded on incalculable harm.

New gender dynamics and domination were also at stake in this new legal and moral environment. In 1996, another representative from a fund told me the first words he spoke to his wife and son when he returned home from work: "Get away from me, I am contaminated!" Kulyk was a mere thirty-eight years old when I met him, but he looked at least sixty. He lay on a living room couch, a kind of centerpiece, surrounded by members of his fund. As he spoke, his wife, Tania, mocked her husband's "stupid sense of duty." She was left to take care of a deteriorating person, "He was a Party secretary, and now he is a skeleton. His stupid sense of duty is now killing everyone!" Tania explained that Kulyk had experienced all the signs of acute radiation sickness: "He frequently lost consciousness; he coughed and vomited blood. . . . He is alive, and that's all I know. I don't want to know what is inside his body." Every village, every housing block, every work collective knew a living bio-robot—or one who had already died.

Many who had done less dangerous labor, like Nimenko, saw these bio-robots as political kin. Unlike Kulyk, Nimenko remained physically and socially mobile. For him, science had social utility. It could be called upon to set a price on survival, to create assets based on that survival, assets that could be used to leverage the state for compensation. Nimenko had mastered a language of symptoms and science. He was also part of a disabled persons fund that mediated the claims of other cleanup workers. He was scientifically literate and had a strong sense of the value of science in empowering him to set the value of his life. He knew how to read cytogenetic tests indicating chromosomal aberrations in his cells. He used the ambiguities of radiation science—and there are many—to facilitate his chances of having his case reassessed favorably for his compensation claim. Referring to a request he had made in 1991 for a retrospective quantification of his internal dose, Nimenko told me:

> The central polyclinic of our ministry arranged a contract with the Institute of Oncology of the Ukrainian Academy of Medical Sciences. I went to the director of the polyclinic and said I want to know my dose

burden. After three months, they gave me a dose burden based on the increase of the level of chromosomal aberrations in my blood, which testifies that radiation activity in my organism is higher than 25 rem. . . . That was five years after the accident. And if you throw away five more years, how much dose I received, *I don't know*. Obviously it was more. Nonetheless there is radiation in my body.

Where ignorance once amounted to a form of repression (in the Soviet period), it is now used as a resource in the personal art of biosocial inclusion. Nimenko based his self-account on an accumulation of unknowns. In this regard, he used scientific knowledge in a specific way: not to know but to circumscribe what he can never know. Nimenko crafted his social identity in terms of what Hans-Jorg Rheinberger in another context has referred to as a "characteristic irreducible vagueness" (1995:48). He politicized what-he-can-never-know as a means of securing his place as a scientific subject and, by extension, as an object in an official exchange relation with the state. In this move, he acquired a name, a document, and a position as an individual "in the rights he enjoys and his place in the tribe, as in its rites" (Mauss 1985:11).

The Unstoppable Course of Radiation Illness

I went to the state's Ministry of Statistics to ascertain the impact these developments in the politics of knowledge might have had on health data. To my surprise, beginning in 1990 (the year the laws on Chernobyl social protection were being publicized by Ukrainian legislators), I noticed a sharp increase in the clinical registration of illnesses under the category "symptoms, signs, and ill-defined states"—Class 16 in the International Classification of Diseases. These states include anything from insomnia, fatigue, and persistent headaches to personality changes, hallucinations, and premature senility. In a sense, people were claiming Chernobyl as *their* ill-defined state.

Table 1
Data on "Symptoms, Signs, and Ill-defined States" (per 10,000)

1982	1983	1984	1985	1986	1987	1988	1989	1990	1991	1992
1.3	1.7	1.7	1.9	2.3	2.7	5.9	34.7	108.3	127.4	141.3

Source: Ministry of Statistics, Kyiv, Ukraine.

International observers, not surprisingly, grew ever more skeptical of claims to a sudden expansion of Chernobyl health effects and strongly criticized Ukrainian scientists for their failure to prove or disprove these claims on the basis of epidemiological criteria of causality. Yet as this book shows, the complex strategies, techniques, and relations that have been engendered within this postsocialist environment are not measurable by scientific criteria of causality alone. Upon these relations of injury and compensation, other risks, particularly those connected with the market transition, are superimposed.

The collective and individual survival strategy called biological citizenship represents a tangle of social institutions and the deep vulnerabilities of persons; it is also part of a broader story of democratizing processes and structures of governance in the postsocialist states. Here the experience of health is irreducible to a set of norms of physiological and mental activity, or to a set of cultural differences. Only through concrete understandings of particular worlds of knowledge, reason, and suffering, and the way they are mediated and shaped by local histories and political economies, can we possibly come to terms with the intricate human dimensions that protect or undermine health. Seen this way, health is a construction as well as a contested way of being and evolving in the world.

Chapter 2
Technical Error: Measures of Life and Risk

A Foreign Burden

Dmytro is a miner from the coal-mining region of Donbas in Ukraine. I met him at the Radiation Research Center where he came to "settle his social matters." Within ten days following the Chernobyl accident, he was one of two thousand coal miners from his region mobilized to carry out work at the disaster site. Dmytro said he underwent an occupational health screening before his mobilization: "I knew I was healthy before going there." Dmytro lacked a special protective mask during his month-long work, which involved digging tunnels under the reactor. Miners injected these tunnels with liquid nitrogen and other gases in attempts to cool the reactor core. Dmytro received five times his average salary for this work.

Since his work at Chernobyl, Dmytro has undergone annual hospital examinations and monitoring at the Radiation Research Center. In August 1996, he was admitted to the center's Division of Nervous Pathologies with cerebral, cardiac, and pulmonary disorders. Dmytro said he had one daughter, born five years before the disaster. He decided not to have any more children because he believed himself to be genetically damaged. "A healthy child cannot come from a sick father," he reasoned.[1]

His documents showed him to be categorized as a disabled person (level three). This meant he was officially recognized as having lost 50 percent of his labor capacity. Before entering the center, Dmytro decided to quit his job and secure full disability benefits from the state. He wanted to qualify for higher disability status, a certification that he had lost 80

34

percent or more of his work capacity. This move would have doubled his pension and allowed him to pay for his medical treatments. Behind his hospital referrals, institutional rubber stamps, dose assessments, diagnoses, corrections to diagnoses, further diagnoses, and other papers conferring his Chernobyl identity was a person who perceived himself to have lost the capacity to father, to work, and to live a normal life. Dmytro complained of emotional stress and gastritis. Like many patients I met at the center, he no longer identified himself as a worker of a state enterprise; he had come to see himself as a "prospective invalid." This was an interesting word choice since the related Russian words *perspektivnyi / neperspektivnyi* were vintage statist terms for deciding the fates of financial investment in Soviet towns and villages. He was engaged in an everyday form of life science to increase his chances of becoming worthy of investment. Dmytro knew the level of internal radiation he had received on the basis of a count of aberrations in his chromosomes. He calculated his lost work capacity and amassed diagnoses. He referred to the radiation in his body as a "foreign burden" (*chuzhe hore*)—unnatural in origin and creating a new locus where "there is no peace." He was but one of many left to assess, but without an exact numerical equivalent for, his foreign burden. His narrative also suggests that technical measures used to define the biological effects of Chernobyl were malleable. They acquired different values over time depending on the contexts of their use.

What is the relationship between individual suffering caused by the Chernobyl accident and the technical measures and scales of expertise used to assess radiation-related biological injury? In this chapter, I trace the work of international scientific networks in patterning initial Soviet remediation strategies and public health responses. I explore key aspects of the initial Soviet management of the Chernobyl disaster and show how definitions of radiation-related injury were informed by an array of international scientific and political interests, and elaborated through a particular set of technical strategies. Accounts of injury were limited to biomedical measures derived from a group of acute accident victims in the first few weeks following the disaster. Such activities limited Soviet government liability for the many populations that were not screened or that were possibly made vulnerable to radiation-related injuries in the future.

Such interventions illustrate the ways experiences of illness are engendered and understood within the technical and political domains where they come to be addressed. With the collapse of authoritarian power, they clearly opened the way to a new form of politics based on the (unaccounted-for) scope of biological injury in the future. Adding further perspective on how this politics could take shape, we must also recognize that among radiation research scientists working in U.S. laboratories, there is considerable disagreement as to suitable parameters for interpreting radiation-induced biological risk in human populations. There is also disagreement among them as to how various experimental data may be unified in terms of a systematic theoretical approach (Chatterjee and Holley 1994:222). This lack of consensus at the basic science level deals a blow to the confidence that inspires expert claims to knowledge in the field. Ambiguities related to the interpretation of radiation-related physical damage subjected post-Chernobyl state interventions and medical surveillance to a variety of competing scientific and political interests. Scientists and government leaders garnered resources on the basis of those ambiguities to make claims for their own legitimacy and to push their scientific research and political agendas forward.

Saturated Grid

Scientist and Soviet political observer Zhores Medvedev has authoritatively detailed emergency measures taken after the Chernobyl accident, with particular emphasis on the first ten days, when officials were acting under the protection of a news blackout (1990:41).[2] In the following paragraphs, I want to convey something of the technical responses that ensued to assess a radioactive Chernobyl plume. The work of estimating its fallout was based upon approximations and semiempirical models. In retrospectively surveying this technical work and its inherent problems, we arrive at a finer map of a domain of anthropological inquiry. I approach this surveying work as a multilocale investigation of transnational, state, and local forces and actions that to some extent framed what we currently know and do not know about the human toll of the Chernobyl aftermath.

I turn first to the question of the size of the plume and how best to image it. Tom Sullivan is the former director of the Atmospheric Release Advisory Capability (ARAC) at Lawrence Livermore National Laboratory (LLNL) in Livermore, California. Sullivan's team worked with the U.S. Nuclear Regulatory Commission to assess the severity of the disaster. When I interviewed his research team in 1997, members were still refining estimates of the height of the Chernobyl explosion's plume.

Prior to Chernobyl, the ARAC researchers compiled meteorological data, satellite photos, wind patterns, and atmospheric activity data to model sizes and movements of nuclear plumes associated with above-ground American and Chinese nuclear weapons tests and the Three Mile Island accident. They developed computer codes calculating concentrations of contaminated material at a certain location; they tracked contaminated plumes for a distance and, based on certain meteorological conditions, estimated concentrations of radioactive contamination at any point in time along a trajectory.

The historical context of the Cold War prevented ARAC from modeling the movements of the Chernobyl plume in real time. Limitations on the sharing of sensitive data between Western and Soviet regimes made it difficult for U.S. scientists to locate the plume in Soviet air space. "The problem was there were no weather charts for that part of the world."[3] Additionally, the source of the plume was difficult to locate, since maps of Soviet nuclear installations were kept secret.

Sullivan's team relied on meteorological data showing the arrival of the plume in Sweden and used Swedish measurements to "invert the mathematics of the calculation. Given the concentration in Sweden . . . we estimated on the order of 2 megacuries of iodine and cesium were being released." Their mathematically generated trajectory showed the source of the plume to be "at or near the Baltics."[4]

After intense international pressure, the Soviets admitted that a catastrophic meltdown had occurred at Chernobyl. ARAC's computers were coded to map plumes within a limited spatial range. Once the team had refined their trajectory and located the source of the Chernobyl plume in northern Ukraine, Sullivan told me, his computer programs "weren't ready" for what they had found:

> We typically operated within a two-hundred-by-two-hundred-kilometer area. This area had been sufficient to model prior releases such as the one at Three Mile Island and American and Chinese nuclear weapons tests. Our first calculations were on a two-hundred-kilometer-square grid. We did the imaging near the Chernobyl plant, but the grid was so saturated, I mean, you couldn't even make sense of it because every place had these enormously high values—*they filled the whole grid, in every direction.* . . . Our codes were not prepared for an event of this magnitude.

Sullivan's team found something "far worse" than a meltdown. A runaway chain reaction of uranium-235 contributed to a powerful explosion, capable of rupturing any modern form of structural containment. "We knew there had been a core meltdown after Swedish scientists sampled the plume. They found mono-elemental particles of pure ruthenium, indicating that a meltdown of the reactor core had occurred."[5]

Sullivan's team conducted real-time atmospheric modeling of hazardous airborne materials. Computer codes were designed to do this modeling within a limited space. Assessment of the situation required a technical upgrade, which the Nuclear Regulatory Commission was ready to support. The team had initially tried to adjust the system to account for a larger territory "to get us into Scandinavia and Western Europe." In the second week following the explosion, there were reports that the radioactive plume had reached Japan. The team decided that they needed a hemispheric model.[6] According to Sullivan, "that was another step in changing the whole system and implementing new capabilities." New technologies allowed them to "drive [their] transport models and model the entire plume as it moved around the Northern Hemisphere."[7]

■ ■ ■

The Soviets rejected Western offers to help assess the meteorological situation. (Tom Sullivan offered his team's assistance through a Swedish intermediary, but his offer was refused.) Within the Soviet Union, a special military radiological service was charged with the task of monitoring radiation levels around the plant.[8] No information was released (Medvedev 1990:46). The service finally presented crude data, indicating the distribution of the plume within the Soviet Union, in its August 1986 report to the International Atomic Energy Agency (IAEA). In that report, the Soviet State Committee on the Utilization of Atomic Energy made a seemingly definite statement:

> None of the populations received high doses that would have resulted in acute radiation syndrome. . . . On the basis of an analysis of the radioactive contamination of the environment in the Zone, assessments were made of the actual and future radiation doses received by the populations of towns, villages, and other inhabited places. As a result of these and other measures, it proved possible to keep exposures within the established limits. (USSR State Committee on the Utilization of Atomic Energy 1986:38)

As Medvedev reported, radiation on the ground "was well in excess of the scales on the available dosimetric equipment" (1990:45). He also noted that "in some spots . . . it killed four hundred hectares of pine forest within a matter of days" (103). Skeptical of Soviet claims that no genetic effects from Chernobyl could ever occur, Medvedev wrote, "Pine trees may be more sensitive to radiation than oak trees, but they are much more resistant than rodents and vertebrates in general" (ibid.).

Buttressed by crude maps, the Soviet truth (as presented to the IAEA) prevailed above and beyond observable evidence and realities of the plume; that truth authorized a domain of government activity and limited intervention. Facts that did not support this domain were either disregarded or eliminated. For example, a follow-up report from the Soviet-American bioscientific collaboration (which I will discuss shortly) stated that "external measurements were unavailable at the time of the accident; they were either not designed for these levels of radiation or were destroyed or lost as a consequence of circumstances associated with this accident" (Baranov et al. 1989:205).[9]

My interview with Sullivan's ARAC team, together with the information detailed above, underscores the constructed nature of the unknown in this setting. A catastrophe whose scale was unimaginable, difficult to map, and "saturating" became *manageable* through a particular dynamic: nonknowledge became crucial to the deployment of authoritative knowledge, especially as it applied to the management of exposed populations.

Institute of Biophysics, Moscow

Information about the radioactive explosion and fire was transmitted to the Soviet Ministry of Health in Moscow. Angelina Guskova, chief radiologist of Clinic No. 6 of the Institute of Biophysics, was contacted one hour after the initial explosion, "on my phone at home, I was in my bed," she told me in 1996. Guskova and her colleague, Aleksandr Baranov, were charged with organizing emergency aid measures, providing biomedical care, treatment, and monitoring for the first victims of the disaster.

Guskova was trained as a hematologist and neurologist; both skills would serve her well in this situation. She has been a member of UN-SCEAR (UN Scientific Committee on the Effects of Atomic Radiation) since 1967, and she worked under Professor L. A. Ilyin, chairman of the Soviet Radiological Protection Board and director of the Institute of Biophysics in Moscow. Since the mid-1950s, Guskova and her colleagues had been engaged in the clinical study of radiation effects in humans. Prior to working at Clinic No. 6, she headed the Neurological Division of Medical Services of the Mayak nuclear plant, a munitions industry complex producing plutonium in the once closed city of Cheliabinsk, the capital of the southern Ural region. This area had been wrecked by two nuclear disasters, both of which were covered up by the Soviet government. The first one lasted a decade, when, beginning in 1951, the Mayak plant began dumping waste from nuclear bomb production into a small lake.[10] In 1957, a failure in the nuclear waste cooling system at the nearby Kyshtym plant released at least seventy tons of waste containing about twenty million curies of radioactivity—roughly one-fourth the amount released in the Chernobyl accident.

Guskova oversaw research involving two hundred individuals who became part of her official Acute Radiation Sickness (ARS) cohort. Until Chernobyl, this group was considered to be the largest cohort of ARS patients in the world.[11] Her clinical experience was multifaceted, reflecting the variety of radiation-related injuries these workers experienced, from direct contact with ionizing sources to inhalation and whole-body exposure. She developed surgical procedures for removing radiation-induced lesions and scars. She established medical classifications and methods for clinical observation of occupational radiation-related diseases. She developed the protocols for clinical monitoring and legal-medical evaluation. In short, Guskova "formulated radiobiological questions which could only be answered by the clinical observation [of man]" (1997:604).[12]

Guskova also formulated what she referred to as a "semi-empirical model" for estimating dose exposures in cases where doses were not known. This model was based on an examination of patients' external symptoms and linked the time of symptom appearance to an estimation of dose. Based on this model, she organized treatments and projected patients' recovery or death.[13] Acute radiation sickness occurs at dose ranges between 200 and 400 rem. At 400 rem, bone marrow failure sets in. Up to approximately 1,000 rem, there is a chance for survival with intensive treatment.

ARS consists of a series of clinical events ("syndromes"). These syndromes include the central nervous system syndrome, characterized by an onset of apathy, lethargy, seizures, ataxia, and prostration, appearing immediately after exposure. The gastrointestinal syndrome is characterized by anorexia, nausea, vomiting, fever, and severe systemic infections. These symptoms manifest within a few days to a few weeks after exposure. The hematopoietic or bone marrow syndrome is characterized by an absolute fall of the patient's peripheral lymphocyte and granulocyte count and by an increase in leukocyte counts. Changes in these blood indicators can occur within the first few hours of exposure; they can keep fluctuating over several months, and, some say, over an individual's lifetime.

Guskova went to meet the first planeload of possible ARS patients airlifted from the Chernobyl accident site and flown to Moscow on April 27, 1986. Initially, over four hundred people were taken from the disaster site to Clinic No. 6. This group consisted mainly of firemen who had extinguished fires in areas around the burning reactor core. Patients described this flame to me as a long green-blue radioactive phosphorescing column. In our interview, Guskova blamed the Soviet radiological service for failing at the outset to provide enough dose-related information for her to make an appropriate assessment of patients' doses. "We had patients expressing symptoms that were the same as symptoms of ARS, but we did not know the radiation situation." She relied on semiempirical models to assess patients' doses. The individuals selected exhibited symptoms of the central nervous system and gastrointestinal syndromes, including fevers, vomiting, and nausea. Changes in the blood composition of these patients were recorded within three days of exposure.[14]

Guskova's high-dose human know-how, for lack of a better phrase, was a unique achievement of Soviet radiation science. Chernobyl's scale and lethality posed challenges that Guskova and her colleagues had not confronted before. Guskova told me that these patients received much higher doses than those she had observed in previous accidents. In one scientific article, she referred to these doses as "overlethal" (1997). An intense graphite fire in the reactor's graphite-moderated core resulted in combined injuries (burns with symptoms of ARS), making categorization of the victims difficult and "complicat[ing] the nature and effectiveness of interventions" (Baranov et al. 1989:205).[15] The majority of deaths in the first three months after exposure were attributed to skin lesions (burns) that involved 50 percent of the body's total skin surface (Wagemaker et al. 1996:29).

Soviet-American Cooperation

In their 1971 monograph, *Radiation Sickness in Man*, Guskova and her collaborator Baysogolov conceptualized the organization of medical services for victims of large-scale nuclear catastrophes. They wrote that a "large number of victims introduces a number of forced corrections and apparently somewhat changes therapeutic arrangements." They considered the introduction of a triage mechanism essential because "detailed investigation is extremely limited in these cases." They also recommended "using more tranquilizers than is warranted under normal circumstances, considering the mass nature of the injuries and seriousness of the psychological situation" (245).

Guskova relied on a higher threshold dose to facilitate sorting patients at the Chernobyl plant in days following its explosion. A threshold dose is the dose limit above which radiation exposure would likely produce long-term biological effects. Symptoms of ARS begin to manifest themselves at 200 rem. Guskova set the dose at which patient recruitment would begin at roughly 250 rem. The use of a threshold generated an on-site social dynamic. For example, because preclinical examinations were limited, some of the initial selections were faulty. Indeed, during fieldwork in the Radiation Research Center, I met one man who had panicked over having to work at the disaster site. He self-induced vomiting and nausea and was among those airlifted to Clinic No. 6. Later he was released and never returned to the Zone.[16]

Such were the semiempirical models at work at the disaster site. Through their implementation, Guskova enacted a procedure, a set of "dividing practices" (Foucault 1984). She limited the group of victims who would be subject to early active therapy and delayed medical

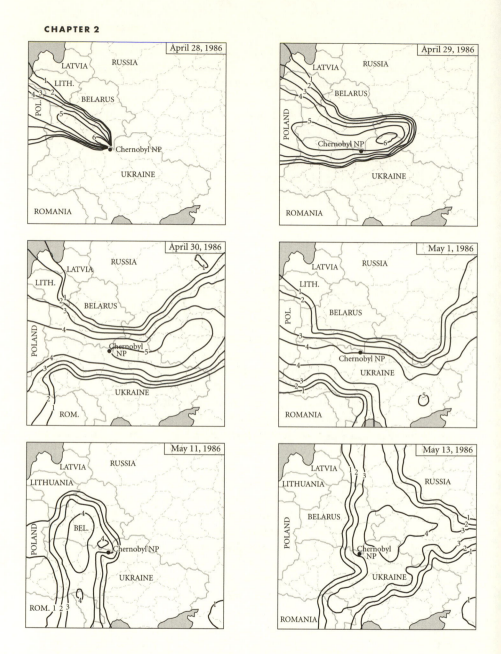

Figure 2. Volume of concentrations of cesium-137 in the air at different moments in time after the Chernobyl accident (month, day, hour) according to an atmospheric transfer model. The increase in isopleth number indicates a tenfold increase of concentration (World Health Organization 1996)

evaluation and therapies for workers who were potentially injured at doses below 250 rem. I met a person who estimated her dose to be 220 rem, 30 rem shy of the threshold, but who was excluded from the ARS cohort and therefore required to continue working at the disaster site.

■ ■ ■

Thousands of people like Dmytro were either voluntarily or involuntarily mobilized to work at the site under perilous circumstances. Administrators simultaneously withheld meteorological information and set occupational standards of radiological exposure artificially high. They also introduced a psychological technique in the effort to control perceptions of risk and interpretations of symptoms for anyone living "beneath" this threshold—evacuees, workers, and inhabitants of unmarked contaminated territories.

Declassified documents illustrate how this technique was introduced.[17] In late May 1986 and at the height of East-West bioscientific collaboration, leaders in the Soviet Health Ministry issued an order to Anatolii Romanenko, then Ukrainian health minister, who had not achieved full control over the activities of local medical personnel. Romanenko was ordered to make sure that Ukrainian republican scientific and clinical administrators used a medical diagnosis, "vegetovascular dystonia" (VvD), to filter out the majority of radiation-related medical claims. This condition is akin to panic disorder in the West, but its etiology is different. It was introduced into Soviet medical classification in the 1960s to account for environmental factors, including "mental factors, pollution, stress, or atmospheric factors," in the initiation of disease.[18] The external symptoms of VvD include anything from heart palpitations, sweating and tremors, nausea, and hypertension to hypotension and neurosis-like disorders, spasms, and seizures. VvD resembles the central nervous system syndrome of ARS, but its cause differs: one is radiation-induced, the other is "environmentally" induced. Romanenko's directive to Ukrainian medical personnel read as follows:

> This directive concerns diagnosing early symptoms of exposed persons who are in clinics and who do not show signs of ARS. Indicate the diagnosis of "vegetovascular dystonia" in the patient's medical record. Also indicate "vegetovascular dystonia" in the medical records of workers who are entering clinics for monitoring and *who have received the maximum allowable dose*. (Emphasis added)[19]

Six months after the Soviet Health Ministry issued this decree, the Ukrainian health minister confidently reported that his medical cadres had successfully fulfilled the command to enter the VvD diagnosis in the

43

medical records of the exposed. He also stated, "In the period following the disaster, 17,500 people have been hospitalized *with various illnesses*. Following the directive of the Soviet Ministry of Health, all persons from the Zone who are being hospitalized and who lack signs of immediate acute injuries *have received the diagnosis of vegetovascular dystonia* [emphasis added]."[20]

This official intervention reinforced a dynamic we have already seen at work with respect to Soviet radiological monitoring. Nonknowledge became crucial to the deployment of authoritative bioscientific knowledge. Technical laxity fit well with this process, as well as with the way the Soviet administrators attempted to adapt a general population to the postaccident situation (this process will be assessed in terms of its impact on individual lives in chapter 5).[21] A Union-wide clinic and research center was established in Kyiv in 1986 to monitor 600,000 children and adults. Romanenko became its acting director and held this position until 2000.

■ ■ ■

I turn now to the initial focus of Soviet bioscientific concerns and interventions and their political outcomes. Within two weeks of the disaster's onset, unprecedented Soviet-American bioscientific cooperation began. This endeavor, an example of high-profile "techno-diplomacy" at the end of the Cold War (Schweitzer 1989), became focused on a limited group of 237 acute accident victims. Their extreme injuries became the measure by which the scope of populationwide injury was defined, justifying immediate remedial actions. International experts used the accident context as a scientific "ready-made," evaluating preparedness for future accidents and accelerating bioscientific research.

This techno-diplomacy was initiated by Dr. Robert Gale, under the auspices of Armand Hammer. Gale was a leukemia specialist at the School of Medicine of the University of California at Los Angeles, who offered to conduct bone marrow transplants on workers who were irradiated in lethal doses and to treat less severe cases experimentally.[22]

Significantly, Gale's five-member team had little background in radiation medicine, radiobiology, or accident management. Richard Champlin was a bone marrow transplant specialist and a specialist in the treatment of leukemia. Paul Terasaki was a kidney transplant specialist involved in researching problems of donor-recipient matching. M. Ray Mickey was a leukemia specialist involved in problems of genetic (HLA) matching. Yair Reisner was a bone marrow transplant specialist researching hematopoietic reconstitution using stem cells and developing methods of obtaining high yields of bone marrow cells from murine models. All were part of a growing international network of transplant specialists, and some were affiliated with the International Bone Marrow Transplant Registry. Angelina Guskova's team consisted of twelve members, medical workers, leukemia and radiological specialists of Clinic No. 6.

Gale considered his cooperative biotechnological gesture a breakthrough in Soviet-American political relations. He felt that both parties stood to benefit: "I had a series of clicks in my mind, which was that, you know, this is exactly what we do every day. These guys don't have the resources to deal with it, and we do." He used the media attention on the Chernobyl affair to get the Soviets to agree to let his team in. "No one was going to believe what Gorbachev had to say about Chernobyl. I convinced them of that [in my negotiations]. . . . They had no credibility." Gorbachev personally invited the American specialists to conduct experimental bone marrow transplants, hoping to improve the image of Soviet remedial actions in the international media.[23] American biotechnological assistance was the only form of humanitarian help the Soviets agreed to accept in the initial crisis period.

Thirteen patients, with estimated doses ranging from 440 to 1,340 rem, were slated for high-profile bone marrow transplants. All had a high risk of dying from bone marrow failure. But there were risks inherent in the transplant procedures themselves. Immunities must be adequately suppressed for transplants to engraft. In clinical settings, adequate suppression is achieved under conditions where the administration of dose is controlled. It was particularly important for clinical examinations and dose assessments to be accurate in uncontrolled circumstances and where the radiological situation was not known. Dose miscalculations lead to misrepresentations of levels of immunosuppression. Inadequate immunosuppression leads to transplant rejection and to a host of unanticipated secondary diseases.

Questions of risk aside, both sides did indeed have much to gain from this short-term therapeutic collaboration. Gale's team and their major financial backer, Sandoz Corporation, got a jump start on the emerging biotechnological market in growth factor molecules that I will discuss shortly.[24] Guskova told me, "Contact with Gale upgraded our hematological department not in the problem of radiation, but in the problem of hematological disease and in the treatment of leukemia. We had contact with Dr. Hammer and needed the American specialists for treatment, equipment, diagnostics."

Yet the American team, unlike the Soviet team, was uninterested in long-term assessments of the health impact of Chernobyl. During our 1996 interview, Gale told me that his interests were short-term, and that the accidental situation offered his team a ready opportunity: "The Chernobyl accident for the firemen at the power plant was exactly what we do at the clinic every day. Potentially, there were patients with [leukemic] cancer exposed to acute whole body irradiation."

Gale told me that the way Guskova selected patients at the accident site was, in part, arbitrary. This arbitrariness generated a group of over four hundred patients. He said that his initial impulse was to help "what was not a clear number of acute radiation victims. . . . Actually, we brought genetically engineered molecules in here that had never been given to humans before, one of these cloned hematopoietic growth factors [rhGM-CSF].[25] We were working with it for about two years, for Sandoz actually." The bone marrow transplants were a venue for testing of a new product. The genetically engineered molecule was believed to be useful for treating bone marrow failure by accelerating the recovery of stem cells and other blood products. "We used hematopoietic growth factors subsequently in an accident in Brazil. The point, another idea I had at the time, was that it wasn't just useful for transplanting. We could use these growth factors for a whole bunch of things." Ethical standards in the United States allow for untried experimental treatments if a patient's life expectancy is minimal. That there was some uncertainty regarding the acute radiation sickness status of patients at the disaster site does raise questions about the ethics of research in this instance.[26]

In the United States, the in vitro activity of GM-CSF had been investigated intensively.[27] Little was known, however, about the activity of this protein molecule in vivo. Animal research had gone from murine to primate model testing. In monkeys lethally irradiated (900 rem), GM-CSF had been shown to promote bone marrow recovery by initiating stem cell growth. The product had not yet been tested on humans because of federal laws banning human experimentation (in this case, subjecting humans to lethal radiation doses). The American team ran GM-CSF trials on patients to see whether the molecule could stimulate recovery where recovery would otherwise be improbable.

When I asked Gale whether he felt that the product was successful, he said:

> It's very hard to say. All I can say is that we had about 499 people in the hospital, 29 died. So we were either incredibly skillful or incredibly lucky. I would favor incredibly lucky. . . . And most of the deaths we did have were not from bone marrow failure, which was the thing we were trying to treat. The deaths were mostly from burns or other injuries, not related to radiation. The same guy who was in the middle of the fire was the guy who got irradiated and who had steam fall over his

head. People don't understand that really, you can save them from one thing, only to die of another, and these things are tending to occur in the same people.

From his point of view, causes of death associated with the disaster except bone marrow failure became scientifically insignificant.

The Soviet-American team published the results of the transplants in the *Journal of American Medical Association*. Out of the thirteen transplant recipients, five died of burns, three of interstitial pneumonitis, two of graft-versus-host disease, and one of renal failure and respiratory distress. Two survived. The Soviet team later criticized Gale's drive to conduct bone marrow transplants. The team published in *Hematologiia I Transfuziologiia*, without including the American participants' names in the list of contributors. The American team had introduced biological dosimetry using biological markers (such as chromosome aberrations of peripheral blood lymphocytes) rather than Guskova's symptom-based markers of estimating dose exposure. The Soviets reported that out of the thirteen, at least two who underwent bone marrow transplants died as a result of the inaccuracy "inherent in estimating doses by the use of biological parameters." Guskova told me that Gale was a "good hematologist but he projects knowing more than he does." The article criticized technological quick fixes and reaffirmed the value of the Soviet clinical model based on long-term observation and treatment of syndromes.

The success or failure of GM-CSF was never commented on directly in subsequent scientific articles. Soviet administrators, as documents show, were worried about sensationalism stemming from this human research (*Chornobyl'ska Tragediia* 1996:214). Judging from the lack of follow-up studies, the whole matter was dropped. But the authority of these initial interventions remained uncontested. A joint meeting in August 1986 between Soviet scientists and members of the International Atomic Energy Agency confirmed the scope of injury as being limited to the 237 cases of ARS. Thirteen patients received bone marrow transplants. Eleven died. In the next months, seventeen more ARS patients died. Two others were reported to have died from injuries unrelated to radiation exposure. By September, the death toll was thirty-one. The joint medical team, in its 1986 report to the IAEA, did not try to minimize the consequences of the accident. By 1987, neither Gale nor Guskova and colleagues commented on the possibly greater general health impact of the accident (Medvedev 1990:165).

In her clinic today, Guskova treats "mainly local skin burns." She also screens claims of radiation illnesses by all nuclear workers throughout Russia. Guskova told me that she was a strong advocate of rehabilitation, and that typically her patients "recovered within two years only if

47

patients help in the process." She expected patients to "react and work." She made a distinction between the workers she immediately registered as sick and the subsequent six hundred thousand workers sent into the Zone. Her original patients could recover. Her new patients "are psychological." She blames these patients for impeding physicians' efforts in the recovery process. "The new patients don't wish to recover." For her, the real cause of their illness is not radiation but the loss of a work ethic and of *lichnost'*—a Russian word denoting a virtuous personality and often associated with a desire to work. She connected the illnesses of these new patients with a "struggle for power and material resources related to the disaster" (1995:23) and downplayed their symptoms as nonradiogenic. She summarized their medical particularities by stating that "there have been no new cases of ARS; but social, psychological, economic problems facilitate psychosomatic realizations that result in light changes in cardiovascular regulation and psychosomatic and neurotic realizations." In Guskova's Soviet model of health, such "realizations" become the readable equivalent of social vice and individual weakness; the desire to work and the possession of *lichnost'* counteract any individual tendencies toward physiological vulnerability.

For his part, Gale went further in annulling the medical significance of the event. During our 1996 interview he noted that with the exception of those initial ARS patients he attempted to treat, from a medical point of view, "Basically nothing happened here. Nothing happened here . . . and nothing is going to happen here."

■ ■ ■

In completing their containment mission, international experts and Soviet administrators had internationalized the problem of radiation protection. In generalizing, they redefined the problem in abstract terms, removing it from the human horror of the immediate context. Only the experts, they claimed, could make objective sense of the situation by constructing parameters of biological risk and safety, assessing levels of individual and populationwide exposure, and, by extension, arbitrating emergent claims of illness. In the process of this internationalization, an internalization process ensued: the narrative of the human effects and the number of workers it took to contain environmental contamination at the accident site was relegated to the domestic sphere of Soviet state control.

The first half of this chapter traced the trajectory of Chernobyl's ill wind, showing how perception of that wind was reconfigured through a series of informational omissions, technical choices, semiempirical models, approximations, dividing practices, and interventions. Combined, these official practices, with international scientific assistance, produced a picture of a circumscribed biological reality. The biological effects of

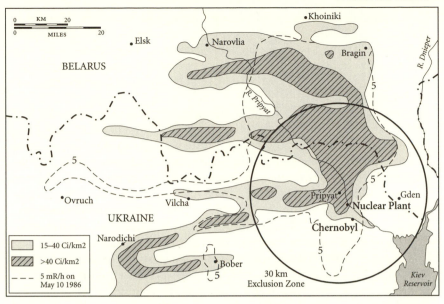

FIGURE 3. Map of 30-km Exclusion Zone, showing levels of cesium-137 contamination as measured in 1988 (adapted from Medvedev 1990)

Chernobyl became inseparable from the political interventions that contained them.

Safe Living Politics

The Soviet period continued to be marked by controversy over the level at which the radiation threshold dose should be set. By March 1989, the first maps of the spread of contamination were published, and a "Safe Living Concept" was outlined for persons residing in contaminated zones beyond the Exclusion Zone in Belarus, Ukraine, and Russia. Under the concept, the threshold dose for populations was set at 35 rem over an average seventy-year life expectancy. Persons living in areas exceeding this lifetime threshold dose were eligible to receive health and housing benefits elsewhere. Throughout the Soviet period, an image of containment was partially achieved through selective resettlements and territorial delineations of contaminated zones.

The Ukrainian state inherited a technically unresolved and socially volatile Chernobyl aftermath. By 1991, it had declared independence from the former Soviet Union and took on responsibility for the maintenance of the damaged reactor and for ongoing containment strategies. The beginning of the Ukrainian administration of Chernobyl was characterized

49

by a dramatic lowering of the lifetime threshold dose. The Ukrainian version of the Safe Living Concept was part of a first set of laws formulated by the new independent Parliament. "We agreed that over seventy years, a person's dose could not exceed 0.1 rem per year."[28] The Ukrainians claimed their own expertise and introduced a new standard for biological safety.

These claims and new standards became part of a politics of national autonomy. Their social effects will be considered in more detail in subsequent chapters. In sum, Soviet interventions sought to provide technical solutions to the problem of political disorder. A relatively high threshold dose regulated levels of state intervention and liability and limited the size of populations considered to be at risk. Below this threshold, clinically observable effects were deemed insignificant. In such a technical universe, key ethical questions about the health effects of Chernobyl were evaded. Those questions concern the uncertainties around the fate of the cleanup workers—the so-called bio-robots—who were not airlifted to Moscow and continued to work in the Zone. They also concern the significance of health effects among people who lived in contaminated areas and were resettled, or who continue to live in contaminated areas.

In the remainder of this chapter, I continue to elucidate the values that are both implicit and explicit in technical responses to Chernobyl, this time by turning attention to the mainly American experts who took part in subsequent assessments of the toll of the aftermath. In the post-Chernobyl context and in meetings with Soviet colleagues, radiation safety experts affiliated with the International Atomic Energy Agency made assessments of the health effects of Chernobyl-related radiation exposure, which, among other things, tended to undercut the veracity of local scientific claims of radiation-induced damage. My concern here is not to reiterate the story of their complicity with Soviet attempts to downplay the scale of the disaster but to reexamine the basis of expert authority more generally. Experts promoted their authority, in part, on the basis of their allegedly firm grasp of what constituted proper evidence of Chernobyl-related damage. One goal of their mission was to instruct their Soviet counterparts on how to evaluate the kind of damage that was considered relevant to expert assessment; it was to turn their disaster-fatigued Soviet counterparts into "valid witnesses" of the disaster's human toll, and to make the witnessing of the uninitiated marginal and invalid (Shapin and Schaffer 1985). I counterpose this expertise with the ways other valid witnesses—namely, basic scientists working in U.S. radiation laboratories, who are less invested in the arts of Chernobyl truth making—think about the human health effects of radiation induction. In this light, I look at scientific constructions of biological risk and safety and situate them in the context of their laboratory production and testing. In the process, we learn about the extent to which ways of monitoring radiation's health effects are contested at the level of basic science research, and how dependent such research is on the political and economic arenas in which knowledge of radiation risk and safety is brokered.

■ ■ ■

The journal *Nature* published an editorial on the tenth anniversary of Chernobyl urging politicians to make funds available for further studies of the unique scientific and medical experiment afforded by that nuclear accident ("Chernobyl's Legacy" 1996:653). Chernobyl's "legacy to science" is knowledge of the impact of radiation on living organisms, and this, according to the editor, should not be lost. Some of the immediate lessons learned, the editorial notes, include the knowledge that bone marrow transplantations for patients with acute radiation sickness are relatively ineffective; that previous calculations of the impact of likely dose exposures were correct (this claim is questionable); and that taking measures to prevent thyroid cancers resulting from radioactive iodine exposure can be effective. Moreover, an alleged absence, to date, of documented cases of leukemia among exposed groups is also consistent with predicted dose-response relationships based on relatively low exposure to cesium in the ground. The editorial calls for continued research on the Chernobyl accident aimed at achieving greater refinement in approaches to nuclear risk management (especially with regard to the massive effort to clean up nuclear facilities in the United States). Supporting arguments are framed in the language of a cost-benefit analysis.

> [The extent of the effort] depends critically on the social acceptability of radiation levels that will be left after the clean-up has been completed. If there is a threshold [dose] below which radiation has no long-term biological effect, will much be gained by achieving complete elimination? Conversely, if no threshold [dose] exists, can the cost of eliminating radiation risks entirely be justified by the likely medical benefits if these are, ultimately, insignificantly small? (653)

Such statements elucidate the capitalist social contexts and values that are implicit and explicit in data-production with respect to radiation-contaminated sites. More broadly, they illustrate how interrelated spheres of scientific, social, and economic production are in the area of radiation safety. In later chapters, we will see in Ukraine how the radiation sciences and safety issues (as applied to Chernobyl) are embedded in particular forms of institutional and individual politics of nationhood, market economic policies, and the welfare struggles of post-Soviet citizens. In the United States (as exemplified by the editorial in *Nature*), the aims of such sciences are similarly multipurpose. They are to refine knowledge about the impact of radiation on living organisms, offer methods for evaluating

51

epidemiological intervention, and, most important, to develop an empirical database for rationalizing the cost-effectiveness and potential medical benefits of cleanup efforts—for all of which, incidentally, Chernobyl is named a "living laboratory."[29]

Within radiobiological laboratories, the impact of radiation induction on experimental animals or human cells is described in terms of a biological event. Indicators of biological events, or "biomonitors" (for example, dosage, type of damage, repair, fixation, cell cycle status, differentiation status, microenvironment, hormonal status, and the age of the organism), help identify stages of a carcinogenetic process in experimental animals and inform an etiology of occupationally induced cancers in humans. These indicators are part of the technical means for monitoring exposed populations. However, values internal to the strategies and goals of scientific institutions often drive the selection of the biological sites considered (for example, a cleft palate versus a genetic mutation on chromosome 2). The particular "site" chosen influences the interpretation of the medical consequences of a radiation exposure event; this interpretation, in turn, may serve as a measure for what counts as normal life and a normal life expectancy in populations identified as being at risk.

In the paragraphs that follow, I describe how the issue of biomonitoring for populations was introduced and exchanged between Western (mainly American) and Soviet-bloc scientists in the context of the International Chernobyl Project (1991).[30]

In October 1989, three years after the accident, the Soviet government requested assistance from the International Atomic Energy Agency (IAEA) to coordinate an international expert assessment of the Soviet Safe Living Concept, which the government had introduced in the previous year, for inhabitants of contaminated areas. A meeting held in Vienna in May 1991 brought the authority of the world's leading scientists and specialists to bear on the expressed task of instilling confidence in the affected populations, with the objective of stamping out the "obscurantism" and "sensationalism" that arose concerning the accident's medical effects. The project had the exclusive aims of radiation protection and the restoration of public trust among unresettled populations; it "sought to provide a sound scientific basis for a decision yet to be made." It noted that a "poor understanding in affected areas of the scientific principles underlying radiation and its effects . . . was the root of many medical and social problems observed" (IAEA 1991a:6). An official report, published later that year, accentuated state-of-the-art measures that were being taken into account in the assessment of the accident's long-term health effects.

On the one hand, the Soviet scientists claimed to have lacked an acceptable system of biodosimetry (a system of internal biological dose calculation and estimation).[31] The United States, on the other hand, had sponsored sustained research in biodosimetry and radiation health effects since the bombings of Hiroshima and Nagasaki, and in the wake of nuclear weapons testing, human experimentation, and various medical radiological procedures. One immediate effect of this scientific collaboration was the transference of Western biodosimetric technologies to the Soviets as part of consensus-building efforts. Another effect of this collaboration was the international confirmation (under severe public criticism) of Soviet selective remediation strategies and the Safe Living Concept.

Some issues remained unsolved, however. How were the scientists to convert the scale of the Chernobyl accident into plausible biodosimetric data five years after the event? Recall that in the radiobiological experimental context, data are unique to the indicators and the biological events that are selected. Similarly, biodosimetric systems are interpretive measures associated with specific radiation exposure events (the first biodosimetric system related to Hiroshima was the result of roughly twenty years of research on human subjects). Not surprisingly, the Vienna meeting was marked by negotiations over the value of individual radiobiological claims. The specifics of where, when, and how researchers should medically interpret radiation induction in biological samples taken from affected individuals became a source of contention and scientific collaboration. This was especially true with respect to the question of how human inhalation of hot particles (radioactive dust and debris from the reactor core) could best be addressed. The following samples of the discussions among the scientists provide a sense of this give-and-take.

E. P. Petryaev of the Department of Radiation Chemistry, State University of Belarus, presented photographs of necrosed lung tissue of Chernobyl accident cleanup workers who were not included in the official patient cohort, and who had died.

> The content of these [hot] particles on the surface varies but attains very high levels, particularly for samples from the Zone where we observed up to 10 particles per cm^2. . . . So far we have studied the autopsy material from the lungs from about 300 people whose deaths were due to various causes. Samples of lung were also obtained after operations. A definite relationship between the content of particles and the concentration of radioactive substances on the surface was found. . . . , hot particles were found in the lungs in about 70% of the 300 samples. (IAEA 1991b:27)

Petryaev's claims were essentially dismissed as *irrelevant* to radiation protection. L. R. Anspaugh of the IAEA and Lawrence Livermore National Laboratory of the United States responded:

> After several trips to the USSR, I am absolutely convinced that 'hot particles' do exist. I have certainly seen many radiographs in several of the laboratories I visited.

> The really important question is: What do they mean in terms of dose and health effects? . . . , the next important questions are: How many of them are there and how much activity is in the lung? (Ibid.)

IAEA experts' dismissive approach should not be surprising as one of their concerns is to advance nuclear energy. But there are ethical issues for which experts need to be held accountable in their readiness to ignore the significance of raw tissue data and then to blame the local scientists for an alleged inadequate knowledge of radiation protection. In this vein, Anspaugh shifted discussion away from the samples to more abstract questions of "counting the hot particles." A. J. Gonzalez of the Division of Nuclear Safety of the IAEA, Vienna, seconded Anspaugh's move:

> At the risk of repetition, I should say that there is a very clear recommendation . . . which basically indicates that a given activity incorporated into a tissue as hot particles carries less risk of cancer induction than the same activity uniformly distributed in such tissue. . . . If the activity is uniformly distributed, the number of target cells will be higher, and therefore the risk will also be higher. The photographs showing tissues with necrosis due to hot particles presented here are very impressive *but have little relevance to radiation protection.* (Ibid.:28; emphasis added)

There was a striking variety in the kinds of evidence submitted by Soviet and Western scientists to support their differing interpretations of the Chernobyl event's health effects. For local scientists, photographs of necrosed lung tissue mattered most. For IAEA experts, it was the number of "potentially activated target cells." Implicit was a consensual valorization of public health, understood in specific terms: a normative notion of risk was quantified in the correct biological contexts (target cells, as opposed to necrosed lungs), with the correct biological value, and in the correct representational form.

The exchange of measures noted above occurred in a context of humanitarian relief established by the United Nations and its subsidiary groups. Accordingly, an international Chernobyl Fund was set up in 1991 to provide monitoring and health care for the people still residing in contaminated zones. Representatives of the World Health Organization who took part in the International Chernobyl Project recommended the following: a long-term epidemiological study, an investigation of the psychosocial health effects, a retrospective analysis of dose intake to sharpen the biodosimetry related to those effects, and the establishment of radiation health data banks.

By 1995, however, the Chernobyl Fund was out of money. The under-secretary-general for humanitarian affairs of the United Nations and spokesman for the fund stated that in most catastrophes, officials can sooner or later see an end to suffering and dislocation. "It is not easy to see an end here. . . . In fact, we don't really know where we are in the process" (Crossette 1995:A11). According to one scientist affiliated with the project, most American life scientists interested in Chernobyl are finding less and less funding for studies related to that accident.

Life Sciences

> Life overcomes error through further trials
> (and by error I mean simply a dead end).
> (Canguilhem 1994:318)[32]

When I first traveled to Kyiv in 1992, I had to consider seriously some of the unknowns related to this ethnographic work, especially the possibility of my own exposure to low-level radiation and related risks. The U.S. State Department's travel advisories made no mention of risk; Ukraine was and is deemed safe for travel. In a 1988 article in *Science*, Anspaugh and colleagues of Lawrence Livermore National Laboratory were already saying: "Probably no adverse health effects will be manifest by epidemiological analysis in the remainder of the Soviet population or the rest of the world. Projections of excess cancer risk for the Northern Hemisphere range from an incremental increase of 0% to 0.003%" (1988:1518).[33] An additional 0.003 percent of cancer deaths caused by Chernobyl among the approximately five billion residents of the Northern Hemisphere would be about 150,000 deaths. When I talked about safety measures with a representative of the World Health Organization, I was told that "flying to Denver was more dangerous in terms of radiation exposure than entering Ukraine." That same year (1993), I bought a personal dosimeter and wore it on my chest all summer. It registered nothing unusual.

Nevertheless, there are currently almost no foolproof measures for ascertaining claims regarding radiation (particularly low-dose) from Chernobyl. Biodosimetric systems have changed over time, depending on the nuclear event. For example, there is one system related to the bombings at Hiroshima, but for the Chernobyl accident, a different system is being devised. The absence of a standard measure of threshold dose and its biological relevance has serious consequences not only for interpreting the medical effects of exposure to radiation released during the Chernobyl accident but also for the acceptance of the medical status of that nuclear event itself.[34] In addition, the absence of an agreed-upon set of biological criteria in experimental organisms makes it difficult for scientists to scale up estimates of radiation effects for individuals and populations. Not only does the mutability of species of organisms differ, "but there are a number of intervening steps that will influence the frequency of mutations observed and. . . . the type of mutation event scored by a particular test will determine the mutability of the genetic endpoint screened" (Favor 1989:844). What is meant by genetic or biological endpoints?

To find out, during spring 1995, I attended weekly meetings of the Radiation Biology Group of the Life Sciences Division of the Lawrence Berkeley National Laboratory (LBL) on the University of California campus. At the time, this group consisted of radiation biologists, radiologists, and biophysicists, whose research methods aimed to represent quantified independent causal realities in the form of linear energy transfers (LETs), and the mechanisms of radiation damage and repair processes in a one-to-one linear model (that is, the dose-response curve). NASA funded the group's study of the health effects of protons and high-energy heavy ions of the kind encountered by astronauts in space travel, and the space agency also supports its efforts to define relevant experimental endpoints for carcinogenetic processes. The group relied heavily on the BEVALAC, a large-particle accelerator and source of LETs for animal experiments on the LBL campus.[35] At the weekly meetings, individual scientists made presentations on their work in radiation biology, cell death, and DNA damage related to cancer formation.

As part of experimental design, each investigator studies what is biologically turned on and off, and the types of genetic products produced, when LETs are applied at a specific rate and dose to experimental organisms, usually mice. LETs at the biological target are counted from the residual range of LBL's eighty-eight-inch cyclotron beam line. The mice are sacrificed, and the necessary biological material is harvested, frozen, sectioned, stained, mounted, and photographed. Reactivity to radiation exposure is measured by observed changes as biological events at selected endpoints: immunoreactivity of proteins and cell kill.

Other important endpoints include mechanisms of DNA repair after irradiation. Radiation induction is known to cause breaks in DNA, and so much of the experimental activity of the radiation biology group focuses on providing information on the induction of DNA damage in patented human cells by exposing those cells to high LETs and determining the extent to which that damage can be modified by natural DNA repair processes. After irradiation, researchers construct a dose-response curve by noting induction, cell survival, damage, and repair of DNA breaks according to LET dose. They measure breaks in the arms of specific chromosomes using techniques such as pulsed field gel electrophoresis and

Southern hybridization. Gene-specific probes are used to demonstrate biological "slow spots" and "hot spots" for repair.

Some of the rationale behind the investigation of DNA damage and repair relates to the current Department of Energy–specified need to identify biological forms of dose monitoring that could be used as a base for designating threshold measures for individuals and populations exposed at lower doses. The model assumes that biological monitors, if identified correctly, can predict future radiation-related health risks in an individual person or human population.

The certainties (considered in terms of endpoints where biological events occur, which can be scored as such) and uncertainties (rooted in assumptions in radiation biology that attempt to make the match between damage at endpoints and diseases in populations) combine so as to make the biodosimetric enterprise a source of proliferating questions through which more resources can be enrolled.

The import of basic research such as the kind sketched above is argued from the perspective of improving the accuracy of population-based epidemiological studies of radiation-related cancers: risk assessment for human carcinogenesis requires determining the levels at which DNA damage produces malignancy (Department of Energy 1993:3). Research into the basic response mechanisms of organisms after irradiation sheds light on unproven assumptions built into epidemiological extrapolations of health risks for nuclear workers, as well as for general populations. Improved understanding of the mechanisms of radiation carcinogenesis through basic research at the cellular and molecular level is essential to valid epidemiological extrapolation (ibid.).

The director of the LBL group is accountable to the goals of the NASA grant. He acknowledges the challenges facing radiobiologists in creating an integrated body of data about risk, noting the increasing volume of primary data. The director strongly encourages his group to produce theoretical frameworks for unifying various experimental data, especially regarding cancer formation. The weekly meetings were instituted to make that goal easier to achieve.[36]

While members of the group say they produce and study DNA and cell damage involved in particular cancer-selection processes, it is also true that individual scientists draw different conclusions about radiation's damaging effects at this level. As one researcher told me, "What one researcher says about radiation is not what another might say." Such differences challenge the notion of a single approach and present opportunities for further research. All the while the links between biological events in laboratories and courses of disease in populations are left unclear; at stake is the more immediate interest of finding legitimacy for one's own individual experimental work.

What is the link between experimental animals and human populations? To ask these scientists to relate their knowledge of the micro-levels of radiation-induced biological events to the macro-level projections of radiation risk for humans seemed out-of-field, although finding those associations was a part of their mission. Conversely, the director asked me several times what bearing his group's experimental investigations had on my work on Chernobyl. Perhaps this impatience points to the fact that his group's work is relevant only in a world of potential radiation exposure events.

Clearly, no coherent worldview, except that of cancer risk, links radiobiological bodies of data. Since 1902, when cancer risks were first attributed to overexposure to X rays, the U.S. government has spent $2 billion on research on the health effects of ionizing radiation, and more than eighty thousand scientific articles have been published on the subject (Yalow 1993:436). The radiobiology that induces illness through a single, direct-acting carcinogen introduced into experimental organisms in order to illuminate the biological parameters for the staging of cancer, and searches for forms of monitoring doses to guarantee a future health, is a science undergoing change. These approaches are no longer accepted as the exclusive grounds for predicting radiation risk to human life; their claims are being rescaled in the face of current developments related to the Genome Project and the growth of molecular biology. It is debatable to what extent such a rescaling has been part of a larger public health process in which there is an increasing institutional gap between diagnostics and therapeutics (Rabinow 1996a:100).[37] Predictive risk models, meanwhile, continue to be developed, transferred, and evaluated for their use or obsolescence.

Interestingly, the editor of a U.S.-based radiobiology journal, *Radiation Research*, recently bemoaned continued cuts in government funding of outstanding basic and applied problems in radiation in favor of support for the genome program at the Department of Energy. The government, the editor noted, has recently been ready to spend large sums of money looking back at studies that involved the development of isotopes, radiotherapy, and investigations of the potential harmful effects of radiation in humans. "It is ironic that there should be great concern about exposures in the past but a marked reduction of funds for research required for improving the recommendations about limits and safety that will protect people in the future" ("Some Material" 1996:145). What kind of matrix for the administration of life is in the making now?

Reflecting on a recent congressional mandate to monitor the effects of low-level radiation among American nuclear plant workers, physician and scientist Ron Jensen writes, "[I]t is clear that techniques are needed to assess the exposure and/or risk of genetic diseases associated with a broad range of contaminants" (Jensen et al. 1994:100). The cell and molecular biology laboratory he directed at the University of California collected blood samples from a variety of persons exposed to radiation, including Russian and Baltic cleanup workers sent to Chernobyl. The lab analyzed these samples as part of a validation study of a new biomonitor indicating radiation-induced somatic mutations in peripheral blood. Both he and his research technician are former associates of Lawrence Livermore National Laboratory (LLNL) where important human biomonitoring techniques related to radiation exposure are being continually refined.

Thus far, the most reliable and widely used technique involves scoring aberrations and their specific formations (translocations) in chromosomes, derived from the peripheral lymphocytes of irradiated organisms and revealed through a technique called fluorescence in situ hybridization (FISH) and chromosome-painting technology.[38] In this technique, a small sample of human blood is obtained from an occupationally exposed worker; lymphocytes are cultured, metaphase spreads are prepared on glass slides, and chromosomes are examined.

When I spoke with the technician about the FISH technique, she described the difficulties associated with its wide-scale application for occupationally exposed populations. According to her, the associated laboratory work is "tedious." To facilitate the task of scoring, the technician travels to LBL to use an automated microscope to help locate chromosomes on slides (at the time we spoke she was working with the blood samples of seventy X-ray technicians). The automated finder is designed to shift around the surface of the glass slide to find and focus on abnormalities and translocations that are highlighted by fluorescent stains of green, red, and yellow. The technician estimates that she scored over 54,000 metaphases (a metaphase is a particular phase of cell division) as part of her job. She continued, "Each worker will have about 1,000 metaphases. . . . They have selected chromosomes 1, 2, and 4 because they are the longest and represent about a third of the total genome." This cytogenetic technique has been transferred to and is being used in medical research institutes in Kyiv as partial support for a diagnosis of radiation-related abnormality.[39]

Risk In Vivo

Can the data obtained from this cytogenetic technique be scaled up to represent the total translocation frequency in the entire genome, as the authors claim? (Straume et al. 1993:176). State-of-the-art research on biomonitoring considers stem cells (vital for ongoing blood cell production) to be the better, if not the premier, internal monitor for representing biological events at low-dose exposures (Trosko 1993). Stem cells provide a different point of reference since the ability of the translocation frequencies in vivo to indicate dose and risk of the individual's developing radiation-induced cancer has not been rigorously established. According to one researcher, molecular biological techniques related to biomonitoring at stem cells are expected to allow for more informed evaluations of individual exposures and compensation claims related to leukemia and other types of cancer among U.S. nuclear facilities workers, provided their blood is stored first.

Such careful monitoring of exposures and claims, according to Robert Gale, the leukemia specialist who worked with Angelina Guskova in the initial Chernobyl intervention, could never be established in Ukraine—not only because of the lack of these technologies, but because political, economic, and social factors conspire to make the identification of radiogenic cancers "impossible." He argues, more generally, that it is impossible to detect statistically the stochastic-related increases in cancer deaths. Gale periodically reviews compensation lawsuits for a nuclear power plant in Sacramento. According to Gale,

> If a person who was exposed to radiation gets leukemia, it's not proof it's radiogenic. We have a terrible problem in the United States right now. We have 600,000 nuclear workers, you can say that 20–25 percent will die of cancer, normally, just like in the rest of the population. And every one of these workers is going to ascribe the cause of his cancer and death to radiation. And there is not going to be any way of convincing any one of them that it's not from that. And every one will be a lawsuit. No one imagined there would be 200,000 lawsuits.

Rather than focusing on those Ukrainians and Belarussians who will get cancer, Gale prefers to emphasize those who will not. "Even if you could show that a person with leukemia got 25 rads,[40] what does that mean? Most of the people who got 25 rads at Hiroshima didn't get leukemia. I think that it does this population a disservice by implying, just because you can prove that it might be possible, that this is a knowable thing."[41]

For the fraction of those U.S. nuclear workers who will get cancer and who might ascribe their cancer deaths to radiation, laboratory efforts to turn radiogenic cancers into a knowable thing continue to find government funding. A collaborative experiment testing stem cells as potential biomonitors is now underway. The links between individual genetic susceptibility and what radiation scientists regard as a known form of radiation-induced leukemia are being examined. The experimental subjects are mice altered by the addition of a specific human chromosome (this chromosome is the location for the individual susceptibility gene for the form of radiation-induced cancer under investigation). Under conditions of irradiation, susceptibility genes of these transgenic mice are turned on, initiating the radiation-induced cancer. Stem cells are isolated, and their ability to respond to increased radiation-induced biological loads is observed and graphed. Through a combination of molecular biological and genomic mapping techniques, these researchers hope to be able to monitor radiation-induced biological events and predict the outcome of radiation-induced cancer in exposed populations, while at the same time examining potential treatment interventions that could be transferable to exposed workers.

This combination of activities—all at the same stem cell site—points to an evolution in the forms of quantifying radiogenic cancer risk, from the monitoring of external radiation dose, to internal biological forms of monitoring dose, to productive internal biomonitors. Stem cells are now seen as holding the key to knowledge precisely because of their fundamental biological function, their inherent manipulability, and their capacity to elucidate the mechanisms of radiation-induced cancers—all in one site.

In the meantime, in Ukraine, the Chernobyl event and its errors constitute a new daily rational-technical reality that has mobilized lawmakers, groups of sufferers, radiation scientists, and health professionals. The deputy director of the Radiation Research Center noted the emergence of a "social Chernobyl"—evidenced by a perceived increase in psychosomatic illnesses and personality disorders among affected individuals and groups, and by an unprecedented increase in the number of citizens demanding medical services. It is important to keep asking which biological values, health provisions, and clinical practices can ethically be brought to bear on the complexity and magnitude of individual and social disturbances.

One immunologist, a senior member of a medical-labor committee charged with registering the connection of illness, disability, and death with ionizing radiation, works daily on the social welfare issues of his neurological patients at the center in Kyiv. He notes a current probabilistic measure:

> It seems to me that from the immunological point of view we have no specific radiation markers—we can only say that the probability of [neurological] disturbances is much higher or much lower. There are patients, though, who insist that they have specific illnesses linked to immunological deficiency, and that this is due to the influence of radiation. I don't know. *Who knows?* The specificity of this influence happens only during the moment of exposure, when radiation makes contact with immune cells or any other cells, membranes, and structures. And what comes after that exposure are the repairs, compensations, adaptations, and decompensations. All these reactions have their usual

rights of order, of physiological order. Say, for example, an evacuee from Prypiat' enters my office. I don't know in advance where he lives and I only have the laboratory tests before me. I ask him: Are you from Prypiat'? He looks surprised and responds, Why do you ask me? Then I respond, I see it, by your immunological report.

The claimant was surprised to learn that through his potentially damaged biology he had been accorded a new social status and identity. Before examining the sociopolitical dimensions of this biological identity, I step back in the following chapter to examine Chernobyl's reception in the immediate postsocialist period, when national politics focused on the reassessment of past Soviet abuses, and the writing of a Ukrainian history was underway. Individual narratives of experiences of Chernobyl critique the role of state power in everyday life. They tell us as much about the ways daily structures of Soviet authority collapsed as about the ongoing skepticism citizens felt toward new national authorities and their political promises to protect citizens' health. Definitions of health and disease move far beyond calculable physiological dimensions and become deeply entangled with historical and political determinations.

Chapter 3
Chernobyl in Historical Light

The sciences, politics, and international cooperations that informed Soviet state responses to Chernobyl produced an image of control over unpredictable and largely unassessed circumstances of risk. My focus has been to consider this absolute model of rational-technical control from an ethnographic perspective, to open that model up to scrutiny, and to identify the state and international processes through which the scale of the aftermath was defined, the ways radiation-related risk came to be a knowable (or not knowable) thing, and how populations at risk came to be identified. What was known or not known about the scale of the disaster was the result of policy choices, supported by a base of scientific knowledge that was provisional at best.

Yet on my first visit to Ukraine in 1992 I saw clearly that among general populations an "absolute" model of knowledge prevailed. Life was perceived to be in the hands of an invisible all-knowing expert, Soviet or otherwise, who arbitrarily gave or withheld information about the real human health risks stemming from the disaster. The apparent arbitrariness of the situation prompted people to search for other resources and clues to render an uncertain and unknowable world knowable and inhabitable in some way. This chapter draws out some of the prehistory of Chernobyl's reception in some aspects of Soviet-era life from the perspective of individuals and families living outside state-designated zones, in a time when bureaucratic lines between sufferers and nonsufferers were just beginning to be drawn, and when other informal structures of accountability regarding state-related abuses were in place. It illustrates how life narratives and family histories reflected a vexed and complex history of

Ukraine, but also how these histories informed interpretations of the Chernobyl experience. Privately held family accounts of war, famine, and Nazi occupation were circulated not only for purposes of mere recollection. They rendered more transparent and predictable the machinations of state power by which family members, because of their ethnicity, social status, or beliefs, were victimized.[1] Hanna Kozlova, an organizer of a group of resettled women who lobbied for additional medical treatments for their children, conveyed the corporeal nature of these historical narratives when she told me, "I am a Chernobyl resettler, my grandmother died fighting in World War II, her youngest sister was cannibalized in the famine of 1932." Her lineage of consumption, death, and exposure references bodies as both subjects and objects of state power. That lineage also attests to an underlying logic of a biological citizenship by which "the bare life of the citizen" is a life exposed to such power and is wholly imprinted by its history (Agamben 1998:9, Foucault 1984:83). While narratives of such life-and-death lineages provide a rationale for a history of state interventions in everyday living processes, they also reflect the insufficiency of language to account for their sheer brutality. From the perspective of one family, what follows is a story about how individuals reached the limits of their ability to reason, narrate, and project futures in the context of an invisible nuclear hazard.

How To Remember Then

It is 1992. The driver promised by Bila-Skala's city government has not shown up at the airport in Kyiv, so I reach the town by overnight train. Bila-Skala is located near the southwest border of Ukraine, and I have come here to participate in an archaeological project. It is not a very simple one, I soon find out. The city officials have opened up their Old City to a group of American students, and I am the first member of the group to arrive. As an architecture student, I plan to contribute my rendering skills to the project.

I am standing with a flashlight underneath a Dominican church and monastery in the center of the Old City of Bila-Skala. The original structure dates back to 1370. City government officials have designated the monastery and the crypts beneath the church as places where archaeological salvaging can begin. The nave of the church is used as a storage facility for carpentry tools and lumber. Humidity causes the remaining frescoes to crumble: they tumble to the ground at the slightest touch. Birds nest in the roof area. The crypts beneath the nave are about five feet high. There is a slender ray of light emanating from what appears to be a chute cut into the stone foundation. My flashlight illuminates adult human skeletons. In some vaults the skeletons appear intact; they are neatly stacked and covered in lime. In other vaults they lie disfigured and strewn around. There are skulls with evidence of bullet holes. I realize that these crypts are both a mass gravesite and a human skeletal dumpsite. Somehow, with the cover of an American college student nosing around, some old men start to gather above the crypt. I show them a skull with a bullet hole, and one man says that the hole is evidence of organized killing. "This person could have only been shot at close range." He tells me that the bones in the crypts were those of prisoners who were shot by retreating Nazi armies in 1943; the bones were moved from a nearby former Franciscan convent. In the thirties, the convent was converted into a Stalin-era deportation center.[2] In the forties, it became a Nazi prison. In the fifties, after World War II, it was converted into a textile factory. At that point, the remains of prisoners were deposited through the chutes and into the crypts of this church. (Bones were moved to other underground sites in the Old City as well.) The "neatly piled ones," as the man referred to the intact skeletons, were those of adults and children who had died in the cholera and tuberculosis epidemics and famine that ravaged this area in the early 1920s.[3] I urge the city officials to construct a memorial here, but they are not interested in the idea.

I abandon my architectural interests and turn to a historical study of the convent. I track down Mr. Pasichnyk, seventy-five years old, who was the engineer hired by the city government in 1950 to convert the Nazi prison into a textile factory. The factory, now abandoned, used to produce clothes for workers of a nearby tobacco factory and a spoon factory. Behind the bushy overgrowth sealing the entrances one can just barely make out a faded fresco of a medieval saint. Pasichnyk takes me to an opening in the building's floor, and he says, "The cellars, the cellars, I had to get to the cellars to build the supports for the textile presses. The foundations were very old, and when we were rebuilding . . . I will show you." He leads me to where he initially accessed the cellars. At this moment, Pasichnyk breaks down, "Dear heart," he says, "there were the cellars. They were laid out in order, all in order. The skulls of adults, the skulls of children. They were exposed for a month. Do you understand? And so I moved them to the cemetery and buried all of this."[4]

Pasichnyk carries a folder with him. After we examine the site, he opens the folder and shows me photos he took of the destruction of a site where the Jewish population in the area of Bila-Skala was executed. He kept careful photo documentation of the city's destruction of a Jewish cemetery, ordered by the city architect, for the purposes of road construction.

When we leave the building, I walk with Mr. Pasichnyk onto a dirt path. He points out a Polish Catholic Church, to which the original convent belonged, at the end of the path. Back in the late seventeenth century, during Turkish occupation of the area, a minaret had been attached to this church; in 1700 the Franciscans returned. This same church was converted into a planetarium during the Soviet period. Its large Baroque-style paintings of saints, hung from the walls of the central nave, were replaced by paintings of Galileo, Copernicus, and Darwin. Where a candle once hung high in the nave—in Catholic churches, a sign of God's eternal presence—there was now a Foucault's pendulum descending to the floor and demonstrating the earth's rotation.[5] Pasichnyk describes how even in the late 1980s, history students were being ordered to move the bones, literally, as "history lessons." Mr. Pasichnyk recollected his protesting upon seeing students do this work.

> The boys were throwing away bones from beneath one of our churches! Somehow, I started to feel faint, sick. I asked, "What are you boys doing?" "Cleaning the church!" they answered. "Are you preparing the bones for burial?" I asked. "They told us not to." Then I said, "You people are of the history department of our university? Ah! Let the man who ordered this cleaning busy himself with toilets. *Toi-lets*!"

The Old City's underground was turned into spaces for displaced, disheveled bones. They are reminders that structures of accountability for tragic historical events—which Pasichnyk himself was implicated in having destroyed by "cleaning" the bones out of the prison—remain hidden.[6] Against Pasichnyk's protest, the boys kept collecting the bones in bags and dumping them through chutes into the underground crypts, without proper burial. When he saw what the boys were doing, and the ill-shaped sacks they carried, Pasichnyk felt himself to be at the mercy of history and at its disposal once again.[7] It was no surprise that the city officials did not want to hear about erecting memorials in these dumpsites, given their recent use.

New City of Bila-Skala

Anna, aged twenty-three, has just been fired from the local institute where she was a much admired lecturer in Russian musical traditions. With a new national government in place, her talents are deemed disposable. She is quickly replaced by a lecturer in Ukrainian musical traditions. I meet Anna on the train from Kyiv to Bila-Skala. Uncertain about the future and angry about her dismissal, she is concerned about what will happen next in her life. Her English is perfect. In the course of our conversation Anna invites me to live with her and her parents during my stay in Bila-Skala.

The Strokat family lives in the "New City" of Bila-Skala where inhabitants reside and work in the city's sugar and brick factories. The textile factory was relocated from the Old City to the New City in the 1970s. Like most other families here, the Strokats reside in the tight quarters of a one-room Khrushchev-era block apartment. The family consists of three members: Vitalii, a Ukrainian and former official in the Soviet Army; Oksana, his wife, an Ossetian woman; and Anna, Oksana's daughter from a first marriage to a Russian man. The lives of Vitalii, Oksana, and Anna are interconnected with some of the last century's worst atrocities: the Nazi Holocaust, Stalinist repression, and the nuclear catastrophe at Chernobyl.[8]

Our so-called kitchen talks take place over the next three weeks. Kitchens are considered "the most sacred place in Russian/Soviet society," where opinions, anecdotes, and private indignations can be voiced (Ries 1997:21). In the context of Chernobyl, even this most sacral and protected frame of reference is exposed for its incapacity to repel what was widely interpreted as a further assault of a state apparatus. Not surprisingly, in that early period of collapse, nearly all the people with whom I spoke counted themselves as victims of the disaster. The Strokats own experiences illustrate the shock of Chernobyl in its lived inescapable sense. In articulating the imprint of this shock on their bodies, their narrative also provides a genealogical context for new kinds of political self-awareness and assertion that are both continuous with Soviet legacies and divergent from them.

Vitalii

Vitalii was forty-six years old when I met him in 1992, Oksana's second husband and Anna's stepfather. A native of Bila-Skala, he returned here after quitting the Soviet Army and the Communist Party in 1978. His English, like Anna's, is perfect. He taught himself by watching American films he received from friends in the military: these provided him with the opportunity to hear the spoken English word, with the out-of-sync Russian dubbing giving him the translation split seconds later. He states that he detests Ukrainians, and points to a picture of his Jewish mother and tells a story of her Ukrainian first husband's treachery.

Vitalii's mother escaped the city in 1941 when Nazi armies invaded southwestern Ukraine. They set up headquarters in Bila-Skala. In an attempt to survive the Nazi extermination of Jews in Bila-Skala, she fled to a village thirty miles to the north, leaving her young son with her first husband. She found refuge in the attic of the home of a Ukrainian woman whose name was Kulchyt'ska. After two years in hiding,

67

Vitalii's young mother returned to Bila-Skala, only to discover that her husband had given away their son to the Nazi prison in the Old City because he feared being incriminated as a protector of Jews. Vitalii shifted from contempt to nervous laughter as he told the story of his half brother's fate. Born in 1946, after the Nazis had retreated, Vitalii recalled that as a little boy he played near this very prison, running the length of its fortified walls and catching folded notes that remaining inmates cast out of small holes in the prison walls. Too young to read the notes, he speculated that they were to family members of the incarcerated prisoners.

Vitalii insists that I speak Russian, and only provisionally allows me to speak Ukrainian in his home. I explain to him that my Ukrainian is much better than my Russian. I was raised in a dual-language household of World War II Ukrainian refugees; they escaped their villages in the chaotic moment when the Soviet armies reclaimed territories of the western Ukraine from the Nazis in 1944. This clash afforded a small window of opportunity for those who felt their lives were threatened. In fact, it happened a day before my maternal grandmother was informed that she and her family would be deported by train to a forced labor camp in Siberia. Many of these war refugees lived in displaced persons camps in Germany and Austria set up by the American military. In 1949, and after rigorous health inspections, they were moved to the United States, where they became laborers in the postwar industrial boom. (As the story goes, my grandfather's first request that his family be moved to the United States was denied on account of his varicose veins.) Others remained in Western Europe or moved to Canada, Australia, or South America.

Stories about World War II formed an inescapable imaginary context for the children of those immigrants. Their stories, however, were overshadowed by the claims of Jewish communities that Ukrainians had participated in Nazi atrocities. Public allegations like these often raised the temperature of immigrants, who identified strongly with their ethnic background. Most of them had escaped with the retreating Nazis, they claimed, to avoid collectivization or deportation by the Soviets.

In Bila-Skala, the issue of language sparks a continuous fuss between the women and Vitalii. Communication becomes stilted, as my Russian is weak. As I recount the story of my grandparents' decision to flee during the war, Vitalii rethinks his essentialization of my identity. He simply asserts, in English, "They were smart." There is a sense of unexpected trust. For the moment, experiences of history are recontextualized to address the present. Here we are, the anonymous fragments of history, contracting that anonymity in English. We arrive at a moment in which both of us can indulge in harmless projections: Vitalii and Oksana were the "survivors" of . . . , and I was an "escapee" who returned to find out about. . . .

Contracts of Truth

Believing implies a pact. The act of believing dissimulation played an important role in the functioning of everyday life in Soviet society. Speaking half-truths became a distinctive practice in a social structure where power rested with a *nomenklatura* class and where, as Kharkhordin has shown, a system of "mutual horizontal surveillance" was put in place that "insured the dominance of the collective and the suppression of individual public disloyalty" (1999:277). By late socialism, the pretense of loyalty was aimed not so much at preserving the collective as at subverting the mechanisms of surveillance themselves (ibid.). I routinely document accounts of how habits of dissimulation turned some Soviets into moral accomplices in the Chernobyl context. One administrator in the Ukrainian republican Ministry of Social Welfare living in Kyiv told me that while she publicly participated in the state's ritualistic denials of the dangers of Chernobyl, she told her pregnant daughter to go to the Crimea for three months, far south of the nuclear epicenter. Another scientist told me how she distributed iodine tablets to friends' children while she was required to behave as if "radiation did not exist" in the scientific institute at which she worked.

In contrast to the public repression of interior states were the private ways that individuals drew together knowledge of historical accountability and truth. Michael Taussig identifies these contrasts between secrecy and truth in terms of the "public secret," or what is "generally known but for one reason or another, cannot be easily articulated" (1999:2). The public secret is about "knowing what not to know" in a social arena where "knowledge is power and the reality of illusion serves the social contract" (104). Taussig draws from an early-twentieth-century account of the Selk'nam who lived in the so-called Land of Fire, or Tierra del Fuego. Every few years, initiated men gathered for performances in which they "became" spirits. Women were conscripted as witnesses to the reality of these spirits (102) such that "men act[ed] as gods, women act[ed] as believers, and men mime[d] their belief of the women's believing" (1993). The penalty for unmasking the fabricated nature of these spirits was death. This theater, whose actors are organized on the basis of sexual difference, holds the key to social order as well as to sanctioned social violence.

In the private context of the kitchen, believing and witnessing are part of a ritualized theater aimed at the preservation of individuality (something the Strokats valued dearly in the context of Soviet society) and dignity. Vitalii consumed most of the attention of his wife and daughter, as well as my own. His passion for American music was our passion. Vitalii's long sermons about the virtues of bodybuilding were our interests. Vitalii became intensely popular in this small town when he single-handedly cleared away the debris from the first floor of a housing block and opened his own weight-training facility, the first one, he claimed, in southwestern Ukraine. He built from scratch, and with the help of a few treasured American bodybuilding magazines, barbells, lifts, and presses. This facility attracted men and women from all over the city and continues to produce self-confident bodies. Often young men and women arrived at the *kvartyra* (apartment) to pick up bodybuilding journals that Vitalii acquired through friends. Vitalii speaks of the bodies he trains with a fatherly pride. Two summers later he would lament the fact that the very people he had trained became heavily involved in mafia activities in the city. As one man told me on the train from Kyiv to Bila-Skala, "We now live under the rule of the physical man."

With Oksana and Anna, I would often sit and watch Vitalii's American videotapes. He was also able to buy Western-looking clothes that were smuggled from Turkey and sold in the market in Bila-Skala. The women often watched Vitalii get dressed in his finest outfits and shoes, in preparation for walking out on the street. As he observed himself in the mirror, we chuckled among ourselves in the kitchen over the time and energy Vitalii expended on this daily ritual. Vitalii admired the images of American bodybuilding journals and films. He thought of these images as empowering, and he wanted to embody them, even if from a distance. But on the main street of the New City, in 1992, he was anomalous and anonymous. On my daily return from the Old City, I would often find Vitalii standing in the street, looking somewhat aimless. No public space was available (except the spaces that he built himself) where Vitalii could feel like the person he wanted to be or felt himself to be. In subsequent years, Vitalii rarely left the house. He perceived his health to be deteriorating. In the context of heightened criminality and hopelessness, Vitalii's "America" became the ruin of yet another dreamed existence.

Oksana

Oksana, Vitalii's wife, was forty-seven years old in 1992. She was born in an Eastern Siberian labor camp. Oksana's father, as a young student in Tbilisi, allegedly vandalized a portrait of Stalin in a lecture hall at the university. He was carted off on a train to Khabarovsk along with five other students, including the student who had informed on them to the

70

state police. Oksana explained that, in a fit of rage, her father and the four others strangled the traitor and threw his body off the train. As Oksana told this story, her daughter Anna kept a stern face and nodded in a matter-of-fact way, while interjecting, "Yes, yes." I inquired about the moral ramifications of murder, but Anna retained her upright posture (her civilized composure) and insisted that her grandfather's actions had been the correct and only course available to him.

Gestures of enactment—Oksana's hands positioned for the act of murder, Vitalii's assortment of poses on the street and in the kitchen—were moral acts that were played out often. The moral "implications" of these enactments, or their verisimilitude, were negligible considerations. Rather, these enactments required believers—silent nods of the head, agreements. These believing acts were part of a familial repertoire guaranteeing access to feelings and desires that were impractical elsewhere.

There were different stakes in my relationship with Oksana. We were both women and operated as women in the household when Vitalii was around. During his absence, we talked about issues related almost exclusively to motherhood and sex. It seemed evident that Oksana and Anna were very interested in what an American woman had to say about these issues. In the course of one kitchen talk with Oksana and Anna, I raised the issue of abortion. "How do women perceive it?" I asked them. "It is common, but no one really talks about it," Anna answered. I asked, "Is it considered safe?" Anna replied, "Women do what they have to do." I realized that Anna really wanted to avoid the issue. But as her mother cooked with her back turned to us, Anna quickly leaned across the table and whispered to me, "She has had nineteen abortions." I whispered back in shock, "What? Why?" I was caught between two worlds—American moral and medical terms ("good or bad," "safe or unsafe")—and the other terms that Anna's "public" lack of response and whispered private response seemed to suggest. But what were these other terms? Anna seemed caught between two worlds as well: the world of the believer, where a history of nineteen abortions was considered acceptable, even normal; and the shock that she shared with me across the table, of knowing that her mother had physically endured so many repeated and often brutal abortions. Oksana reasoned that a good sexual rapport was important to a stable relationship; she refused to use contraceptives. (This is what she told me, but I had been told by her daughter that contraceptives were not available in Bila-Skala.) Abortion is the only form of contraception, and access to it is easy.[9]

Often, Oksana and Anna engaged in verbal fencing. Oksana often joked that she had never wanted Anna, that Anna was a problem child. Anna, a prolific reader, reminded Oksana how often she misunderstood Russian literature. When the question of children came up, we exchanged opinions about bearing children (how many? when? the right man?). Oksana seemed to want to steer the conversation and offered advice based on her experiences with men and marriage. After divorcing her first husband, Oksana had married Vitalii. Oksana was proud of the fact that Vitalii had accepted Anna "as his own." I asked her, "Have you ever thought of having children with Vitalii?" Oksana answered self-assuredly, "Never." I asked, "Why not?" She replied, "Because I didn't want him to love our child more than Anna. I didn't want instability or conflict within this household."

Oksana continued now in a somewhat moralizing tone and asked me, "Do you know how many abortions I have had for this?" I took a chance and answered candidly, "Nineteen." Oksana responded, "Almost twenty." She had made her very personal bargain with her own body public. I doubt that Oksana's assertion had any relation to the pervasive hero-mother image in Soviet ideology. Instead, she was telling Anna and me not to pass secrets in the kitchen. We had violated a public code of conduct: a contract of consensus aimed at preserving dignity. (This discussion would never have happened in the presence of Vitalii; Oksana told me that he simply does not know.)

Anna

In the course of a kitchen conversation, I asked to see pictures of the family from previous years. Pictures of the family's life in Irkutsk, where Vitalii had been stationed, were strewn all over the table. All three family members were present. From this mound of photos, Anna selected a picture of herself as a young teenager. I was struck by this image—Anna had deep-set blue eyes and long braids falling to her waist. After commenting on how stunning she looked, I asked Anna, "Why did you cut your hair?" Anna became uncomfortable and replied, "I didn't cut my braids, I pulled them out of my head with my hands the day of the Chernobyl incident." Her hands mimicked the motion of pulling hair.

She continued, "At the time we did not know what caused this. I stood in this kitchen as we are now, with my braids in my hands." Anna cupped her hands as if holding her braids. Vitalii left the kitchen with a look of disgust. Oksana kept a stern face and nodded in a matter-of-fact way while dutifully preparing food. It was her turn to believe and to act in accordance with a public code. Then the nods of the head and the upright posture disappeared. She turned away from the stove, leaned over the kitchen table intently, and advanced the open palm of her hand toward her daughter's face, saying to me, "Do you see what *they* have done?"

There was a long pause after Oksana's incriminating assertion. What had Oksana invited me to witness? Before the Chernobyl nuclear disaster, it had been more clear who *they* were—the Soviet state apparatus. After the Chernobyl disaster, *they* entered a private zone. *They* had made their visible mark on Anna—there was no choice but to witness. At the moment when Oksana asked me compellingly to see what they had done, it was not only an accident that she was talking about. She brought into relief her own life, her costly efforts to keep the household stable and guarantee Anna a father. Chernobyl undermined the ability of this internal culture to foster and preserve the dignity of its members. In this instance, that culture of belief was revealed as a "monstrous nothing" (Kristeva 1989:223), inadequate to keep the system out.

Oksana and Anna began to argue over the precise cause of the accident.

"Who are *they*, who is to blame?" I asked. "Scientists were performing an experiment at the Chernobyl plant, they were testing its capacity, and it blew." Anna responded matter-of-factly, overriding her mother's skepticism about the state's role in the accident. Anna argued until she prevailed (meaning she silenced the witness). Her arguments were based on what she had seen on television, which contradicted initial allegations that the accident was the fault of an incompetent Ukrainian technician (Dobbs 1992:A12). Anna needed believers, in this case her mother and me. She wanted us to participate in the established structure of familial belief. Within this structure, Oksana and I were supposed to act as believers, and Anna was to mime her belief in our believing.

I was the first "outsider" to whom Anna told this story. Oksana was silent while I held the look of disbelief. Anna's task was to make a believer out of me, to incorporate me into her world. We arrived at a moment when the violence of Chernobyl could have been absorbed and normalized within the *kvartyra*. My presence at the scene deprived Anna of the possibility of making sense of this traumatic event in the way her parents could make sense of theirs.

Political and economic conditions in the post-Soviet era continue to lead individuals to neglect their bodies in exchange for something: the stability of a household, authority over the "facts," survival. Such forms of reasoning are elementary to the life of public secrets. They involve striking bargains and making them public in the kitchen. The price of this bargain fluctuates depending on whether one is a man, a woman, or a child. It is dependent on available symbols of, for example, what it means to be a good mother or a potent man, and the personal costs involved in becoming those things.

In the case of Oksana, however, motherhood acts as a cultural medium that diffuses the activity of hurting one's body, a hurt that is inflicted by a culture which, to some extent, relies on the commonplaceness of that hurt. But Anna, who experienced a loss of control over her body at the time of Chernobyl accident, can directly relate her lack of control to a catastrophic instance that is indiscernible in its future effects. Anna's experience is socially and symbolically new; she has not chosen this for herself as her mother has chosen to have repeated abortions to "save Anna." Anna had no culturally available symbols to lessen her pain, to protect her emotions. The affirmative nods-of-the-head disappeared. With the effects of radiation still unknown, invisible, and the responsibility for the accident unclear, who or what is Anna to bargain with?

Anna's life had come full circle in a historical sense. It was her unfortunate turn to become both the subject and the object of a familiar life-and-death lineage. This repetition of destiny—its truths and pains—constitute a road on which we can trace the tragic force of Anna's narration of the Chernobyl incident.

■ ■ ■

The explosion at Chernobyl occurred on April 26. Official governmental announcements of the explosion came on May 14. Vitalii described the plans his family had made to travel to Kyiv in order for Anna to undergo a kidney operation the night of May 7. (No medical treatment was available in Bila-Skala for Anna's nephritis.) The Strokats boarded an overnight train to Kyiv. No word about the disaster had reached Bila-Skala. The nuclear plume began to pass over the city on May 1. In Kyiv word had already spread in the form of very brief reports published in and around the Zone, by word of mouth from administrators and Zone cleanup workers to family members, through foreign reports, and from European tourists who were told by their embassies to evacuate. The Strokats, traveling eight hours from a remote southwestern corner of Ukraine, said that they had no idea of what caused Anna's hair to fall out when it did, nor did they imagine that by traveling to Kyiv they were getting closer to the alleged source of their misery.

Such differences in access to information between the tourists, for example, and the average Soviet citizen speak to a radical disconnectedness between rational-technical knowledge and social conduct at the time of the disaster and thereafter. Only in hindsight did the Strokats link Anna's sudden loss of her hair with radiation. But even here their judgments were off. It was later determined that a chemical explosion occurring at approximately the same time as Chernobyl in the southwestern town of Chernivtsi caused the hair of many local people, particularly children, to fall out. Absences of information such as these illustrate why for people like Anna, the more information they believed the government to have withheld, minimizing the scale of the Chernobyl catastrophe, the larger their own sense of potential injuries loomed. Anna's conclusions are not symptoms of farfetched beliefs and obscurantism, as some observers would have it (IAEA 1991), but part and parcel of the faulty policy decisions those observers legitimated.

■ ■ ■

Upon their arrival in Kyiv's central train station, the Strokats encountered total chaos.

"Stay on the train!" one woman shouted to Vitalii as his family descended the steps of the train. Oksana recalled people pushing and shoving on the platform to get on a train, any train. Yet Vitalii said he was skeptical in the face of this hysteria. He recounted his reaction to it: "What is going on? Hah! These people are fools! The government is trying to fool us again! Before it was Americans attacking us, now it is a nuclear disaster!" Vitalii was convinced that the people "have all gone mad" (he used the Ukrainian word *zdurily*). As an ex-military man, Vitalii claimed he had firsthand knowledge of the often bizarre population management tactics of the former Soviet state. Vitalii refused to be manipulated by them. The family decided to press on, as Anna's surgery was critically needed. Vitalii led the family as they moved resolutely through the panicky crowds.

Oksana explained what the family saw in the main Bassarabskyi market hall in Kyiv. In her usual way, she mimed the event, inviting me with her gestures to witness what she had seen. Pretending to hold an abnormally large strawberry, she hooked her hand toward her gaping mouth, reminding me of Eve in the primal biblical scene, the prelude to Adam and Eve's expulsion from paradise to a nomadic life on earth. I continually recollected Oksana's enactment after I had returned to the United States. The Strokats refused to believe in the chaos all around them. This refusal to believe and to witness was a virtue that had insulated them from political machinations before. But here that virtue led to disaster.

Should they have stayed on the train? The family returned to Bila-Skala aware that the consequences of their actions were unknown. Their lives were overwhelmed by new uncertainties. Their history entailed a refusal to succumb to old authorities that victimized their families and their progeny. That same mode of reasoning was exposed for its insufficiency; it could not protect them from further assaults. After Chernobyl, the Strokats saw themselves—their bodies, their sense of reason and known survival tactics—rendered obsolete. The blinding light delivered by Chernobyl has become a consuming hole of the present. In history's place stands the reason of the witness, the pictures inside Mr. Pasichnyk's head.

Requiem for Storytelling

In the course of the next few years, questions of how to adjust to the new economic order continue to overwhelm Anna. She worries about her inability to have children, a condition that she blames on her kidney disease and on radiation. She organizes music classes for children from local rural areas. As I visit Anna over the next couple of summers of my evolving research on Chernobyl, we form a friendship. The following is a brief summary of her attempts to build a life for herself in a postsocialist environment, her struggles against the barriers posed by compounding social and economic crises (and the mental health challenges that result from such crises).

By 1993, Bila-Skala comes to feel increasingly hopeless and dangerous for the Strokats. Their relations with an emerging local mafia become perilous, particularly because Oksana, who comes to privately own a small clothing boutique, resists paying "roof" to protect her shop from being torched. Local police, in what she perceived to be a partnership with the mafia, arrest her and throw her into jail for three months.

Oksana and Vitalii begin to envision moving to Israel. Their hopes are temporarily thwarted because Oksana cannot obtain the death certificate of at least one parent that is required for her to emigrate. Vitalii jokes to me that he is so fed up with life in Ukraine that when he arrives in Tel Aviv, he wants a "stretcher waiting for him at the airport to transport him to the local hospital."

In 1994, Vitalii and Oksana move to Israel and expect Anna to join them. Anna postpones leaving. She enjoys the bliss of living alone in an apartment that for most of her life has been cramped. In less than one year, and in a surprise move, her parents return from Israel. Vitalii reports feeling discriminated against and "like a second-class citizen." Upon his return, he becomes increasingly depressed, possessive of Anna, and physically abusive. During the ensuing year he rarely steps outside his apartment. He is preoccupied with fears of cancer. He is angry that I do not bring treatments from an American pharmacy for what he believes is prostate cancer (his Soviet medical records do not indicate this diagnosis). He becomes preoccupied with intruders and stores weapons in the apartment. He assaults Anna when she expresses her desire to move to Kyiv, away from the family. For a month she remains in a local hospital, which also serves as temporary safe haven from Vitalii. After she returns home, Anna overdoses on tranquilizers. Oksana returns from work one day and finds her daughter unconscious. Oksana violently shakes her daughter out of her overdosed stupor.

In 1996, Anna decides that she desperately wants to leave Ukraine by any possible means. She places her photo in the on-line catalog of an international marriage agency and attracts a fifty-year-old suitor from Montana. She travels twice to Kyiv to meet him. On the second visit he proposes. A month later he ends the relationship, conceding Anna's beauty but claiming that she is "too depressed." Anna's dream of living away from her stepfather is realized in the summer of 1996, when she makes enough money from her music classes to move to another apartment. She marries a local man and tells me she is able to have children. The move from her parents' home seems to have broken the spell of infertility. She is successful in making the break with family constraints and the violences of the past, both imagined and real. The reengineering of life by trial and error becomes her everyday challenge.

In 1996, I encounter people who speak of a time in the not-too-distant past when "there was room for storytelling." I hear the words *istoriia* (history), *baiky* (fairy tales), and *ekzotyka* (exotica) in reference to the personal discourses, sensibilities, and historical family accounts that circulate privately and publicly in the first years following the Soviet collapse. Such words reflect not only a change in moral valuations of history but also a transmogrification of the languages and codes used to express everyday distress in the context of heightened economic and social uncertainties. I turn to an example of the latter type of change in the context of an emerging Ukrainian state administration of Chernobyl, increasingly defined by bureaucracy and legal and medical categories, and where distinctions between populations of sufferers and nonsufferers were beginning to emerge.

■ ■ ■

In 1994, I was invited to attend a meeting, in the parliamentary commission building, of the then much admired minister of Chernobyl, Heorhii Hotovshyts, with a group of five mothers whose children had developed thyroid cancers. Hanna Kozlova, a former leader of a Komsomol (Young Communist League) in Prypiat', led the group, whose members had been evacuated from the Chernobyl zones to governmental housing in Kyiv.

When I first met them (the day before on a Kyiv street where they were informally organizing), the women were consumed with fear and anger over what had happened to their children's health and what to do next. They had learned by that time about scientific studies which had shown that the sharp rise in child thyroid cancer was attributable to the inaction of the Soviet administration in the initial crisis period. Potassium iodide tablets, had they been made available in that critical period, would have blocked radioactive iodine and cesium from being absorbed into their children's thyroids.

Studies of prior fallouts suggested that thyroid cancers should be expected to appear between eight and twelve years after the Chernobyl fallout. Instead, they appeared after four years.[10] Simple and unsettling questions lie dormant beneath this datum: What will happen? What is happening? And how do we *know* what is happening? What forms of inquiry, imagination, pain, and self-assertion are related to this sudden fact?

The mothers had little trust in the new government's ability to protect their children. Hanna expressed that distrust by requesting my assistance in taking their children abroad. "This will give them hope and health," she said, "for at least a few months, I would be so grateful." In their conception of the world, "going abroad" was synonymous with "getting healthier." "Let the host family send children to my home. I will thank them for taking my child away from here."

During the meeting with the minister, the mothers argued that the state's schedule of compensation and criteria for defining sufferers did not correspond to the actual distribution of the disaster's health effects. Hanna stated that children treated for thyroid tumors should receive priority in terms of compensation. More should be done to guarantee their access to medications. Hanna and her group wanted to make sure that children with surgically removed tumors were guaranteed lifetime prescriptions of thyroxine (thyroid hormone) to prevent recurrence.[11] Each woman was given a chance to speak at the meeting.

"My child and my husband are sick, we have no money, how am I to live?" asked one woman. She broke down in tears and said, "I have no future. I want to die."

"Promise to put your emotions aside," said the minister, who was born in what was now referred to as Zone Two of contamination.[12]

Suddenly she stopped, and her demeanor became businesslike; she used terms that were more legally accurate: "I am a mother of a child who is a sufferer. I am an evacuee from Zone Two. My husband is a Chernobyl worker, Category One."[13]

The others followed suit, presenting their cases in a similar fashion. The minister asked them whether their children's thyroid glands had been measured. "There is no thyroid in my child anymore," one woman answered. Instantly, the minister, famous for his goodwill and compassion for affected persons, decreed, "All children suffering from thyroid disorders will automatically be viewed as having the status of sufferer under Ukrainian law." He told them up front, "The state has no money." He urged the group of five to form a "fund" (*fond*), a nongovernmental civic group representing and advocating for sufferers' rights. "There are many out there," he said. "Draft statutes. Give us your preliminary documents. You work for a month, and we work for a month." The mothers drafted statutes and received official approval for their new organization. Though the state could not provide resources, it gave the mothers something more significant from a social standpoint: the freedom to associate, to represent themselves, and to act on their own behalf.

The Institute of Endocrinology and Metabolism in Kyiv monitors cases of thyroid cancers in the predominantly rural contaminated zones. The vice-director of the institute, Dr. Valerii Tereshchenko, told me that lack of early ultrasound monitoring systems, the paucity of capable professionals, and the poverty of rural families have exacerbated the spread of thyroid cancers. Consequently, the institute's physicians see only the most advanced cases of thyroid cancer in children. Tereshchenko said that although some surveillance technologies are available, there is yet another problem: "No endocrinologist wants to live in a contaminated area, for the sake of his/her children."[14]

I visited wards where mothers from contaminated rural areas sat with children waiting to undergo surgical excision of their thyroid glands. One room contained four girls aged twelve to fourteen. One of the girls had already had her operation; the three others were awaiting theirs. Out of the three mothers who accompanied their daughters to the hospital, two of them had the characteristic U-shaped scar on their necks, indicating that they had also been operated on. One of the girls said that three in her class of twenty-eight in the Kyiv region had been operated on. Another girl from the Chernihiv region said that out of thirty classmates two had been operated on. The girls came from areas representing the map of Chernobyl fallout in Ukraine. The "technogenic" dimension of their experience was palpable in this room.

Ira had just undergone a second operation. She told me that her mother had the same type of cancer, and that recently "the doctors found a 'knot' (vuzol) in my little sister's thyroid as well." Ira, like the other girls, marked the progression of her disease by counting the number of "knots" forming in her throat, chest, and neck. "The doctors tell me how many I have at a given time," Ira said, as if she was engaged in a ritualistic form of anticipation. In this ritual, she was also attempting to symbolize her being in light of the course of unrelenting biological events taking place in her body.

Those biological events are influenced by social conditions. The thyroid gland regulates the release of hormones necessary for normal human physical, mental, and sexual maturation. Children and adults became dependent on shipments of thyroxine from humanitarian aid organizations abroad. The ward was scheduled to close during the summer, owing to the lack of state funds and humanitarian shipments. Even with thyroxine, the normal function of the endocrine system (including ovaries, adrenal glands, and pituitary glands), particularly important for the sexual development of these young teenagers, was permanently upset. In other words, these girls knew from the experience of neighbors that their suffering didn't end with a simple surgical excision—rather, a different form of suffering and dependency began. Their biological existence was now predicated on a complex medical and legal structure. The girls told me that they believed their growth would be stunted, and that they could not have children. They translated their experiences and sense of impossibility into images of nonreproduction.

Alina, aged fifteen, had arrived at the institute a week earlier. She had been diagnosed with thyroid cancer in 1992, and her thyroid gland had been completely removed. She had just undergone a second surgery to remove knots that had spread to her trachea. Alina wobbled her head, straining to find ways of resisting the surgical pain. In spite of her delicate state, I was surprised to find out that she "had just spoken to journalists that day." Alina thought I was a journalist and was once again ready to occupy her public role as citizen-patient, attracting media attention and possible medical resources. We sat in a separate room; her mother sat near us, listening.

"What are you thinking about after this operation?" I asked her.

"I have to live . . . I was afraid of this second operation. The nodules can still spread into the lungs and to the brains. If they go into the brains it will be too late; it will be almost impossible to save me. But if the nodules spread into the lungs, they can still save me." She wanted to be saved. "But everything is normal right now," she reassured herself. "I have to drink iodine and take daily doses of thyroxine. If I don't have that hormone I'll be faint, and I won't be as lucky."

Alina learned of her thyroid cancer when she went on a trip to Sweden with other children from the contaminated zones. She attributed her condition to the Chernobyl disaster: "We all relate it to Chernobyl." "Why did it happen?" I asked her. "Because of an explosion. It came as a cloud upon, well, on a lot of cities and villages. The cloud left its trace in my city too. I can say that the trace in me is this scar." She gestured the shape of her scar and said, "In others, other traces."

Alina displayed a sense of her own fragility as she translated the disaster into a concrete set of images. "Do you dream?" I asked. Alina said that she had once dreamed of a magician, "long ago, when I was still small. But I knew what the dream was supposed to mean." The magician wore a black overcoat and a black hat; he carried a thin cane. "He poked a girl's eye." Alina immediately related this poking action to a transmogrifying event. "She was of normal growth, like me, and suddenly she became small, like a little doll." Alina was implicitly preoccupied with her growth and sexuality. The experience of the disaster made her dreams literal—she became a "little doll." A little doll for whom? Alina continued with her dream interpretation: "And now I can see that indeed my dream came true because now children don't grow." Indeed, the loss of the thyroid function can lead to growth problems. "They become smaller. They remain the same, just as they were at birth." She looked to her mother as if to receive affirmation from her.

Alina's gestures and words suggested that she envisioned herself as bound to her infancy, and to a complex compassionate tie between daughter and mother, patient and doctor, child and state. "There is a girl in one of the rooms here," Alina said. "She's eleven, but she is small, an infant." Alina referred to Sveta, an eleven-year-old girl who suffered from an underdeveloped thyroid—the wrinkled, aged, and mute being had not grown beyond the size of a one-year-old child. As we looked at the playful little big girl, Alina expressed her fears and anxieties about her future. "When I see her, I think 'this cannot happen.' Earlier it was in my dreams and now it is real."[15]

The clinical space became a space of images, bodies, traces, and dreams through which Alina portrayed herself to the visitor as irreversibly transformed. Alina considered Sveta kin, not by blood, but by fate. Was she aging normally or aging too fast? The simple question lying dormant beneath Chernobyl's indefinite biological metric preoccupied this girl. Alina didn't know what would happen next.

Chapter 4
Illness as Work: Human Market Transition

City of Sufferers

Since 1986, over 500,000 people have been resettled from contaminated regions to virtually all areas of Ukraine. Contaminated territories are divided into four "zones" according to levels of cesium, strontium, and plutonium contamination. The Exclusion Zone is managed by the national government's Zone Administration, which also monitors the Chernobyl plant; Zone Two is an area of compulsory resettlement; Zone Three is an area of guaranteed voluntary resettlement; and Zone Four is an area of heightened radiological monitoring. Ukrainian state law guarantees resettlement to persons living in territories where existing conditions could be expected to exceed a 0.1 rem (or 7 rem over an average seventy-year life expectancy) threshold limit.[1] The law also guarantees the demarcation of new zones should their ground contamination reach radiation levels beyond those designated for a particular zone.[2]

In November 1996, I took a trip with a geophysicist who worked in a provincial unit of the new state's Chernobyl Ministry. His unit is responsible for administering contaminated areas in the Zhytomyr region (*raion*), northwest of Kyiv. We traveled north from the town of Zhytomyr, Zone Three, to Narodychi, Zone Two and located twenty kilometers west of the Chernobyl plant, where Evhen Palatyn planned to review the accounts of a collective farm to see whether its manager had used ministry monies properly. Under the state's Chernobyl social protection laws, the manager was required to procure and add heavy metals to cattle feed. As Palatyn explained, cesium is slow to penetrate into the soil, especially if the soil is unworked, and stays near the surface. Cesium-binding minerals such as ferrocinum are made available through district agricultural departments. Injected into the animal's abdomen, they have the effect of binding radionuclides and removing them through natural excretory processes. Under the new acts, the manager was also required to provide special clothing to protect tractor drivers from airborne radioactive dust, and to add a host of mineral-based "radioprotectors," to foodstuffs—cow's milk, for example.

As we passed the dusty city of Korosten', we observed people walking on the streets. "The whole town consists of sufferers," Palatyn commented. He used the legally accurate term for sufferers—*poterpili*, or "those who have suffered." Korosten' was situated in Zone Three. These zone demarcations seem arbitrary from the ground, almost like state lines in New England but without the signs telling you which state you are in. Inhabitants of this zone live in an environment that contains at least twice the accepted normal levels of background radiation. All of them carry "dosimetric passports." These passports contain information about the person's dose that is registered in a statewide dosimetric registry system, and certify an individual's identity as a sufferer. Once his or her dose exceeds the maximum allowable annual dose set by the state, the person is eligible to move to free government housing in areas deemed ecologically clean. Most of these people, Palatyn told me, have stayed. They "pay half their rent, have free public transportation and free medical assistance."

Since 1991, the Ukrainian finance ministry has spent a significant portion of the country's pension and social protection monies on sufferers of the Chernobyl disaster. Yurii Shcherbak, former environment minister and an author of the Ukrainian laws, admitted that protective laws were informed by a certain "legislative euphoria" during the democratic inception. The law placed "environmental controls over the whole territory of Ukraine. . . . Exact scientific criteria laid the groundwork for laws that address the issue of protecting the populations of areas that have endured varying levels of soil contamination by radioactive cesium, strontium, and plutonium" (1992:508). As Shcherbak noted, "Life, however, shows that the adoption of laws—whatever good they do provide—cannot solve all environmental problems. The task of simultaneously putting laws into practice and taking into account the given economic, social, moral, and mental situation in a state is the most complicated problem" (ibid.).

This is an understatement. Under the law, suffering became the new social leveler. Rural workers, industrial workers, professionals, intelligentsia—laborers of unequal status under state socialism—became part of a novel national collectivity of Chernobyl sufferers transcending class, educational, and employment categories.[3] The state established a

Chernobyl welfare system and a health services sector as autonomous subdivisions of the state's social welfare services and public health ministry. Pensions and free medical care, among other things, were authorized to approximately 3.5 million sufferers.[4]

In a previous chapter, I showed how Soviet medical laws sought to contain the human consequences of Chernobyl. The deployment of centralized administrative power went hand in hand with an intensification of legal-medical processes meant to control the definition of legitimate injury. In this chapter, I focus on what has been termed an "epidemic" of disability in post-Soviet Ukraine. Given the unknown long-term effects of radiation and overall economic crisis, the line between sickness and health is a highly politicized one. In the absence of sufficient state health care financing, state laws on the social protection of Chernobyl sufferers have turned suffering and disability into a resource affecting family, work, and social identity. Traditional forms of Soviet social organization—particularly the labor collective (Ashwin 1999, Kharkhordin 1999)—are being replaced by a new architecture of welfare claims, privileges, laws, and identities. Politics has moved into medical realms; health sector activity has once again become crucial to the legitimacy of state power. I examine these transformations from the clinical perspective of medical doctors and health administrators, and the bureaucratic and legal machinery through which claims of suffering and disability are formalized. The latter half of this chapter is based on interviews that I conducted with health administrators and patients at the Radiation Research Center in 1996.

The Chernobyl population is stratified in terms of categories of sufferers. The first category indicates how different Ukrainian criteria for judging injury are from their Soviet predecessors'. It includes 50,000 people who were rendered incapable of work and/or contracted some form of acute radiation sickness (ARS). The second category contains 350,000 people who were involved in the cleanup activities in 1986–1997 and/or who were evacuated and relocated from the compulsory evacuation area. The third category includes 550,000 people from among the cleanup crews (1988–1990) living in the compulsory evacuation area and the guaranteed voluntary evacuation area. The fourth category includes approximately 1.2 million people currently living or working in the zones.[5]

Benefits are graded according to category. Those labeled "persons disabled from Chernobyl" for example, receive much higher pensions and greater privileges than sufferers. Those electing to work in the zones are typically paid two or three times what they would normally receive doing the same type of professional work outside the zones. Everyone in the system knows that a disabled person is much better off than a sufferer. Sufferers are arguably more secure than some unemployed workers who have no claim on state social protections. Built into the system is the possibility of sequentially transforming oneself from a sufferer to a disabled person. For both groups, it makes little sense to drop out of the system since the state provides no better alternative to this form of social protection. The sufferer's position, and the work required to keep that position, constitute an investment for life.

One clinician working at the Radiation Research Center, the epicenter of these biopolitical transformations, summed up the situation succinctly: "Here, the worst is to be healthy." Her words suggest that in this moment of political and economic crisis, individuals give greater importance to the material benefits of social organization around illness than to their rights and responsibilities to be "healthy" citizens. Socialist societies tried to guarantee universal access to a minimum standard of living. A system of social protections including state-provided education, health, pension benefits, and basic food subsidies lowered living costs. What was the Soviet health sector is now either severely curtailed in its services or is privatizing, leaving significant health care issues unaddressed. The clinician's wry observation suggests that being "healthy" today means being left alone, abandoned by the state, left exposed to the market, and without social supports. "Illness" provides some measure of protection against the vagaries of joblessness and social disorientation. People were converting themselves from Soviet citizens into biological citizens in their driving efforts to maintain a tie with the state and to avoid abandonment.

■ ■ ■

Leaving Korosten', we drove through fields, and Palatyn commented that radiation had settled unevenly on the land. He pointed to a valley bordered by a row of trees, "On that side it's really contaminated." He pointed to the left and said, "There's nothing here." He spoke about the difficulties of measuring plutonium: "You measure it here one day, and it's here. You measure it the next day, and it's somewhere else. That's why there is no map of the plutonium." As we drove from Zone Three to Zone Two, we passed Ovruch, where five buses were parked, ready to take local children on their annual field trip to a sanatorium in Zhytomyr, in Zone Three.

Palatyn explained that the radiation content of milk, berries, mushrooms, fish, potatoes, and other foodstuffs is monitored in local radiochemical laboratories. Particles such as cesium-137 transfer from soil to milk; ingestion of contaminated milk results in increased internal doses. Palatyn said he encouraged local villagers to use filtering devices that reduce the cesium content in milk, but many villagers refused to use such

85

devices. "They complain the milk loses its fat and is then impossible to sell," he said.

While state workers like Palatyn discourage increased exposures, the dire economic situation (combined with legal privileges) *encourages* dose exposures—that seemed to be Palatyn's quandary. Why do some people choose to stay in the zones rather than resettling? Why do people elect to drink the contaminated milk rather than decrease risk through filtering devices? These questions raise a number of other troubling questions about the future of government in these zones. Palatyn seemed to be nagged by an ethical question: Should the government simply "give up" on these people and let them govern themselves? Indeed, by 1996, new amendments to the social protection laws stopped some resettlement and cut all social privileges to inhabitants of Zone Four. Yet whole cities of sufferers remain.

■ ■ ■

I culled the following exchange from a local Zhytomyr newspaper published for inhabitants of Zone Three in October 1996. The author, an unnamed civil servant, singled out individuals who had returned to their resettled villages. He chastises them for disobeying government norms of safety and for violating the "pledge" they had implicitly made to the state to protect their own lives.

> Think about this, good People! We have learned that several families, resettled from the village of Kalynivka in the perilous Zone Two, returned to their former home. It is an especially bitter fact that, along with families Petrenko and Kuzmenko, Natalia Mudrak and her four children have broken their pledge. The state has taken on the responsibility of giving those families the opportunity to live and breathe in an ecologically clean area and to drive the perilous Chernobyl threat away from them, including their four children. People are deciding their fates injudiciously. They have sold the new homes they received by resettling, and have returned to their deserted house, where danger awaits them in every corner. This is because everything around them is seething with radiation: the grass, the garden, and the water in their wells. What explains their behavior? *Ignorance or simple disregard of the deadly menace* [my italics] of the Chernobyl monster that breathes, carrying death for all who are alive? Good people, come to your senses, spare yourselves, or at least spare your children.[6]

The author of this public notice, Volodymyr Shatylo, works with Palatyn in the Zhytomyr unit of the Chernobyl Ministry. A journalist by training, he conceded the warning to have been a bit dramatic, but believed "that is the way to reach our people" (it apparently wasn't). Shatylo's main work consisted of informing the public about strategies for mitigating risk, coordinating resettlement, deciding whether people qualified as sufferers, and monitoring dosimetric passports. In general, he made sure the bureaucracy of this new welfare system was running smoothly.

Shatylo showed me a column appearing in a newspaper weekly called "They Ask—We Answer" that he and others in the local ministry unit edit. Inquiries were representative of those Shatylo receives daily:

A widow inquires about legal procedures for obtaining a larger apartment after the family breadwinner dies.

A man writes that he participated in the Chernobyl cleanup as a worker of the Ministry of Internal Affairs. "I lost 10 percent of my work capacity," he writes, "It's been two years and I can't get an answer. By law, who is supposed to compensate me for this lost 10 percent?"

A man writes that in January 1987 he worked on the construction of the city of Slavutych (Zone Two). "I worked twenty-four days. After this experience, my eyesight got worse. Do I have the right to become a sufferer?"

"Examination of the laws," the respondent wrote, "shows that the answer is no. Only people *who permanently reside* in Zone Two are eligible as sufferers."[7]

Shatylo's response, paradoxically, reinforces the idea that staying in the zone improves citizens' rights. By the same token, people have become quite masterful in culturally appropriating their own suffering.[8] When zone inhabitants come to Shatylo's office for procedural advice about becoming sufferers, he tells them, "You *especially* must work." He advises his fellow men to fight the morally debasing aspects of the law and to defy the "sick role" (this issue will be discussed in detail shortly). He implores them to undertake not just any ordinary work but a moral purging. He tells them to "work until you sweat, until you've raised your metabolism high enough that you feel your exhaustion."[9]

Shatylo is not delegitimating their claims as sufferers but is offering an empathic moral response to processes of medicalization and victimization that he knows are inevitable. "Their souls need to be treated," he said. He also knows that the state's legal controls have engendered a whole new environment where illness has become work.

Maria Ivanivna, a collective farmer who had achieved a secondary education, was one step removed from becoming a knowledgeable agent of her own illness. I interviewed her at the Radiation Research Center, after I had returned from my trip to the zones. She told me that prior to coming to the center, she had had a difficult time "collecting my spiritual strengths to apply with the documents. I have a psychological barrier."

On the advice of her neighbors, she took a two-hour bus ride from Narodychi to seek added social protection based on illnesses she had developed while living in Zone Two. She conveyed a desperate, beleaguered, and confused sense about her physical symptoms and those of her son, a confusion that she made clear was not of her own making.

Ivanivna had been resettled twice. Her native village, located in the Zone of Exclusion, was evacuated in June 1986—"liquidated," as Ivanivna said—and declared off-limits for human habitation. Her family was moved into temporary housing in a village called Radcha, Zone Two. Though Soviet officials promised Ivanivna and fellow villagers that they would return, "we knew we would never return." After two years, and realizing the risk of contamination, Ivanivna's in-laws left Radcha to live in government housing in an ecologically clean area in Belarus. Ivanivna and her husband decided to stay. They weighed the uncertainty of finding a job in their new settlement against the indefiniteness of the radiological situation. Her husband had already found work in the local forestry service. The couple and their two children later moved to the nearby town of Narodychi. The town was just six kilometers from Ivanivna's native village—confusion went full circle. "Well, what can I tell you," Ivanivna said. "We did not go much further."

Ivanivna's anxiety about living in a contaminated area was overshadowed by her general mistrust of government. At first, "We didn't believe in radiation. We thought it had dispersed." Like other local villagers, Ivanivna was recruited to carry out "disactivation" work. She was routinely driven out to the reactor site, along with military regiments stationed in her new village. For five years, she raked and shoveled pieces of the reactor core—radioactive graphite—scattered over a vast area. She said, "They cleaned and showered us at the military headquarters" when she returned at night.

Ivanivna did not exhibit any observable signs of distress about the danger she might have encountered during this work. She was mistrustful of a sign that "stood at the edge of our forest warning not to enter, not to pick the berries or the mushrooms." Radionuclides are known to build up in forest floors, especially in the upper layer of soil, in moss and lichen, needles, and in twigs and branches. She said a dosimetrist told her that her resettled village was more contaminated than her native village. "Maybe it was all a swindle (*obman*)," she said, suggesting her frustration with conflicting representations of Chernobyl's danger.

Yet one issue was unambiguous to Ivanivna. Her entire family had been affected. Her husband was "Chernobyl disabled." Her eleven-year old son's health was poor. "By the time he was ten, I knew something had fallen on him." He experienced fevers, rashes, allergies, thyroid problems, and leukopenia (a blood ailment); moreover, according to Ivanivna, he "lost his ability to walk, his leg functioned abnormally, as if something is not letting that leg walk." In her conception, the leg was autonomous, controlled by an unknown, external force.

Ivanivna began to rely on clinics made available by the new welfare system, but she could not keep up with medical terminology. During another conversation, she expressed her confusion by making associations between symptoms and medical classifications that did not seem to make sense. For example, she used a phrase that literally translates as "leukemia of the knee joint." This confusion in language suggests that Ivanivna had reached the desperate limit of her own ability to reason. In spite of reaching that limit, Ivanivna could detail every symptom, skin reaction, trip and fall, out-of-socket knee, headache, irregular blood indicator, blurred vision, lymph node inflammation, recurrent allergy, and thyroid disturbance her son ever had. Throughout our conversation Ivanivna literally grasped for words and gasped for breath, suggesting that the boy's production of symptoms had outpaced her ability to adjust to them. "Upon initial examination, the boy's leukopenia diagnosis was confirmed, and my God, we went to three professors, to two doctors at the ambulatory, and to a third one, an endocrinologist we drove him to in Kyiv. His lymphocytes started to normalize and they sent us to hematology for a consultation." As she described the unfolding of her son's symptoms, his travels to specialists, emergency rooms, and radiological research centers, it became clear that Ivanivna, a lowly collective farm worker, had learned much about elite systems of medical care. The boy had apparently learned to find solace in the hospital.

When I asked her how she handled her own fear, she said that she initially "avoided melancholy" and "winding herself up" about radiation. "I threw these thoughts away. Our people were not even strung up about this." In emphasizing her calm, she also wanted to project a sense of being in control, fighting to preserve her dignity in the confusion. Moreover, as a mother of a sick son, wife of an invalid, and laborer, Ivanivna could not afford the luxury of getting sick.

Ivanivna's expressed resistance to the idea of becoming sick also had its roots in Soviet work culture. In that culture, social tensions related to labor discipline were often negotiated through illness, or what Talcott Parsons called the "sick role," an exemption from normal social responsibilities and labor obligations on account of illness (Parsons 1991:76, Turner 1987:40). Under the pressure of extreme forms of labor discipline, for example, Soviet workers tended to justify work tardiness by resorting to medical excuses (Field 1957). The Parsonian equation "to be sick is to be not at work," however, included one more level of social negotiation in a context in which labor was often in short supply owing to uncertainties related to socialist production (Verdery 1996:22). In an effort to counteract a "cult of nonwork," state enterprise and collective farm managers often threatened workers who exercised the sick role with sanctions in the form of uncompensated sick days. According to one sociologist, "Although Soviet citizens [we]re guaranteed the right to work . . . , they [did] not enjoy any corresponding right to choose *not* to work. The right to work was no right at all, it was a 'legal obligation,' and any able-bodied citizen of working age who 'follow[ed] a parasitic way of life,' [was] liable to criminal prosecution" (Teague 1988:278).[10]

Against this background, Ivanivna struggled to translate her condition into a legally authorized form. An incapacitated worker (or his or her family members) had to engage a highly bureaucratized, penalizing, and at times criminalizing process in order to be granted sick days. To be sick meant that one *had to be equally motivated* to work to obtain permission to be sick. This work folded organic and social processes into what might be called a sick role sociality.

■ ■ ■

I want to return to Ivanivna's life to understand how "confused" personal and intrafamilial processes (not to mention the fact of her exposure to radioactive debris) inhere in this new sociality. Her genuine confusion becomes the foundation upon which Ivanivna affirms a new public agency through sickness.

In 1994, while working as a collective farm hand, Ivanivna developed a cardiac condition and back problems; she began losing her memory, routinely fainted, and experienced paralysis in her legs. She continued to work, "hiding her physical weaknesses from her husband" and maintaining an image of health. In May of that year, her son was interned at a local clinic for possible knee surgery, something he adamantly refused and feared, but he asked his mother to leave him alone in the clinic. Judging from what follows, her banishment produced a new set of events that forced her to reimage herself. "Well, that was about the son," she told me.

While returning home on the bus, Ivanivna recalled that she suddenly lost control of her body. "I felt so sick, it took hold of me." That "it," that force that controlled her son's leg, now controlled her speech. She said that she "spoke like a drunk, it was hard to speak. And when I got to a store, my heart was racing. My legs felt cut off. And I thought, God! Soon I will lose my consciousness! I will be ashamed in front of all these people for having lost my strength!"

When she got home, the neighborhood doctor "shot [her] up with something" and said he would try to help her to get "treatment and social protection." Worried neighbors advised her to consult a neurologist or cardiologist. They provided real help when they introduced her to a visitor, an evacuee who had returned to the region to visit his family members' gravesites, an annual tradition called *hrobky* or "day of the graves." (Evacuees are entitled to return to their empty villages once a year for this occasion. They receive special passes, and the state pays their travel expenses.) Ivanivna referred to the visitor simply as an "important functionary."

The neighbors brought this functionary back to Ivanivna's house. She recollected her sense of surprise when she learned that "he was sick too." In this moment of recognition, Ivanivna seemed to have authorized her own sense of sickness; at least that was what she conveyed to me. As she lay on her couch at home with neighbors leaning over her, she told the functionary that she "didn't want to fall into a panic," but that "*no one tells me what is happening with me.*" She continued, "Living is hard for me, I can't work anymore. My strength has left me and I do not know from what."

By recounting this scene from her past to me, Ivanivna narrated her transformation from being a "confused," overworked, and disenfranchised rural woman to becoming a knowledgeable agent of her illness, a disabled citizen. The functionary referred Ivanivna to the Radiation Research Center, where we met. Ivanivna subsequently underwent medical-legal examination for disability status. After returning home, she wrote me a letter about the results of her examinations. She said, "The doctors are giving me level three disability for the rupture in the spinal column." Perhaps recalling the years she spent shoveling radioactive graphite, she wrote that she now "had the right not to work." She spoke of this right as an achieved status.

The tone of her letter suggested that she had just returned from a ceremonial feast of sorts, where medical gifts were bestowed on guests. In the process, symptoms had shifted from being intrafamilial matters to legal matters of personhood. Through this new distribution, Ivanivna had found her social position in an exchange with the state, outside her family relations and obligations. In justifying her decision to occupy the sick role, she wrote that she understood her struggles "as spiritual tortures. I could not see any other way to live."[11]

Ivanivna attained her disability status because of a chance encounter with a functionary, through a network of agents, concerned neighbors, and physicians. Her account suggests that the state system for transforming radiation-induced illnesses into a claim of disability is an institution unto itself. The new state defined itself not only by introducing a new system of environmental controls but also by generating and subsidizing a system of compensations and exemptions from work for people working or living in environmentally compromised areas. To address the growth of Chernobyl-affected populations, the state's social welfare system expanded. Eleven regional medical-labor committees (*Ekspertiza*), attached to local dispensaries and clinics, were established to decide claims of Chernobyl-related disability.[12] These committees are more like clinical courts. For workers like Ivanivna, and in a world where levels of employment and the real value of currency have dropped, they are precious gateways that allow individuals to transit from states of disenfranchisement into disabled social states. In the next section, I illustrate how such transitions are also generative of new resources, both financial and material, for the institutions involved. My focus is not on the question of corruption per se. Rather, I aim to show how economic paralysis (which has stemmed the flow of resources such as gas, electricity, and food that are basic to the functioning of institutions) breeds codependencies in which compensation is no longer simply moral repayment; it also serves as a stimulant to new and at times exploitative forms of accumulation.

Capitalist Transition

These practices of expanding claims have a resemblance to a phenomenon anthropologist Marilyn Strathern has noted in the context of economic activity in Papua New Guinea following Australian pacification in the 1950s and 1960s, during which time the value of local currencies (shells in this instance) suddenly plunged. In this inflationary context, natives correspondingly "scaled up" demands for compensation in traditional exchanges involving clan displays of wealth, dowries, and tribal war payments; and in exchanges with the state involving tribal property sales and clan assertiveness expressed in terms of losses suffered during battles (1993:2). This same notion of inflation as both macroeconomic reality and occasion for local expansions of compensation claims can be applied to this post-Soviet/Chernobyl context. The uncertain economic climate has affected the scale of Chernobyl-related disability claims.

Following the liberalization of the market in 1992 in Ukraine, household financial savings were wiped out by hyperinflation (at 10,000 percent in 1993).[13] Russia and other countries of the former Soviet Union experienced similarly dramatic price inflations. As the Soviet industrial framework fell apart, "a half or more of the industrial labor force faces a dead end in their present enterprises. Their firms will be sold, restructured, or simply closed down. There has been no experience in economic development this century during peace-time to compare with the labor upheaval in today's FSU countries" (*Ukraine Human Development Report* 1995). Across the former Soviet Union social protection systems are overburdened and inadequate to address these fast-paced changes during which a core group of long-term poor have emerged. As of 2001, 50 percent of the Ukrainian population lived below the poverty line.

I turn to an examination of the role of the Exclusion Zone in an informal Soviet economy and capitalist transition, and to the ways workers micromanage inflation with a sick role sociality in their everyday lives. The state pays two-thirds of all Chernobyl allowances as wage bonuses to workers in areas of radiation contamination; it has maintained the real value of compensations and privileges for these workers.[14] Throughout the transition, many Zone workers realized that they faced fewer chances for economic survival outside the Zone; they considered themselves to be unhirable because of their work history. The state became a protector, not only against exposures accumulated through work or residence in the Zone, but also against the worst effects of the market.

One such worker lived in Kyiv and traveled to the Exclusion Zone to work in multiple two-week-long shifts (*vakhta*). He worked for an organization overseeing medical care and monitoring of persons working and living in the Zone.[15] It was relatively easy for him to have access to the center. His wife directs the only polyclinic in the Exclusion Zone that refers Zone workers for medical-legal assessments at the center; she is an invalid herself and regularly interacts with the center's physicians. A physician by training himself, Dubinin said he received double his normal salary by working in the Zone. He received an additional 25 percent of his already doubled salary because he elected to work with radiochemicals, "which involve more risk." All in all, he earned the equivalent of three hundred dollars a month, about three to four times the average worker's salary. When I asked him whether his coworkers want "to get out of the Zone and into the market"—that seemed to be the way to formulate his economic situation—he responded, "No, they hang on to the Zone."

In formulating the notion of the sick role, Talcott Parsons drew a connection between definitions of sickness and labor requirements in the United States in the post–World War II economic expansion. "In capitalism, health becomes a commodity like other commodities in the market place. . . . there is a permanent tension between the requirements of the economy and the requirements of a healthy existence" (Turner 1987:172). Dubinin's ultimate goal was to *leave* the Zone, but only under conditions whereby he would be socially protected by the state. He was preparing to assert his right *not* to work, to use Ivanivna's words. But in the meantime, he had to keep track of his symptoms and injuries, much as Ivanivna did. In this way, he was also preparing to enter the market as a competent sick person, as a disabled person, whose labor is a cancelled commodity.

Dubinin's reasoning reflects the resources available to workers in the Zone and other affected individuals to guarantee themselves a place, albeit a negative one, in a democracy and in a market-oriented form of social reorganization. Ironically, the resources tied to disability here are much more than many communities in the former Soviet Union can currently "command," particularly in rural and indigenous areas. The right to disability status and the search for protections become part of the highly orchestrated procedures reflecting the devastating effects of the capitalist transition (Verdery 1996:10). They are not idiosyncratic peculiarities of this postsocialist state or culture. They are part of the "human engineering, not to mention violence, chaos, and despair [and] hidden costs of establishing nation-states," capitalism, and "free markets" (ibid.). In this context democracy is both a possibility and a prison. Such procedures also represent an institutionalized exercise of democratic freedom, a "practice rather than a state, as that which can 'never [be] assured by . . . institutions and laws' but 'must be exercised' " (Foucault 1984:245, quoted in Brown 1995:8). To gain protections, a patient must be willing to participate in a complex medical game. How does the Ukrainian state emerge through its own conception of protection and redistribution of protections? What role do work exemptions, clinical courts, suffering, and trade in diagnoses play in the broader economic transition from a command economy (where money was relatively unimportant) to a market economy?

Nothing to Buy and Nothing to Sell

"There's no way of making money in the village. If I got a Chernobyl pension, I could at least buy some bread." Pavlo Strakhota was one of over 140,000 workers—military, technicians, miners, police officers, drivers, engineers, and physicians from all over Ukraine and other Soviet republics—who were recruited into the Zone as part of the construction of the Sarcophagus, beginning in September 1986. By that time, the government had announced that radiation no longer posed any threat. Rumors spread throughout the villages telling a different story, however. Strakhota's regiment was one of several stationed in Ivanivna's village. As Ivanivna recounted, "rumors circulated, and after a half of a year of working in the regiments, one of these military boys was saying that his brother's godfather was excused from the regiment and had already died. That is, they started to die." Among Zone workers, the Chernobyl death toll was perceived to be considerably higher than the thirty-one-person toll cited in scientific reports.

Strakhota was an uneducated, semiliterate collective farmer from the Transcarpathian region along the western border of Ukraine. He did not want to tell me his name. His medical files indicated that he had received an invitation from the Radiation Research Center to undergo a physical examination. Strakhota told me that he had "shoveled six inches of soil around the plant into buckets" as part of decontamination procedures in the Zone. He also "drove the dosimetrists around the Zone." He characterized his state of health while working in the Zone thus: "The head hurt, the mouth was dry; we walked around like drunks." Like Ivanivna he drew on the image of a drunk to convey his radiation intoxication.

He was selected as a Zone worker from a host of village youth. His recruitment story was an elliptical indictment of a social system, peppered with local lore. "It happened right in the middle of *koliada*, the night of January 8, 1987," he said. *Koliada* is a period of celebration after Christmas characterized by traditional house-to-house caroling—groups collect money for charitable organizations such as a local church or, in this case, the collective farm administration. That night, the administrator received military orders to organize a regiment of Zone workers.

Strakhota recalled being brought to the local military recruiting station (which had been set up in the collective farm manager's office) after the long and cheerful night. He said, "The boys escorted me to the station where those designated to work in the Zone gathered. . . . The boys were singing religious carols. When we got to the farm manager's headquarters, we saw army officers there." In a half-drunken state, Strakhota was approached by a colonel. "He gave us uniforms, and next day we were in the Zone."

By that time he had learned that his fate was sealed because he "didn't know how to organize *blat*." *Blat* is a system of informal exchanges and favors that became a normal part of the Soviet environment of chronic shortage.[16] *Blat* was also important for getting exemptions from military service or conscription, getting jobs for friends and relatives, arranging appointments with well-regarded doctors who might in turn provide access to hospital beds, or obtaining sick-leave permission slips (Ledeneva 1998). Strakhota referred to the manager as "the cashier" who "took all the money and settled his accounts."

Dubinin, on the other hand, was more highly educated and conveyed a different sentiment about recruitment. "I went to work there with joy," he said. "In 1988, after the army, I finished the medical institute with my wife. They placed us in the public health epidemiological station in Donbas. We got an apartment, then I worked in the mines, for a year. Then friends told me I could make some money. They asked if I wanted to work in Chernobyl; they said there was good money, food, and you worked in two-week-long shifts. I did the same work and got paid almost three times as much money."

By Strakhota's and Dubinin's accounts, we see that recruitment and work in the Zone became embedded in a set of complex economic arrangements, both old and new. Benefits and pay for military leaders and professionals began to increase. Documents retrieved by historian Natalia Baranovs'ka from the archives of the Communist Party of Ukraine and other administrative bodies indicate that between 1986 and 1990, a full-scale Zone-related economy emerged.[17] A number of requests to the Soviet Finance and Energy Ministries were made to "raise the salary for the military," "compensate for the material losses of evacuees," "send more back-up contingents," "expand material compensations for cleanup workers," "provide additional financing to scientific research work," and so on (*Chornobyl'ska Tragediia* 1996:225).[18]

Through interviews with workers from various occupational strata, I learned that depending on whether one was a professional or a nonprofessional, Zone laborers were compensated differently for exposure to the same types of risk. My informants were acutely aware of these discrepancies. As Ivanivna and Strakhota indicated, the least educated and those with no *blat* (in the sense of protection, money, or social networks) were required to perform the basest of tasks. "You are the ignorant one (*durak*), I am the boss (*nachal'nyk*)," was the way another military conscript characterized the social distribution of occupational risk.

A recruited cab driver driving an army general to make inspections of the burial pits (*mohyl'nyky*) was paid significantly less than his military counterpart.[19] A professional coal miner excavating for new water-cooling channels under the burning reactor received large bonus salaries and an early pension. While a conscript might have faced a military tribunal, loss of work, or possible imprisonment for refusing to work in the Zone, professionals like Dubinin could choose to go, and would receive roughly three times their normal salaries. This open disparity brought the question of the value of life into constant focus. Shouldn't different laboring classes be compensated equally for incurring the same types of risks? Why do I consent to a system that treats my boss's life as more valuable than my own?

Stefan Laschuk was part of a brigade charged with erecting a barbed-wire fence around the reactor site in the first weeks after the explosion. Military commanders implemented Soviet leaders' directives to contain radiation contamination and, based on accounts that I have collected, were given free rein to decide how long recruits would work in the Zone, regardless of their levels of exposure and established threshold standards. According to Laschuk, "the military commanders told us that after being exposed to 25 rem we would be replaced by other workers. But we weren't replaced. There wasn't 25 rem, there was 125 rem, 225 rem," Laschuk told me.

"They promised us, 'You build the ten-kilometer fence around the reactor and then you'll get out of here.' It turned out that we put the fence up quickly. We wanted to get out. Then a general showed up, wearing gold stars on his shoulders, and he told us, 'Boys, do your accounts this way: better bury one thousand than one million.' " Military commanders, many of whom were unfamiliar with radiation protection strategies, projected the valuelessness of their recruits' lives by suggesting that it was more expedient to expose and dispose of their bodies than to call in more recruits.

Significantly, the same experts who gave international credibility to Soviet radiation protection strategies never aggressively questioned Soviet authorities about these careless and dangerous practices. Laschuk said he worked under conditions of entrapment in the Zone: "If you left the Zone, you were against the government. You were against the law. You were nowhere." Like Ivanivna and Strakhota, Laschuk used the state and medical laws that controlled him to control his own future. Their narratives anticipate a new social contract based on establishing the legal, medical, and moral value of their lives in the new state.

By 1989, a massive Zone-related bureaucratic apparatus consisting of on-site workers, incoming workers, and a research institute was established. The Soviet Union's moment of collapse exposed the political calculations involved in defining lives of those working in the Zone as being more or less valued. One former Ukrainian republican administrator and biophysicist who was also a native of the rural Zone, Ivan Los, recalled how desperately he had lobbied for funds at the Soviet state economic planning committee (*Hosplan*) in Moscow, to ensure that cleanup work in the Zone continued. He referred to Moscow as the "center," as was common.

> The regions got money for their problems from the center. To get that money, one had to go to Moscow and argue how that money was needed for this region or for that region. Ukraine understood this very well. There was a nuclear accident on our territory, and we were not to blame too much. . . . Ukrainian Party leaders understood that the quicker and the stronger they latched on to Moscow's coffers and showed how serious the radiation problem was in Ukraine, the larger the central budget that would go to Ukraine. And the better we could stop this situation. But everyone descended upon Moscow, for money. But there was no money because of the economic collapse.

By 1989, the prospect of a weakened Soviet state made way for the emergence of a Ukrainian administration of Chernobyl. By 1990, members of the Parliament of what was still the Ukrainian Soviet Socialist Republic took the independent step of proposing a set of laws on state protection and compensation for *all* workers in the Zone. Getting the "Moscow center" to agree to such a proposal was a major political victory for Ukrainian cabinet and Party members, who were now under the pressure of domestic professional trade unions, Zone laborers, and their families to create such laws.[20]

In an interview, one of the laws' sovereignty-minded authors told me, "For the workers in the Zone, we put in all the benefits we could think of. We searched the books on compensation for war invalids. We included telephones as compensation, even cars, everything."[21] The proposed laws guaranteed these Zone workers higher salaries, bonuses, and privileges, and compensations for illnesses, disability, and death. A new Chernobyl Fund would derive its monies from the Soviet *Hosplan* but would be administered in Ukraine. The not-yet-independent republic positioned itself as a life-insurance agent, guaranteeing cash transfers to a large group of workers whose laboring bodies were used up and "thrown out" without adequate compensation.

But by 1990, the Soviet Finance Ministry withdrew the funds necessary for containment, payment, and monitoring of Zone workers; and the Soviet atomic authorities quickly relinquished responsibility for the Zone. Social protection laws existed only on paper. This withdrawal, however, created a vacuum of authority in the Zone, turning it into a kind of Soviet no-man's-land, and had immediate deleterious effects. As one official in the Ukrainian Parliamentary Commission on Chernobyl recalled, workers in the Zone started to loot.[22] According to him, "Everything was stolen, starting in 1988, 1989, and until 1990." Subject to theft were contaminated helicopter parts, combines, tractors, building materials, cars, and trucks found in the Zone, as well as anything left behind by evacuees in housing blocks and private farms, such as valued icons, furniture, and farm animals. Plunderers, disregarding the destructive consequences of their acts, bought, sold, and circulated contaminated goods at large.

Workers of the Interior Ministry, the army, and the local militia who manned dosimetric checkpoints along the borders of the Zone were also implicated in and profited from this period of no authority. Their work included checking levels of contamination in materials being transported out of the Zone. For example, if the surface of a car registered contamination beyond the permissible levels at these checkpoints, decontamination procedures (hosing with water in most cases) would proceed. If the object in question was thoroughly contaminated (such as forklifts and trucks used in the decontamination of soil or demolition of buildings), it was to be sent back to be interred in the burial pits. Increasingly, there was less reliable dosimetric control around the edges of the Zone, as bribery of checkpoint personnel became routine practice. Contaminated equipment could now pass through easily. These practices highlighted the fictive nature of Zone boundaries.

Ukraine "inherited" radiation-exposed populations, including resettlers and inhabitants of the zones, and their ready-to-be-deployed democratic claims when it declared sovereignty in 1991. Had republican lawmakers reneged on promises to provide social protections, they told me, their actions would have amounted to political self-sabotage. Their sense of constraint attests to the importance of entitlements as part of a legacy of a Soviet welfare state. Yet the ongoing social and technical challenges of Chernobyl offered even less choice as they framed their solution to its aftermath. At the moment of sovereignty, the enormous costs associated with Chernobyl left the country less socially stable and dramatically poorer than it already was.

To subsidize the new laws, a 12 percent Chernobyl tax was levied on all Ukrainian workers' salaries. Of these resources, 60 to 80 percent was spent on social problems, on subsidizing legally established benefits and compensations, health care costs, and pensions, and on the construction of new housing for resettled persons.[23] Monies for technical management, most crucially for engineering work to stabilize the Sarcophagus, would be procured in the context of international cooperation, joint ventures, loans, and technical assistance programs. With almost no funds available for such programs, Ukrainian politicians would continually refer to the country's large number of Chernobyl victims to dramatize the need for foreign aid.

The question of who would own and manage the Exclusion Zone also played an important part in the staking out of sovereignty claims. In one of its first acts of territorial sovereignty the republic seized administration, declaring itself "competent" over all economic and scientific activity in the Zone, and establishing sole rights to cooperative contracts with foreign countries and international organizations.[24]

Along with sovereignty claims, leaders introduced a new system for registering exposed territories and populations. In a resolution entitled "The Concept of Inhabitation," Ukrainian deputies declared their entire national territory "a Zone of ecological calamity." The Soviet administration was denounced for its "willful disregard of the safety of populations living and working around and in the contaminated areas" (State Declaration 1991). In addition to acknowledging the urgent need to protect workers in the Zone, it also made the task of collecting "systematic knowledge" and the identification of exposed populations a top priority.

The Ukrainian approach differed radically from the Soviet one in terms of politics, economics, and public health. Where the Soviets had made the fate of a select cohort of lethally exposed firemen the center of their concerns, the state focus was now on individuals and populations whose doses were unaccounted for in, and partly a result of, the Soviet approach. According to the State Declaration, obtaining "positive identification of an exposed individual would be a difficult task because knowledge of doses received by the general Ukrainian population immediately after the blast was lacking. The reconstruction of this dose is critical."

Another difference between the Soviet and Ukrainian approach concerned the placement of research emphasis, or the level at which radiation-induced biological effects should be detected and monitored. Where the Soviets focused mostly on deterministic effects among their affected cohorts, Ukrainians emphasized both deterministic and stochastic effects. Deterministic effects occur when levels of absorbed radiation doses produce clinically observable pathologies; these pathologies can occur only above a designated threshold dose. We have already seen how constructions of threshold dose can be politically determined. Stochastic effects, on the other hand, are not threshold-dose dependent. They are based on gene damage of which the probability of harmful effects increases with increments of dose exposure, regardless of how small those increments are. Stochastic effects are of particular concern to individuals who are continuously exposed to low doses (doses that are below an allowable threshold dose). Stochastic effects are nonlinear in the sense that they are not governed by any strict dose-effect relationships.

What we see in the transition from a Soviet to a post-Soviet management is the assertion of two very different biological models of risk that, in turn, legitimate two very different political orders. The differences between these biological models as they affected individual case histories and courses of illness will be discussed in the following chapter. It is enough to note here that the new Ukrainian accounting of the Chernobyl unknown was part and parcel of new strategies of knowledge-based governance and social mobilizations. In the Ukrainian version of reality, a significantly lower threshold allowed more citizens to have a stake in their symptoms, if and when they appeared, as Chernobyl-related. A state medical publication illustrates the inclusiveness of such an approach. "The world of post-Chernobyl is a present existing reality. This world is inhabited by millions of people. The main content of this world is radiation, with a place and role in daily civil life. The existence of this world requires constant consideration and reconsideration of what occurred" (Loganovsky and Yuriev 1995:1).

Scientific and biomedical forms of accounting for the biological effects of Chernobyl were once again inextricable from the political processes they legitimated. A state manipulation of thresholds of biological risk has generated in and of itself a political and rational-technical reality to which an increasing number of people belong. The locus of politics would decisively establish itself in clinics, the now contentious sites where patients, activists, health workers, and administrators would debate exposure levels, definitions of injury, and individual eligibilities for Chernobyl-related compensations and medical care.

By the fall of 1991, any person possibly exposed to any levels of irradiation by being present in the Exclusion Zone or the surrounding contaminated zones for short or prolonged periods was likely to undergo clinical monitoring, to put his or her name and medical history in a national registry of sufferers, and to claim his or her entitlement to compensations, including preferential and free medical care and examinations at specialized radiation centers and special Chernobyl hospital wings. Cities, territories, and villages were designated as "protected" by the new state.

Cash transfers, particularly to the historically neglected rural people living in these territories, occasioned what one scientist referred to as an "indexation" of suffering on the basis of what was not initially openly admitted about the scale of the catastrophe, and a configuration of the scale of payments to be extracted from the state. "The laws confirmed the understanding that 'I suffered,' " Mr. Los explained. "The people remember that the state never hands out money for free, meaning, 'the state is paying money, very little though, compared to the damage that is really awaiting me. Meaning, I suffered very strongly.' Remember, they are reading between the lines."

Public spending continued to be directed to the Chernobyl sufferer throughout the 1990s. Various institutes of the Ukrainian Academy of Sciences continued to receive state funding to conduct important scientific research in the zones, to monitor and map contamination, and to arrange international scientific cooperations. Over two hundred new medical facilities provided specialized medical help in Ukraine.[25] Hospitals established special Chernobyl wings with separate funding from the Chernobyl Ministry. In some cases, these special wings were visited by foreigners and attracted vital foreign resources. An expansive sanatorium system was devoted to the treatment of Chernobyl sufferers. Special stores were built to provide sufferers with environmentally clean foods. The sum total of sufferers who underwent monitoring in the Chernobyl welfare system rose from 347,252 persons in 1990 to 1,536,270 in 1991, when the laws on social protection were passed, to over 3,500,000 in 1996. Although these numbers reflect socioeconomic changes of the period, they also indicate the increased role of physicians, bureaucrats, and medical-labor committees as intermediaries of state assistance.

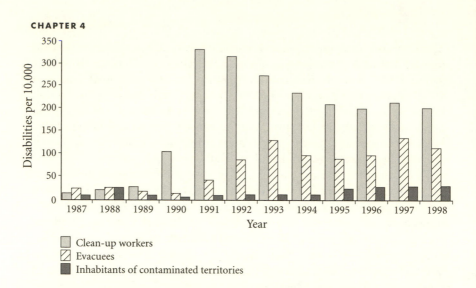

FIGURE 4. Incidence of Disability among Chernobyl Sufferers (per 10,000). Source: *Indicators of Health*, Ministry of Health. Kyiv, Ukraine.

Medical-Labor Committees

Medical-labor committees were established throughout Ukraine to handle the growing number of claims of disability related to Chernobyl. These committees were mandated to "register the connection of illness, disability, and death with ionizing radiation." Such registration (and its supporting documents) is referred to in Russian as *sviaz po bolezn'iu*, literally meaning "in connection with illness." Such "ties," as I will call them, tie or connect disability to occupation-related diseases, in this case to those diseases that are considered to have a Chernobyl-related cause. Ties authorize a host of privileges and social protections for the disabled and his/her family. Before 1990, information regarding the medical and financial privileges associated with illnesses "contracted" in the Zone was classified. By 1990, "the word about compensation soon spread," according to Ihor Demeshko, a former obstetrician, who worked his way up from a provincial hospital to membership in the prestigious medical-labor committee of the Radiation Research Center. This committee was charged with the task of coordinating new criteria of Chernobyl-related disability and for the authorization of so-called ties.

The Radiation Research Center is situated in the forests of one of Kyiv's leisure park areas (Russian: *zona otdykha*) about a mile from the village of Derevo.[26] This village marks the border of the government-designated Zone Four of radiation contamination. The center is set amid a number of health sanatoria, specialized health centers, and an internment facility (Russian: *dom-internat*) for severely mentally disabled adults.

In the Soviet period, Demeshko explained, disability could be claimed through the acute radiation sickness diagnosis alone. Dr. Guskova had restricted the use of that diagnosis to a select few who showed immediate clinically observable signs of radiation injury. Yet radiation injuries can be long-term. Under Ukrainian state laws, a new table of illnesses alleged to be associated with the Chernobyl accident was drafted. This new table was the work of a committee consisting of physicians, representatives of trade unions (most notably those of coal miners, who had intensified their collective demands for compensation), and representatives of the Ministries of Health, Social Welfare, and Labor, and the Chernobyl Ministry itself. Other institutions from which Zone labor was expropriated cooperated too, including the Ministry of Internal Affairs (the state security forces), and the Ministry of Defense (the military). In the last draft of this table, produced in 1996 and circulated for approval among these ministries, I counted more than fifty diseases that the medical-labor committee of the Radiation Research Center recommended should be associable with Chernobyl-related disability.

In 1989, 15 men had been considered for disability in the center; by the end of 1989, 130 men; by 1990, 2,753 cases had been considered.[27] In 1990, Chernobyl disability was granted to the following categories: neurological, 50.4 percent; therapeutic (general) 19.6 percent; and cardiovascular, 11.7 percent. The neurological, as is evident, was a key gateway into disability status. The number of "ties" accorded to specific labor sectors also reflected degrees of political influence of each of these sectors: 34.2 percent were drivers by profession; 27.1 percent were workers of the Ministry of Internal Affairs; and 14.4 percent were coal miners. Under the Chernobyl laws, pension benefits for the disabled differed in important ways from those of average workers. Demeshko explained the difference to me:

> In the former Soviet Union, if you got sick on the job, there was one simple pension for you, for all illnesses. A level three disabled person received 15 percent of his wage. A level two received 30 percent of his wage. With the addition of a professionally related pathology, for example, lung cancer for a mine worker or spinal problems for a tractor driver, a level three disabled person received 30 percent of his wage. A level two received 50 percent of his wage. With the addition of a Chernobyl-related pathology, that same level three disabled person in 1990 received 30–60 percent of his wage; a level two received 50–80 percent of his wage. There is a difference.

Dr. Nestor Mudrak is Demeshko's coworker. He formerly directed a blood transfusion center in a Kyiv military hospital to which Zone cleanup workers were admitted for treatment. Today he is the manager of the Radiation Research Center, responsible for generating resources to run the Clinic. Demeshko screens prospective cases of disability and then sends any individuals he believes have social or economic resources to Mudrak. Mudrak deals "with questions regarding all legal documents that come out of this Clinic," and puts the final stamp of approval on a person's disability status.

In his role as manager, Mudrak engaged in a variety of techniques for accumulating resources, including *blat*, favors, and bartering. He entered into complicated sets of exchanges with well-endowed patients (in energy-related enterprises, for example) and collective farm bosses to ensure steady supplies of food, electricity, and gas to his Clinic. "You know how the Soviet system was," he said. "We didn't have to buy anything. The system provided. There was no need for a manager. The state was the manager. These obligations have automatically transferred to the head of the hospital, me. I have to look for money." He said he had recently negotiated with Derevo's collective farm to supply sugar for the Clinic's cafeteria, in exchange for preferential clinical access for the collective farm's members and administrative staff.[28] He said he was unable to pay the Clinic's phone bill, and worried that the electricity would soon be shut off.

He complained that money derived from the Chernobyl Fund feeds bureaucracies rather than affected citizens. "All citizens (*iurydychni osoby*) of Ukraine pay into the Chernobyl Fund, but the money doesn't come this way." Mudrak explained that the money collected from this fund moves from the Ministry of Finance, to the Academy of Medical Sciences, to the Chernobyl Ministry, to the Ministry of Public Health with its own Chernobyl divisions. "By the time it gets to us, the financing is miserable. For example, I am supposed to get some money for elevators. If I don't pay the bills, the elevators will stop working. The patients with cancers, respiratory problems, and leukemia are on the fifth and sixth floors. The Ministry of Energy disconnected the gas and water on the tenth anniversary of the Chernobyl accident. With some personal negotiation, they eased up and gave us hot water. And our situation is relatively better than in other hospitals because we are a Chernobyl hospital."

Mudrak is a competent observer of the demoralizing effects that laws guaranteeing sufferers' rights, together with economic collapse, have had on governance and the politics of ill citizens. He compared the Ukrainian laws on compensation for Chernobyl sufferers to systems of compensation associated with other nuclear disasters. He noted several social conditions that made Ukraine's compensation system unique. The collapse of a centralized system of national productivity and health care, unemployment, and loss of state guarantees have led to a worsening of social-economic living conditions. He associated the state's compensation system and the illnesses that make it available with a "bicycle"—that is, a mundane vehicle necessary for negotiating daily life. He told me,

> Administrators did it differently in America at Three Mile Island and with the *hibakusha* of Japan, paying the victims in one lump sum.[29] But we're inventing a new bicycle here. The law is so rationally unresolvable. A lot of people are being thrown out of work. People don't have enough money to eat, to buy medicines. The laws are written so that Chernobyl people are supposed to get them for free. But the state doesn't give out the medicines for free anymore. Drug stores have become commercialized.

He likened his work to that of a bank, settling accounts and "issuing money."[30] "If a person needs medicines, a person needs money. The diagnosis we write is money."

The importance of these diagnoses to everyday people cannot be stressed enough. "There's pressure from the invalids to write a Chernobyl-related diagnosis. The demands on the state are increasing with every instant. People working in the zones who have high-risk jobs sign up for work knowing about that risk. They reason, 'I get sick, I get this much money. I die, my family will get this much money.' "

The Chernobyl Division of the Ministry of Health keeps records of how many people request Chernobyl-related disability in every region of Ukraine, and how many requests are denied. Mudrak told me that "the ones we turn away will come back again, in waves." As a professional with medical and legal powers, Mudrak conceded that he was a "rationally unresolvable" link in the current state distribution mechanisms. In his view, physicians had become ethically compromised in their assessment of disability:

> The worse the illness the better it is for the sick person. Maybe this person doesn't even have an illness, but the doctor will see this is an unfortunate person, and that he needs medicines. Maybe from my side this is strange, from another side, you understand. From one side, he should write an honest diagnosis. It's not honest to write an illness that does not exist. But from another point of view, there is the sick person. . . . We have to protect him. The state does not pay, the state is not fulfilling its legal duty. We doctors don't get our salaries for three to four months at a time. We do not get the money. The integrity of the diagnosis is corrupted.

He suggested that physicians should not "be blamed too much" for this suspension of medical ethics, where a trade in diagnoses and symptoms has developed. His superior, the deputy director of the center, linked the epidemic of disability to inflation and workers' loss of purchasing power.

105

He said, "Inflation is so high and the purchasing strength of every person in Ukraine is so low that people cannot guarantee their own future—even for a month." He also felt that an important component underlying the attraction to the sick role is the fact that workers have become unpaid laborers. "Factory workers don't get paid for three or four months, and even that salary is lower than the minimum these workers should make. Workers who live here are literally giving away their labor to the state for free."

This deputy also described the use of the medical system as a form of "market compensation" and as an individual survival strategy.

> If people could improve their family budgets, there would be a lot less illness. Now, people are oriented toward one thing. Only through the medical system, only through the constitution of an illness, and in particular difficult illnesses, incurable ones, can they improve their family budget. The gap between the state, the enterprise, and the family is so large that this "discoordination" will continue to destroy our people.

Such orientations speak to the importance of clinics and sick roles as means of negotiating social disruptions and insecurities. Yet the goal of this sick role is nonrecovery. Only through nonrecovery can the sick guarantee a stable influx of privileges. One patient justified nonrecovery as a way of counteracting unstable laws on social protection and welfare. "Today the law, tomorrow no law," he said. Illness has become a master narrative of the state, according to Demeshko, "We can't stop the illness in this population. Our clinical structures are necessary, vital even. The mechanism of compensation does not depend on us anymore. *The whole state is already integrated into it.*"

In this integration of unstable law and individual economic weakness, clinical structures have become prime sites of social production and power. The social networks built around them compensate for acute social dislocation associated with labor losses and crime. Illness has not only a social course but an "unstoppable" one. How can we account theoretically for this new "speed" of illness? In the social course model (Kleinman 1986), social relations are central to the analysis of symptom causality. The social course model makes allowances for complex states of interdependence among individuals, family, and social and state institutions; it allows us to think of health and illness as anchored not only in the personality of individuals but in their often marginal positioning vis-à-vis broader social forces and institutions (Ware 1998).[31] Other medical anthropologists have shown how experiences of illnesses, particularly those linked with mental illness, are shaped by changing political economies of welfare (Estroff et al. 1997); a biologization of mental illness based on patterns of scientific research underlying the formation of bio-

logical claims (Young 1995); or global economic reorganization impact-
ing family psychodynamics and role allotments (Scheper-Hughes 1979).
These works examine the interplay of institutions, medical knowledge,
and changing economic situations; they point to the patient's becoming a
skilled and knowledgeable—not to mention desperate—practitioner of
his/her illness. They offer important ethnographic ways of understanding
organic, legal, economic, social, and scientific factors as they combine in
specific local contexts of patienthood. They also provide ethnographically based perspectives on universal diagnostic categories such "malingering" or "factitiousness" that reduce certain forms of patienthood to
the exploitation of others.

In my analysis, I examine how claims to disability are embedded in a
complex and productive biosocial reality linking individual lives with the
political economy of the state, the unknown biological impact of Chernobyl, and the history of its technical and political managements. These
elements combine to keep producing an unstoppable dimension of illness.
This process is analyzable beyond individual symptoms or interactions
between doctors and patients (although that level of analysis remains
key); it is coextensive with a new social production of value around the ill
and the heightened role of the state to define or obstruct the terms of their
treatment (Rabinow 1999). While illness after Chernobyl has become the
great social leveler, providing access to citizenship for some, the gates to
this democratic pasture open and close at random. The randomness of the
law (in the form of denials of access, exclusions, postponements) combined with economic instability is precisely what ensures the system's du-
rability and a collective drive toward illness.

Disability Claims

Demeshko allowed me to take notes and to ask questions of claimants
entering his office. By 1996, the laws on procuring the Chernobyl tie were
getting more restrictive. The following office interactions are intended to
capture a flow of appeals and the repertoire of patient strategies. Many
female clients, for example, staked their claim to privileges on the basis of
deceased husbands, or children or grandchildren alleged to have been in
utero at the time of the disaster (in chapter 6, I present a detailed clinical
case of one such claim). Many male clients invoked the number of days
they had worked in the Zone, or the number of days they have not
worked at all, to indicate their degree of illness. Many of the claimants
lived on less than forty dollars a month—the official poverty line in 1996.
Their names and their family members' names were registered in a state-
operated registry of Chernobyl sufferers. Some wanted to discontinue

work in the Zone and receive disability status (these workers tended to have disproportionately high salaries). Others who had already worked in the Zone wanted to ascend to a higher disability grade to increase their pension. And others wanted to register their children or grandchildren as disabled.

We can also observe how the sick role and privileges were allocated and/or denied, and the effects these allocations or denials generated. Allocation in one case was based on the wealth the client could pass on to the research center in a diagnosis-for-resources exchange. In another case, Demeshko perceived the claimant to be "on the border with death." Denials were often based on poorly documented evidence of exposure, or on the count that claimants' illnesses developed beyond the limits of acceptable timetables. But in essence, few formal rules guided the allocation of these privileges. Some clients had to beg for them; others were given advice about informal clinical procedures to expedite their claims.

The mother of a child in utero at the time of the disaster enters Demeshko's office. Her husband is a level three disabled person; she is a level two. She claims that her daughter is "not developing properly." The child "used to be quick, now her legs hurt." She has thyroid cancer.

Someone's head peers through the door. Demeshko says, "A decision has not been made for you yet."

A middle-aged rural woman walks in. She was evacuated from her village located in Zone Two. When she says that her daughter was pregnant at the time of the disaster, she starts to cry. "The little girl," she says, "now ten years old, has a dry mouth; she's weak, her thinking is slow, her thyroid is swollen, her legs hurt, her blood is poor." The woman says that the girl will be interned in the gastroenterological ward of the Clinic for monitoring. She needs to elicit sympathy from Demeshko, who will eventually decide whether the girl will become a state-protected invalid on the basis of her diagnostic paperwork. Demeshko interrupts the grandmother and tells her that she is in the wrong place and should go to the Chernobyl children's hospital for the evaluation of the child's status.

The woman remains seated. A man in his mid-fifties enters. He says that he has worked at the reactor site since 1978, and that he regularly interns himself at the center and at the local clinic of the Chernobyl plant for monitoring and treatment. The man keeps careful records of his illnesses. He shows documentary evidence of his dose, a high 73 rem. When I ask him why he is seeing Demeshko now, he says, "I'm sick." Demeshko then asks him, "And before?" The man answers that he was sick, but that he "hid it." When I ask him why he hid it, he answers, "So I could work in the Zone, I'm used to working." "How much do you make?" Demeshko asks him. "$270.00 a month." He then turns to the seated woman: "How much do you make?" he asks, and her answer is "$27.00

a month." When I ask the worker whether he can say more about what brought him to the Clinic, he answers in a cynical way, "A spinning head."

A tired-looking elderly man comes in and throws his documents toward Demeshko, who then asks him where he works. The man replies that he does not work, and that he lives on a pension. He says that he evacuated people from the zones when he worked for the city taxi service. Demeshko doesn't accept the documents and tells him to go to another hospital.

A man in his mid-fifties walks in. After Demeshko inquires, he says that he worked in the Zone "for one day, on May 18, 1986." He doesn't know his dose. The man worked as a driver and claims to have fallen ill in 1995, nine years after the disaster, with rheumatism, stenocardia, cardiosclerosis, and arrhythmia. "They gave me the Chernobyl tie because of my heart arrhythmia," he says. He also says that he no longer works and has been living on a disability pension that provides him with $27.00 a month. The man wants to ascend to a higher Chernobyl disability rank. When he leaves the office, Demeshko guesses that the man "bought" the tie. He says that the claimant's illnesses appeared "after the acceptable timetable for arrhythmia. . . . His disability status will expire and he won't be able to renew it." The man's physical condition, regardless of whether it is Chernobyl-induced, allegedly prevents him from working. His having based his claim on one day of work at Chernobyl means either that the man is driven by desperation or that his expectations of compensation are unrealistic, or both.

A well-dressed man enters and without introductions reports that he was previously a patient in the cardiology ward. He says that he worked in the Zone for six days in 1986, "building the *Sarkofag*." In 1993, he allegedly fell ill with stenocardia. Demeshko asks him where he works. He says he is a director of the lucrative Kyiv Energy Company (KyivEnergo). He gives an account of his lost work capacity, "I haven't worked twenty-six days in five weeks," and says he thinks he can't work any more. Demeshko tells him "to go see the center's manager, Dr. Mudrak."

After the man leaves, Demeshko says that his stenocardia appeared after the acceptable timetable for stenocardia. The limit is five years. "He got his illness seven years after the disaster. He got sick too late. By law, we can't give him disability status. But because he is a director, we might be able to get some *humanitarka* (a donation or payment) out of him." That is Mudrak's job.

A woman enters, a widow, representing her deceased husband. "I submitted his medical documents last year," she says. "A decision hasn't been made yet on your husband's matter," Demeshko answers. She leaves, saying little else about her case. Demeshko apparently knows her situation and is delaying decision making.

A middle-aged rural woman enters the office. She says that her "husband-invalid" (*cholovik-invalid*) died three days ago, and that she is seeking additional social protections." Her husband, a driver by profession, worked in the Zone in two-week shifts.[32] She lives on a pension of $26.00. He collected a pension of $75.00 before his cancer-related death. Demeshko then asks her, "Was there a Chernobyl pension already calculated in his regular pension?"

"Yes, an added $16.00 a month for work in the Zone," she answers.

"Did you get compensation for his death?" Demeshko asks.

"Just for his funeral," she says.

"What do you want here?" Demeshko asks.

The woman answers, "My husband said to me, 'When I die, get the Chernobyl privileges.' "

In this case, the deceased calculated in advance the benefits to his family of his Chernobyl-related death. His wife "inherited" his medical documents, and with them she is advocating for more social protections from the state. She claims his disability is linked to his death (*sviaz po smerti*, or "in connection with death," hereafter "death tie").

A man enters the room. He says that he worked for two weeks in the Zone, cutting down the surrounding contaminated forests, in June 1986: "Our whole factory went," he says. He says he doesn't know his dose. He receives a pension of $26.00 a month as a sufferer. He says he needs disability status so that he can pay for his thyroid operation and treatments of thyroid replacement hormone. He seems desperate, depressed, and resigned to the vagaries of bureaucracy. Demeshko accepts his documents for review.

A woman enters and says without any introduction, "My husband was a disabled person (level one), a professional. He died of kidney cancer. His dose was 25 rem. He received $325.00 in pension payments." She wants the death tie. When she leaves, Demeshko says, "This woman isn't going to get any more money. The Ministry of Social Welfare has already given her money for his funeral."

A man enters. He is receiving a pension of $32.00 and wants disability status. He says that his wife, a Zone worker, died recently and he needs to "protect himself." He doesn't know his dose.

A woman enters. She is wearing a black dress and a black scarf. Her husband died three days ago. She wants the privileges associated with his Chernobyl-related death. Her husband worked as an engineer. His dose was an extremely high 180 rem, and he died of lung cancer.

A woman enters. She was evacuated from Prypiat' on April 27, 1986. She was laid off from work at a bread factory, where her salary was

110

$37.00 a month. She lists her illnesses for Demeshko. In 1987, she was diagnosed with vegetovascular dystonia and discirculatory encephalopathy (nervous disorders). She has three children to support.

"Can you protect your family?" Demeshko asks her.

"No," she says.

"What will you do next?" I ask her.

"Trade, sell whatever I can. The state doesn't pay anything."

Demeshko sends her to the local polyclinic. "Go there and they will write a referral to the neurological ward here. *That will get you the Chernobyl tie.*"

A man enters. He shows Demeshko documents from a specialized examination that the medical-labor committee required him to undergo. The man worked at the Chernobyl plant for eight months starting in May 1986. He wants his disability. He alleges that he has eczema, and invokes the authority of Dr. Angelina Guskova when he claims that his eczema has "turned into acute radiation dermatitis—diagnosed in Moscow." Demeshko tells him that there are no privileges associated with acute radiation dermatitis. The diagnosis he will need to be considered for disability is skin cancer. After the man leaves, Demeshko explains that Guskova repealed any acute radiation sickness–related diagnoses in 1988. "In general, disability is no longer given for acute radiation sickness. However, if a person shows complications from the effects of acute radiation sickness, he would be entitled to consideration. *Skin cancer would count.*"

A man enters; he looks sallow and exhausted. He puts a document on the table that shows evidence of his dose. "Here's an estimation of my dose based on the routes that I traveled in the Zone. I worked in the *mohyl'nyky* (irradiated materials dump sites)." He says that he suffers from hypotonia and has had two heart attacks. Demeshko asks him to show documentation of his hospital stays starting in 1990. The man answers that he failed to have his diagnoses registered from year to year. "You will get no tie," Demeshko tells him. "But people are busy harvesting their potatoes now," he added, "so maybe there's a bed available for you in the neurology ward. You can get a diagnosis there." The man leaves; Demeshko tells me, *"He's on the border of death*, we have many like that."

Depression, exhaustion, and defeat fill this newly renovated office. So many women in black dresses make the same claims—their relatives or spouses have died. The legacy of Chernobyl is being remade as an intractable marriage between life and death. Yet the Chernobyl death has no distinguishing biological markers.[33] What distinguishes it is the life that preceded it. That life has a specific medical profile and a specific relation with the state. It is subject to a particular type of experience of citizenship

111

and social inclusion. By the time of his or her death, the Chernobyl sufferer will have been the subject of a massive amount of writing. He or she will leave behind a stack of mostly illegible medical records, hospital referrals, signatures, institutional rubber stamps, dose assessments, diagnoses, corrections to diagnoses, more diagnoses, and other papers conferring his/her Chernobyl identity.

A woman enters. Her husband has died, and she wants the death tie. "He was only fifty years old, an operator of a bulldozer," she says. "He worked for seven months at Chernobyl, 1986–1987. He showed no signs of illness and died suddenly of heart failure. I was at my mother's," she says. Demeshko asks her whether her husband had been categorized as disabled before his death. He had not been. Then he asks whether she has an autopsy report. As she hands it to Demeshko, the woman recounts that her husband's body was in the morgue for seven days. She leaves the office. The autopsy report reads:

> The corpse of citizen Malohub was found in a decomposing state. The forensic examination of the corpse of citizen Malohub did not indicate signs of bodily injury. Blood chemical analysis showed white stains indicating a higher than acceptable level of blood alcohol. Given the corpse's stage of decomposition, it is impossible to know with certainty whether this concentration of ethyl alcohol was excessive and what role it played in the death of citizen Malohub because of possible synthesis with anaerobic bacteria in the decaying processes. The death of citizen Malohub, Anatolii Anatoliievych, fifty years of age, was caused most directly by acute coronary insufficiency, made apparent by the shape of the coronaries, evidence of sclerosis, a diffused cardiosclerosis, an overwhelming heart attack, followed by swelling of the lungs and brain.

In a country where the incidence of alcoholism is one of the highest in the former Soviet Union, Demeshko tells me he has developed his own calculus to determine the role of alcohol, as opposed to radiation, in the processes reported by the medical examiner.[34] He doubts the woman's story and questions the medical examiner's conclusion for the following reason: "The autopsy report says that 30 percent of the sclerotic tissue of the heart's arteries (appearing opaque in an X ray) blocked out the rays." If the tissue blocked at least 80 percent—Demeshko's standard—"then we would have 100 percent certainty that the death occurred from heart disease alone—the woman would then get the tie and the Chernobyl cash benefits for her husband's death. The woman will present the documents, she'll circulate in the bureaucratic networks, but she won't get the tie. Her husband drank and brought on his own death."

Illness for Life

In the ever widening gulf between the exact and inexact sciences, probable and improbable causes and, exact and inexact criteria of blame, an entire social transformation took place and occasioned new forms of desperation and bureaucratic dependence.

The center's medical-labor committee members examined over three hundred cases in October 1996. Members typically convened three times annually, but given that salaries were not paid on time, many of the members deemed such work unprofitable drudgery. Some occupied their time selling medical services, while others simply foot-dragged on their committee duties, which resulted in postponements of disability-related decisions and long anxious waits on the part of potential candidates.

I examined one hundred of the approved cases stacked on Demeshko's desk before his secretary opened the office door to the line of people waiting to retrieve them. Of these one hundred, fifty-four cases were approved for Chernobyl-related disability on the basis of cardiological problems related to hypertension, sclerosis, and heart disease; five on the basis of cancers including myeloid leukemia and colon and thyroid cancers; four on the basis of respiratory problems related to chronic lung obstruction; twenty-seven on the basis of neurological disorders, including functional disorders of the higher nervous system such as stroke, encephalopathy, brain damage, and posttraumatic stress; and four on account of endocrinological and autoimmune disorders. Six other cases were put forth by individuals who wanted to obtain a tie on the basis of a family member who they claimed had died from work in the Chernobyl Zone. Causes of death confirmed as Chernobyl-related included organic brain damage, heart disease, and prostate cancer. A last case was that of a man who had worked in the Zone until his death from a stroke.

It is difficult to know whether any of these cases would have come to light in one form or another as Chernobyl-related, and compensable, in a Soviet model of intervention. Given the strict biomedical criteria embedded in that model, it would be safe to say that they would not have. What is clear is that different rational-technical interventions (and the scientific measures and biomedical categories they introduce) used in different political contexts produce strikingly different pictures of the toll of the aftermath. These differences underscore the extent to which interventions have framed bureaucratic actions as well as the status of suffering and its modes of objectification.

Opinions about the fate of the Chernobyl sufferers and the disabled also serve as a kind of barometer of the country's shifting moral fabric.

113

People outside the system held mixed views about the compensation system. Some felt that the very inclusion of Chernobyl sufferers in a state welfare regime meant that the state could still be held morally accountable for socially protecting at least a part of its citizenry. Among rural inhabitants who typically were on the bottom of the socialist redistribution ladder, views tended to be more favorable toward their struggles. Many of these poor farmers and elderly people thought that their inclusion in a regime of compensation made the state somewhat accountable to the needs of other segments as well. Among inhabitants of Kyiv and other urban centers, there was a growing consensus that the sufferers were "parasites of the state, damaging the economy, not paying taxes." The sufferer stood for a sociality made obsolete by an emerging capitalism. Many young people who were evacuated from the zones said that they didn't want to be associated with Chernobyl. They felt that the label stigmatized them and made them unhirable. Many of the sovereignty-minded nationalists and unionists who drafted the social protection laws stopped fueling and participating in compensatory politics; they came to see the Chernobyl compensation system as a dire mistake that unintentionally produced a quasi-socialist population. Funds and activist groups are now indeed supported by socialist and communist leaderships who lobby for continued aid in a divided Parliament. Meanwhile, international agencies such as the World Bank cite the Chernobyl social apparatus as a "dead weight" burdening Ukraine's less than ideal transition to a market economy (World Bank 1996). International monetary agencies are so ill disposed toward the system that they have made its quick extinction a condition of future loan contracting. In response to such pressures, in July 1998, for example, the Ukrainian president ordered the halving of government contributions to the state-run Chernobyl Fund.[35] Soon after, the government issued a press release stating that Ukraine's budget deficit had dropped from 3.3 percent to 2.5 percent of the gross domestic product. Such numbers were presented as evidence of Ukraine's adherence to the International Monetary Fund's main market reform requirements. The presentation of this numerical evidence cleared the way for a $2.2 billion loan from the International Monetary Fund.[36] As others interpret the value of Chernobyl victimhood, the city of sufferers seems firmly entrenched as a critical space of political negotiation and personal survival—and one where so many individuals have gained their illnesses for life.

Chapter 5
Biological Citizenship

Remediation Models

Table 2 illustrates the different kinds of radioactive particles that were released during the Chernobyl disaster, how much was released, and when they (will have) disappeared. The half-lives of these particles have a startling range—anywhere from 1.4 hours, to 285 days, to 24,400 years.[1] The table gives a sense of the virtually infinite incubation period of Chernobyl-related illnesses (UNESCO 1996).

In the United States, issues of environmental liability have generated a legal industry concerned with attribution of costs of pollution and legislation of the forms that remedies and remediations should take. In many contaminated zones that are beyond remediation (in Ukraine and elsewhere), current legal issues often involve weighing the health costs of exposures to environmental contaminants against the costs of cleanup of those contaminants. In sorting out these dilemmas, American legal and corporate analysts have introduced remediation models based on cost-effectiveness. These models balance knowledge of the health effects of ionizing radiation against economic feasibility of cleanup and levels of social acceptability of the radiation levels that will remain after cleanup (Hamilton and Viscusi 1997, Steele 1995, Schroeder 1986, Berkovitz 1989).[2] "Levels of social acceptability" is a highly contingent and relative term, however. Such levels can be determined with or without the participation of affected groups, depending on their economic resources, degree of political influence, and level of scientific literacy regarding radiation health effects (Bullard 2000).

Table 2
Released Particles and Their Half-Lives

Nuclide	Half-life Hours	Days	Years	10x Half-Life	Less Than 0.1 Left	Amount Released PBq[6]	Ci
Zirconium-95	1.4			5.8 days	May-86	196	5,297,297.30
Neptunium-239		2.4		24 days	May-86	95	2,567,567.57
Molybdenum-99	67			28 days	Jun-86	168	4,540,540.54
Xenon-33		5.3		53 days	Jun-86	6500	175,675,675.68
Tellurium-132	78			32 days	Jul-86	1150	31,081,081.08
Iodine-131		8		80 days	Jul-86	1760	47,567,567.57
Barium-140		13		128 days	Sep-86	240	6,486,486.49
Cerium-144		33		330 days	Mar-87	196	5,297,297.30
Ruthenium-103		39.6		396 days	Jun-87	168	4,540,540.54
Strontium-89		52		520 days	Oct-87	115	3,108,108.11
Curium-242		163		4.6 years	Oct-90	0.9	24,324.32
Cerium-144		285		7.8 years	Feb-94	116	3,135,135.14
Ruthenium-106			1	10 years	Apr-96	73	1,972,972.97
Cesium-134			2	20 years	2006	54	1,459,459.46
Plutonium-241			13.2	132 years	2118	6	162,162.16
Strontium-90			28	280 years	2266	10	270,270.27
Cesium-137			30	300 years	2286	85	2,297,297.30
Plutonium-238			86	860 years	2846	0.04	945.95
Plutonium-240			6,580	65,800 years	∞	0.04	1,135.14
Plutonium-239			24,400	244,000 years	∞	0.03	810.81
TOTAL							295,486,675.68

Source: UNESCO Chernobyl Programme, Document: Living in a Contaminated Area, 1996 (Data originally derived from OECD).

Ukrainian legislators have consistently rejected the American and World Bank models of cost-effectiveness. Chernobyl represents a risk in which the damage has already been done. Application of abstract principles of social acceptability of risk is simply irrelevant here. Rather, state laws have individualized access to the legal mechanisms by which citizens exercise their rights to claim harm. In an area of heightened risk, this individualization also suggests personal responsibility for the legal management of one's body, one's fate, one's health—a paradigm that is very distinct from the Soviet collectivist paradigm. Ukrainian laws presuppose an active legal subject engaged in the mechanisms of complaint (*skarha*).[3] The *skarha*, a time-honored tradition in Soviet and Ukrainian life, makes the Ukrainian response in one sense highly culturally specific. Yet at the same time, by empowering people with what they allegedly know how to do well, complain, these same mechanisms of *skarha* do the work of making risk socially and culturally acceptable by making exposure to risk an avenue of economic survival, even profitability. Politics, culture, irreversible harm, and scarcity combine to produce and normalize a particular vision of risk's social acceptability. In this model, risk is not something to be limited or simply denied (as has been tried in the Soviet model) but rather something to be turned into a resource and then parceled out.

Challenging this politically productive but rather *un*cost-effective model, proponents of structural reform have insisted that Ukrainians adopt a more "objective" attitude to the inventory of Chernobyl's health effects. Ukrainians have been criticized for their "improper management" and "deep emotionalism" with regard to Chernobyl's consequences. They have been charged with failing to use "modern epidemiological methods and a reliable data system" that can "quickly and at relatively low cost prove whether or not [illnesses other than cancer] are linked to the radiation from Chernobyl. . . . Right now virtually any disease is attributed to Chernobyl, and no effort is being made either to prove or disprove these claims that would satisfy standard epidemiological criteria of causality" (*Managing the Legacy* 1994:VII-6).

Ukrainian legislators, on the other hand, have given indeterminacy a central place in the official state narrative of the health effects of Chernobyl-related radiation exposure. Ukrainian scientists claim that radiation's effects—particularly in low doses—are especially indeterminate. Roman Protas, a biochemist, expressed a majority opinion when he asserted that "for low doses, the dose-effect curve is not one-to-one." The effects of higher doses similarly follow a nonlinear pattern: "Whereas one person will become ill with an immediate dose of 100 rem, a similar illness may not appear in a neighbor until he has received 200 rem" (Marples 1988:95). Many legislators maintain that specification of biological indicators for radiation-induced illnesses can't happen until all symptoms are known (or have had a chance to fully reveal themselves). Given that the half-lives of some of the particles released are virtually infinite, an exhaustive list of biological indicators is out of the question. Thus state officials argue there is no objective biology that can index the human cost of Chernobyl. The calculus of cost and criteria of injury are by definition open-ended matters.[4]

This understanding of reality as open-ended has led researchers and clinicians to shift scientific course: from laboratory-like attempts to correlate levels of radiation dose with significant biological effects, such as cancer in populations (the generally accepted method, with inherent limitations: see chapter 2), to a more general inventory of symptoms presented by patients in state radiation research clinics. This cumulative approach fits well with the way scientists have conceptualized the effects of low doses—"not as pathology, but as pre-pathology." Protas added, "Drops of water hitting the stone eventually cause the stone to crack."

Ukrainian scientists are basing cost calculations on a model of probability as much as causation. Irregularity, uncertainty, and exception become rules as important as those of lawlike necessity in the assessment of the causes and outcomes of Chernobyl's health effects. This choice of rules expands the productive scientific base and influences the social organization of collectivities of sufferers, who are *also* invested in such rules. On the basis of claims to scientific uncertainty, citizens connect those elements in their lives (measures, numbers, symptoms) to a broader history of technical mismanagement and this can afford them a probability of entitlement—at least in the short term.

In short, in rejecting a cost-effectiveness model, the Ukrainian state is privileging its role over that of abstract indicators (economic, social, scientific) in determining the size and style of government of exposed populations. In line with its Soviet predecessor, the state perpetuates its paternalistic role as the giver and taker of social resources and as life insurer. Institutional legacies and models of power and of scientific training interact with economic crisis to reproduce a known form of bureaucratic dependency. Such interactions also give people the means of enacting a radically new role: biological citizenship.

In this chapter, I continue to explore the experiential and political aspects of this role in individual and collective lives. Specifically, I am concerned with the relationship between an emerging medical classification of Chernobyl's ill effects and the social process of distribution of disability entitlements. The socialist system was imbued with informal exchange networks and relations. Apart from official rations and privileges allocated by the state distribution system, every laborer had a particular kind of access that could be "traded" through networks of *blat* (Ledeneva 1998). Access to clinics, diagnoses, and entitlements continue to be influenced by traditional socialist informal procedures. In many cases, that access is lent, borrowed, or exchanged between persons of unequal experience and resources within informal networks. What kind of experiences and social initiatives have emerged between state medical classification and the redistribution of social welfare goods?

I present the cases of Rita, Lev, and Kyryl, all of whom initially stood little chance of getting state compensation, but who took part in the opening and reconfiguation of the political process through their biological conditions. They negotiated state protections with varying degrees of success, using knowledge of injury, scientific literacy, and bureaucratic influence. They continue to cultivate associations, levels of influence and powerlessness, health and sickness habits, and specific ways of relating to medical doctors and clinical knowledge in the management of their own symptoms. The reader will see the kinds of social identities they acquire within a medical bureaucracy that has legally framed their conditions, and the work they do to maintain members in a postsocialist polity whose interests and needs are recognized by the state.

In this chapter, I use the word "environment" in two senses: as a scientific arena in which the indeterminacy and unknowability of radiation effects is the rule; and as a political opportunity structure where knowledge claims are made and social action takes place with respect to such rules. I am interested in how such environments organize individual realities, and the way they are narrated, contested, and lived as social trajectories. In both Soviet and post-Soviet scientific and political regimes, such trajectories are also anchored by specific state conceptions of biology that in turn influence modes of social control and action. Such biosocial interactions suggest that there are variable ways of relating social worlds and biological processes, such that those processes become particularized (Aronowitz 1998, Lock 1993). Soviet science has been instrumental in shaping Soviet life. The extent to which that interaction is particularized in interpretations of biological processes is illustrated in the following section.

Normalizing Catastrophe

Soviet ideologues sought to control interpretations of biological processes as a means of social regulation (Gerovitch 1999). Trofim Lysenko, a Ukrainian-born Soviet agronomist, epitomized this type of control and spearheaded what many Western and Soviet interpreters have referred to as a "catastrophe of Soviet biology" (Graham 1993:4). During the 1930s, when the agricultural revolution based on modern genetics in the West was underway, Lysenko denied the existence of the gene and advocated methods of accelerating crop growth and yields through a process called "vernalization." Lysenko's methods were unsupported by convincing empirical evidence and ultimately failed, setting Soviet agriculture and genetics back substantially. Yet as historian of Soviet science Loren Graham has argued, Lysenkoism, as flawed as it was scientifically, had "psychological value" for a society undergoing rapid transformation. Lysenko's scientific beliefs provided important social impetus: "The fact that Lysenko was simultaneously denying the existence of the gene, that he was discarding all of modern genetics, meant less to these people than the fact that he was actually getting Soviet peasants to work in the fields and that crops were being harvested" (Graham 1998:21). Every peasant who participated in Lysenko's projects, argues Graham, "enrolled in the Great Soviet Experiment" (20). Lysenko's singular brand of scientific practice had pragmatic intentions of fostering social transformation.

119

Through it, every peasant could find his or her place as an agent of, and a person within, the emergent Soviet system. With its influence upon Soviet sciences lasting well into the late 1960s, Lysenkoism formed part of the "disciplinary grid" of socialist society.[5] As tens of thousands of scientists died under its auspices (Graham 1987:4), socialism's vitality could be continually asserted as not simply originating in the lives of individuals themselves, but as being engendered in complex interactions between individuals and their environments. Soviet people by their very nature were seen as adaptive to and socially conditioned by "reflections of objective reality" rather than made by an "idealized" and independent set of biological truths.

Under catastrophic conditions, efforts to maintain this same ideological dependence of biology on the environment were attempted. Lysenkoist influence can be detected in the Soviet radiobiological work that influenced the Soviet management of Chernobyl. This work is marked by an absence of specific biological description. For example, in her monograph *Radiation Sickness in Man*, Angelina Guskova observed radiation as initiating "adaptive-compensatory processes" in the organism. The organism performs a set of "dynamic rearrangements." It masks, excites, provokes, stimulates, adapts, compensates, or decompensates (1971). Reinforcing a hierarchy of environment-organism relations, Guskova referred to biological processes as *biostrata*. The appearance of these elusive *biostrata* is regulated. They "awaken" at the moment when the organism has "exhausted its own capacity for self-repair," when "the degree of injurious influence starts to supersede the capacity of repair." Biology (as *biostrata*) becomes an artifact of the organism's exhausted capacity to repair itself. It is there only to perform its own death, so to speak. Injury is never measured in terms of independent biological criteria or markers.

Rather than acknowledging the biological effects of Chernobyl, the state introduced new environmental measures. The measures reduced the "autonomy" of biological expression and made its reality contingent upon a set of external norms. This Lysenko-like practice can also be observed in Guskova's manipulation of the biological threshold dose. Prior to the Chernobyl accident, she had established the threshold of the body's response to radiation (the "value of dose for the appearance of responses") at 0.01–1 rem (1971:42).[6] When faced with the "single largest cohort of acute radiation victims" in 1986, Guskova, in inventorying the disaster's health toll, raised the relevant threshold of the biological response to radiation to as high as 250 rem.

This readjustment of external measures exemplifies the importance Soviet administrators placed on the environment as a political tool to "normalize" catastrophe. The "environment" continued to enroll citizens in a "great Soviet experiment" while biological processes remained under-scrutinized as a matter of official policy. The next section details how that normative environment influenced life stories and medical case histories. I consider the types of experience and association that evolved as a result of a lack of coordination between experiences of individual symptoms and their normative environment.

Suffering and Medical Signs

Rita Dubova was fifty-six years old when I met her while she was interned in the acute radiation sickness (ARS) ward of the Radiation Research Center in 1996. She was born in a village in the Urals. She has worked in the nuclear industry for twenty years, first in Cheliabinsk and later in Chernobyl. She was married twice and is currently divorced. She said that both of her ex-husbands (a KGB officer and a nuclear worker) were incurable alcoholics. Having lived in Ukraine for the past fifteen years, Rita speaks Russian only. She currently lives on a pension of seventy-five dollars. "Half of my pension goes for medicines," she said. I met Rita several times over a period of two months. Within that period, she recounted the details of her life, disaster experience, family and economic hardships, health and treatment practices, and medical history.

Rita was convinced that her life was nearing its end, and that she urgently had to do something to economically secure her son and grandchildren's future before her death. This was the second time she had interned herself in the ward that year—she was fighting to upgrade her disability status from level two to level one based on an ARS diagnosis that had been given to her but later revoked (the pension increase would have been significant). Rita tried to convince the head of the ward, Dr. Nina Dragan, to press for her case at the next medical-labor committee meeting of the Radiation Research Center. Rita complained of heart pains and was being treated with an intravenous infusion thought to filter toxins out of her blood.

She planned to use her increased pension not only to buy medicines and support herself but also to support her son, a former worker at the Chernobyl plant. He has two children and suffers blindness in both eyes from an occupational radiation accident that happened in 1984, prior to the major explosion. While he was working as a welder, a steam channel exploded and sprayed his face with radioactive steam. He and five other men worked to seal up the exploded channel. The boss told the workers to work four hours, where they would typically have worked fifteen or twenty minutes, until the steam channel was completely sealed. Rita's son was never compensated for the routine mishap. The incident was officially denied, and he was fired. Rita's benefits would automatically transfer to her son and her grandchildren after her death, provided that she prepared the proper documents in advance.

Rita had worked as a gatekeeper in central gate security at the Chernobyl power plant, several hundred meters away from the wall of the reactor. She occupied her post at 8:00 A.M. the morning the plant exploded. "The explosion happened at 1:40 A.M. A first, second, and third rotation of firemen arrived and fought the fire from 2:00 A.M. and partially contained it by 6:00 A.M." When I asked her why she went to work knowing the risks, she told me that she had been more concerned about losing her pension and social benefits had she not shown up for work. Rita was given no protective gear and observed a powerful machine in pieces: "There was white steam, burning graphite from the reactor core everywhere on the ground, reinforcement bars on the concrete of the roof hung over like bent strings, what a force."

Rita called the head of gate security by telephone. "He said, 'What disaster? We'll send out transport.' " She mocked her boss's swift but feeble denial of the event. As for some of Rita's coworkers, "They insisted on staying until the leadership arrived." The transport never arrived; neither did leadership. The entries in her medical records from this date forward indicate the influence of state policy on the shape of her biological experience. These entries foreordained present possibilities and impossibilities of social action.

After thirty-five minutes of waiting for the bus, three members of the collective, including Rita, left. Rita took a train to Moscow, where friends from an orphanage, as well as one of her former husbands (the KGB officer), lived. She told me that some members of her work collective had already died. "Halia died in Moscow, Ivan died a year and a half later." She does not know the fate of Anna Kirilivna. Anna Petrovna went to a hospital: "They say she is alive." She knew that her boss was still alive; she needed him to confirm that she had been at the disaster site "so that I can have my official dose registered." But he had not replied to her request.[7]

Arriving in Moscow on April 28, 1986, Rita signed herself into a hospital affiliated with the Institute of Biophysics. She knew that firefighters and other members of the cleanup crew had been airlifted there. At first, hospital officials denied her entrance but later, upon her insistence, accepted her. Rita reported vomiting, diarrhea, bleeding, and memory loss. Bone marrow damage was also indicated in her records. After the examination, the hospital staff referred to her as an unequivocal acute radiation sickness case.

In June 1986, Rita readmitted herself to Hospital No. 7. During a three-week hospital internment, Rita recalled "giving a lot of blood." Her medical records indicated that immediately following her arrival, her acute radiation sickness diagnosis was changed to vegetovascular dystonia (VvD). To some degree, the visible symptoms of this disorder approximate the central nervous syndrome of ARS, but they are dissimilar in terms of causality (see chapter 2). One endocrinologist likened VvD to a "game of the blood vessels, producing symptoms, and reacting to external factors." It is an "unspecified premorbid state between two functional states of the organism, one normal and the other pathological," wherein a person exhibits "tendencies" toward subsequent pathological developments.

Rita's symptoms, especially her low leukocyte counts, easily matched those of an ARS patient. Yet her exit records designate her condition as less organic: a "neurotic state based in a residual organic background and vegetovascular dystonia." With each subsequent hospital visit, possible evidence of her radiation exposure would disappear (blood cells repopulate, wiping away traces of organic evidence). New external symptoms would appear that would easily fit a "psychological" mold. In a sense, environmental structures conspired to eliminate forensic traces in Rita's body. The "cause" of her biological activity was removed. Her symptoms were reinterpreted in a psychological frame. The word psychology does not refer to a strictly mental phenomenon in this context. It is material, the result of bureaucratic interventions and medical practices and decisions that shape the course of her future illness experience.

Rita organized her medical records extremely well. She was very knowledgeable of the way she had been medically accounted for over the ten-year period since the disaster. Inflation and growing personal economic powerlessness made accurate accounting even more crucial to her survival. Rita often directed my attention to areas in her medical documents where she felt diagnoses contradicted her experience, symptoms, and knowledge of pain. Her documents made me aware of an "aesthetics" of state intervention.

During my engagement with her, I was struck by her assertion that all members of her collective had died. Had there been a different accounting system set up in Kyiv, outside the control of Moscow administrators? Clinicians at the center directed me to an elderly pathologist doing work at the accident site. Unfortunately, the first time I reached him by phone, he insisted that "there were no other casualties" except for those officially registered by the Soviets. He agreed to meet with me, but when I called back to make an appointment with his secretary, she said the doctor would be "out sick" the following week. When I called the next week, she told me he would be "out sick" again.

I was then directed to the main city morgue—incidentally, located just across the street from the Babi Yar, the site of the notorious Nazi

123

massacre. I asked the taxi driver who drove me to the morgue why this site appeared concave rather than flat. In the 1950s, he explained, some years after the Second World War had ended, the site began to sink, and engineers planned to fill the site with sand and gravel to make it flat. They were channeling sand from the bottom of the Dnieper River when suddenly the water channel broke, sending tons of rushing water into the mass grave and flooding a city district. This story reminded me of other stories I had heard about how evidence of mass genocides carried out during the war were quickly "cleared" (see chapter 3). The area was subsequently landscaped over to create a memorial park dotted with innocuously thin deciduous trees.

■　■　■

What I found at the morgue was more evidence of an aesthetic approach. A medical examiner showed me a document from a short study that the then Ukrainian minister of health had ordered the local Bureau of Criminal Forensics to carry out in July 1986. The reason for the study: the minister wanted to confirm similarities between ARS and VvD symptoms because he had concerns about credibly carrying out the Soviet Health Ministry's order to use VvD in Ukrainian state clinics (see chapter 2).

The study focused on the interpretation of symptoms based on medical documents from 427 persons—men, women, and children—in an apparent effort to get a broad sample.[8] The report gave no other information about who these persons were, where they were from, circumstances of exposure, their work, or health status. Questions focused on the classification of signs of radiation damage based on age group: what kinds of internal doses of ionizing radiation are to be found in these persons? are there any skin lesions? how does the radiation-related skin damage appear? is there internal injury? and what is the estimated role of other factors, such as mechanical and thermal forces, in that injury? how should degrees of severity of injury to the body be characterized?[9]

Symptoms were scrutinized for their short-term course. According to the document, 148 cases showed clinical signs of ARS. The document evidences concern with the validity of comparing ARS and VvD. The author writes, "The symptoms of these 148 cases were poorly defined and *looked similar to those of vegetovascular dystonia* [my emphasis]; those symptoms were accompanied by short-lived fluctuations of blood indicators."[10] Researchers confirmed that once these fluctuations disappeared, ARS without such fluctuations could simply be diagnosed as VvD.

The use of VvD was widespread in the early (five-year) period following the disaster. This "factitious ordering" of symptoms, however, caused more symptom disordering. Doctors, afraid of being singled out as disobedient of health ministry rules but acknowledging widespread suffering in one form or another, started to apply vegetovascular dystonia indiscriminately. One Ukrainian cardiologist, noted for her adamant support of Soviet norms and critical of a subsequent epidemic of Chernobyl-related claims, wrote, "[VvD] was used to account for improbably related ailments such as gall stones, osteochondrosis, and persistent lesional infections" (Khomaziuk 1993). Ironically enough, the indiscriminate use of VvD produced a *counterenvironment* of symptoms and a proliferation of "Chernobyl-related" illnesses that, under the "false" cover of VvD, went unacknowledged in the Soviet administration of the disaster. In the Ukrainian administration, VvD patients knew that the symptoms they experienced could potentially become compensable and hence socially significant.

Rita left Moscow and returned to Ukraine five months later. Her city of residence, Prypiat', was evacuated within a week of the accident and became permanently off-limits to former residents. She was allowed to return once with a busload of evacuees from Kyiv, to pick up photo albums and some clothes from her apartment (families had to leave their contaminated possessions behind, some of which were looted later). Rita had few social ties outside Prypiat', a multiethnic enclave housing Chernobyl nuclear workers. In the meantime, she lived in Kyiv with her son and in hospitals until her employer found her a one-room apartment on the periphery of Kyiv.

Subsequent hospital visits produced more diagnostic confusion. In Kyiv, she registered herself at a hospital mainly used by workers of the Interior Ministry. This hospital, I learned, kept a separate and unpublished registry of additional ARS patients. Based on her poor blood indicators, Rita was rediagnosed as having acute radiation sickness status. But when she returned to the hospital again in January 1987 (this time with pneumonia), suddenly the ARS diagnosis was removed and the VvD diagnosis *reappeared* on her medical protocol. Her medical records read, "Pneumonia, vegetovascular dystonia accompanied by signs of asthenic-hypochondriacal syndrome and loss of hearing." She developed a high fever and readmitted herself. The diagnosis upon that hospital admittance record read, "Vegetovascular dystonia with astheno-neurotic syndrome." Rita also showed signs of cardiovascular irregularities during that visit.

In October 1987, she developed intestinal problems and was consigned to the gastroenterological ward of the Radiation Research Center. Her medical history thus far follows the course of the ARS syndromes. But her exit diagnosis reads, "Vegetovascular dystonia." Indeed, Rita claimed to have absorbed at least 220 rem at the accident site. "There was 380 rem per hour of radiation. If I was there for thirty-five minutes, count, I got

125

220 rem." Guskova's threshold was slightly higher than what Rita calculated her dose to be.

In 1988, she said that a physician from a Japanese medical entourage touring one hospital told her (after she had inquired) that given her estimated dose and based on data obtained from Hiroshima, "No more than five years for you." That was in 1988 (our interviews took place in 1996). By 1989, Rita was beginning to lose her eyesight. An electrocardiogram showed a slight deviation in her heart function. By 1990, records indicate cerebral arteriosclerosis and high blood pressure, and she was at risk for a stroke.

Domestic Neurology

In 1991, the Ukrainian Ministry of Health took over the management of the medical aspects of the Chernobyl disaster. A new nosographic approach was implemented. Vegetovascular dystonia and the persons who were diagnosed with it became subjects of new medical scrutiny. The country's health minister, who had implemented the widespread use of the diagnosis, continued to serve as the director of the country's central Chernobyl medical-labor committee.[11] The country's new minister of health, a psychoneurologist by training, gave specific instructions to Ukrainian medical-labor committee members to consider vegetovascular dystonia (and any symptoms associated with it) a medical condition deserving compensation from the state. He wrote:

> A specific point needs to be made about the registration of vegetovascular dystonia in the period 1986–1991. The diagnosis should not deter [medical-labor committees] from relating its manifestations to the negative factors of the Chernobyl disaster [and hence, to determine whether a person should be considered disabled by the disaster]. The diagnosis should always be taken into account when observing the evolution of patients' somatic illnesses, including hypertonia [high blood pressure]. Absence of somatic manifestations is acceptable if the illness is accompanied by paroxysms [spasms and convulsions] and recurring crises [*krizi*, or traumatic increases in blood pressure]. These crises have several forms, the epileptic, the conversional-hysterical, and the vestibular-vascular form. (*Chornobyl'ska Katastrofa* 1995:459)[12]

Neurological and neuropsychiatric disorders began to predominate in the nosological picture of the Chernobyl aftermath. Fatigue, dizziness, severe headaches, losses of consciousness, and other ill-defined states were now ostensibly a part of the effects of Chernobyl.[13] Interests in the "low-dose clinic" emerged with respect to the several populations of sufferers (ibid.). A new normative environment emerged where symptoms were to be exposed and medicalized rather than hidden and unaddressed.

The head of the neurological and neuropsychiatric section of the medical-labor committee at the Radiation Research Center drew a sketch for me representing a pattern of physiological reactions observed between 1986 and 1996, a pattern that Ukrainian clinicians started to refer to as the "Chernobyl syndrome." This syndrome consisted of functional changes in vegetative organs—the kidney, heart, liver, gastrointestinal tract, nervous system, and brain—which led to morphological changes of these organ structures and/or lesional effects, particularly in the brain. Diagnostic machines—reoencephalogram, electroencephalogram, ultrasound, and computerized tomographic (CT) scanner—were fundamental to the mapping of these phased changes.

Between 1987 and 1989, the incidence of registered neurological and neuropsychiatric disorders remained stable. Between 1989 and 1990, it roughly doubled for these disorders, which were now subdivided as psychiatric, neurological, cardiovascular, and digestive. The numbers of cases of vegetovascular dystonia, however, showed a conspicuous twelve-fold increase. Between 1990 and 1991, a population of neurological and neuropsychiatric cases continued to be identified. In this next period, their numbers tripled, quadrupled, and even quintupled for all subclasses *except for* vegetovascular dystonia (*Chornobyl'ska Katastrofa* 1995:174). This sudden halt in the incidence of VvD was explained by the fact that Ukrainian physicians saw it as a mere "gateway" to subsequent manifestations of the more serious and widely underdiagnosed acute radiation sickness (ARS) as well as its manifold syndromes. By 1990, VvD was understood as "unmasking" itself in particular somatic forms. In short, a Soviet pattern of medical underdiagnosis was being replaced by an emerging "domestic neurology" of Chernobyl's ill effects.[14]

Several administrators and physicians publicly objected to the sudden legitimation and spread of these new disorders. For example, the cardiologist Inna Khomaziuk denounced the indiscriminate use of VvD; she implored physicians at one conference "to be concerned with truth" (1994:46). She singled out VvD as especially "proliferative." She interpreted this disorder as deriving from "a vicious circle of psychogenic and somatic interactions"; she called it a "mask for unrecognizable and illegitimate illnesses." She characterized the social spread of VvD as dissimulating in nature, calling it the "chameleon illness" and an illness "that accepts the face of other illnesses." She also warned neurologists not to "overestimate the psychogenic factor in their analyses." Dr. Khomaziuk insisted that there was only one reliable test for the

127

diagnosis of VvD pathology: visible morphological changes in organs proven by echocardiograms, ultrasounds, and computerized tomographic scans.

■ ■ ■

Rita said that by 1992, "she was going to all the specialists." Her illness followed patterns similar to those of illnesses experienced in the rest of the new Chernobyl population. Yet she recalled more disjunction between her symptoms and medical recording: "In the patient's complaints section in my medical protocol, they started to write 'headaches,' and not once did I say I had headaches!"[15]

But by this time, this lack of coordination between symptoms and diagnoses had a productive side effect. Financial interests began to dictate the ways some physicians evaluated clinical indicators and distributed entitlements. Rita, who said she refused to engage in bribery, continued to insist on her truth: that her symptoms were those of ARS, not VvD. In the following account, she realizes the cost of her own insistence.

Rita took her documents to the center in mid-1991, mistakenly expecting a second chance to authenticate her ARS claim in the independence period. She was interned twice that year for medical evaluation. Asked to give blood twice on each occasion, she left without ever hearing of a diagnosis afterward. She became suspicious. Rita explained how, during one internment, she "entered the cytogeneticist's room and read the list of surnames of persons who had given their blood. Maksymovych, Vorobov, *Dubova* [her surname]." The lab technician had circled her name and then crossed it out.

Rita's suspicion turned into dread. The woman with whom she had been sharing a hospital room, to whom Rita had told everything about her experiences at the disaster site, and who knew that Rita was an acute case, had a bulky bag tucked under her hospital bed. "I looked into it when she left the room. Coffee, cognac, chocolate candies." What else could she conclude? "They gave my blood indicators to somebody else!"

The next day she confronted the deputy director of the ARS ward, Sveta Fimova, in the physicians' office: "[Fimova] was drunk with cognac and eating those American chocolates. The neuropathologist who was sitting with her told me to come see him for a consultation. He wanted to know who I was. I had already been for my psychiatric consultation, I told him." Then he patronized her. "Rita, look around you, here the doctors treat, there aren't any divisions among us here. Regardless of what diagnosis you get, you will have to come to this clinic twice a year for monitoring in order to maintain your disability allowance."

The physician threatened to make it hard for Rita to get her renewed disability if she told anyone what she had witnessed. "I didn't return to that clinic for three years. I didn't say anything to anyone. . . . Now it's all done with money."

That newly independent medical-labor committee reconfirmed Rita's "Chernobyl tie" on the basis of an "organic lesion of the central nervous system of a mixed type, persistent lesion, cerebrasthenic syndrome, osteochondrosis." Her decompensation (*dekompensatsiia*), a Soviet clinical term characterizing a loss of physiologically adaptive responses, would be compensated within certain physiological parameters established by the committee.

Between 1991 and 1994, the period of hyperinflation, Rita's pension sank. She was losing money. "The acute gets $325.00 a month. I get $75.00 a month. That woman knew what she was doing," she told me, referring to the woman who Rita alleged had bribed her way into the acute category with Rita's blood.

By 1994, she resolved to pursue her claims once more and returned to the center. Rita had been interned three times, each time for a three-week period, between 1994 and October 1996, when I first met her. Sveta Fimova had been fired as the physician in charge of the acute radiation sickness ward and demoted to a position in a less prestigious ward. The center's administration replaced Dr. Fimova with Dr. Dragan, a staunch critic of the emergent epidemic of Chernobyl-related disability and uncompromising in her support of Dr. Guskova's work. Dragan's recent volume on the health of ARS patients had reaffirmed the Soviet version of the disaster's medical aftermath and suggested that even most of the 237 constituting the official cohort should already have recovered. Her view was that they currently suffered primarily from psychologically induced or psychoneurological disorders. With Dragan's appointment, Rita sensed that her window of opportunity to make her ARS claim was closing for good.

■ ■ ■

In 1995, Rita obtained an assay of her peripheral white blood cells (fluorescent in situ hybridization, or FISH). The cytogenetics laboratory had received new equipment to test the accuracy of FISH on acute Chernobyl accident victims (via collaboration with an American research team). Her 1995 chromosomes indicated a dose of 32 rem, not enough to put her into the acute category.

That same year, Rita tried to circumvent Dr. Dragan's authority by appealing directly to the Ministry of Health. She wrote a letter indicating her leukocyte counts and dose based on the documents she had collected, and sent it to the ministry's director of the division on Chernobyl matters. Rita heard nothing for almost a year. The director finally sent the letter to the deputy director of the center, who then sent it to Dragan, who, in turn, wrote Rita a letter telling her that she needed to show proof that her leukocyte count had been four thousand in 1986 and 1987. Assuming the absence of that proof, Dragan said that she would "issue a conclusive diagnosis" and reject Rita's claims. Rita responded by showing Dragan medical documents proving that her leukocyte counts met that standard. Dragan suddenly changed the standards and required Rita to show that she had had a leukocyte count of two thousand in May and June 1986.

The new standard, according to Rita, would have been impossible to meet with empirical evidence. "They said to me that I should have two thousand leukocytes. And I said, 'What do you think, that I would be standing before you, alive, now? It's been ten years, I know that people with two thousand leukocytes have already died.' " In the Soviet environmentalist tradition, Dragan readjusted external measures. Rita's biological processes remained underscrutinized as a matter of official practice. She described the end of her odyssey this way: "The clinic will kill me," she said. Rita would have to die (as most of the people in her labor collective had already done) before her claims could be pursued any further. When I was preparing to leave Ukraine, Rita told me, "If I am not here, ask the granddaughter what happened."

Disability Groups

The center is affiliated with a network of hospitals and clinics with specialized Chernobyl wards and medical-labor committees throughout Ukraine. Standards of medical care and diagnostics vary from location to location. The center sets standards and acts as the final arbiter of cases of persons who have been denied claims elsewhere. The decisions of its medical-labor committee can override decisions of other medical-labor committees.

It took me time to build up a network among clinicians and invalids who could afford me access to this medical facility. Although Rita's experiences were wrenching, she was already a step ahead of those who weren't even in the system, without networks, or missing documents and diagnoses. In this section, I describe encounters I had at one of the first places I visited when I began my yearlong fieldwork in January 1996; there I started to notice how difficult it was for people to become part of the system, and how patients formed networks to facilitate their inclusion in the state's system of social protection.

The Kyiv Psychoneurological Hospital comprises several wards. Ward 1 confines the city's severely mentally ill. Alcoholics, addicts, the depressed, domestic abusers, and the domestically abused are treated in Ward 2. A third ward was added in 1993 to serve the emotional and medical needs of the city's Chernobyl sufferers. There I met Lev and Kyryl, individuals who had experienced two different trajectories through the system during the period I followed their stories. Both were categorized as level three disabled persons. Their status, which they received in 1991, automatically expired after five years, in 1996. Lev was singularly determined to upgrade his disability status to level two and knew the routes to success. Kyryl managed to extend his level three status for five more years.

The psychoneurological hospital is located south of Kyiv in the small town of Hlevakha; it is situated on a street named after the great pathophysiologist of autonomic nervous function, Ivan Pavlov. Locals refer to this hospital as the Pavlova. The doors of Wards 2 and 3 are open day and night. In contrast to the locked wards in which severely disabled persons (psychotics and epileptics) undergo prolonged stays with antipsychotic medication and physical treatment, these wards house individuals with borderline and neurotic states who receive medication and are free to stay or leave at their discretion. Sufferers developed close and quasi-familial relationships with physicians. They came to the Pavlova for a variety of reasons. One common reason was "to get some treatments" (*pidlikuvatysia*). Others came because they were out of work and wanted to begin the process of procuring medical evaluations and specialist referrals in the attempt to become candidates for disability status. One of the Pavlova's main technological assets was its computerized tomographic (CT) scanner. Patients were regularly screened on the CT scanner for evidence of organic brain damage. These screenings provided valuable medical evidence for the pursuit of disability claims.

Upon my initial visit to the Pavlova (and after receiving the necessary permission from the Ministry of Health's chief forensic psychiatrist), I had little idea of what the psychoneurological meant or could mean in a still predominantly Soviet context. As I have shown, it had an administrative and normative function with respect to the way the exposed populations were managed after the disaster. Psychoneurological diagnoses in the form of vegetovascular dystonia or radiophobia were used to filter out the majority of Chernobyl-related claims. But in the first days of my fieldwork, before I was able to perceive the disciplinary dimensions of the medical categories at work, I asked much simpler questions, such as, are there people who have gone crazy as a result of the disaster? This question seemed too extreme even then. But if so, what did that mean? I was advised by a trustworthy acquaintance, a physicist who until 1992 had

131

worked and enjoyed a cosmopolitan professional life beyond the borders, in Algeria. Having returned to Ukraine jobless, she turned to cleaning the floors of a dormitory where I had lived in the summer of 1994. She told me to go to the Pavlova if I wanted to understand what she referred to in Ukrainian as the disaster's "little golden center" (*zolota seredynka*).

February, 1996: Like any local train leaving Kyiv, the one to Hlevakha is loaded with rural women and men returning from selling their goods in Kyiv. On the way into the city, I saw many hauling two-wheeled hand-welded pushcarts. These so-called *kravchuchky* (little Kravchuks) were named after the first Ukrainian independent president, Leonid Kravchuk, a former Communist ideologue. During his tenure, rampant inflation hit, forcing people to brave the free-market world for themselves. Today, these pushcarts are stuffed to capacity with dried fish, nuts, fruits, eggs, meat, cabbage, carrots, milk products, and domestic cheeses. On the way out of Kyiv, they carry any of the essential goods that could be found in the city: car parts, paintbrushes, coats, ropes, hammers, and so on. The trains were favored places for beggars and for vendors: sellers of the Kyiv newspaper dailies, the more specialized criminal and astrological chronicles, and health products, especially bottles of *bal'zamy*, herbal tonics imported from Vietnam and China allegedly helpful in stimulating the immune system. "If his *bal'zam* worked, then we would all be cured!" a woman sitting next to me yelled.

The morning train in the middle of February was cold and dark: windows were frozen from the inside, soot-blackened on the outside; seats were made of plywood planks covered with worn ripped brown or forest-green vinyl. Every other seat was vandalized, the hardened foam torn away. Big X's drawn with black permanent markers started to appear on every seat to discourage citizens from stealing state property.

People joked about the vendors on the train, compared salaries or pensions, and discussed how much each could afford to spend on medicines, bread, clothes—this kind of social intimacy was easily established. It stood for a kind of reality checking in the new economic environment. Women talked about the need to sew clothes, to tear old clothing apart and sew new (old) attire. "If we have two hands, how can one not afford to sew these clothes. We are not handicapped!"

Disembarking from the train in Hlevakha, one is met by a raised concrete platform with pieces of concrete missing. Down the metal steps (covered in ice and slush), one enters an open market area with long tables set up for mass-produced American, Polish, and Turkish chocolates, colorful hairclips, shoes, eggs, and bread from local factories; baby carriages are used as portable storage units for fried foods and homemade sausages. Nearby, in the Vasylkivskyi region, there is a village resettled from the Chernobyl zones.

To get to the Pavlova, one had to carefully negotiate a highway with no pedestrian crosswalks. Once on the other side one passes down a long country road, with rows of five-story concrete apartments to the left, and chickens and stray dogs running around. The hospital complex is on the distant right across a field of thin, tall, almost black, leafless trees. As I approached the compound, a sallow-faced man stared at me from the open second-floor balcony of the ward. At the open door, someone had placed a bowl of milk for the stray dogs. I stepped up to the second floor, where I assumed the patients were. The man who had been staring at me was seated in an open dining area, eating split pea soup with bread. He asked me if I wanted some. I said no. He recognized that I was a foreigner and said, "The Germans came here a few days ago, took our pictures, and promised to send them to us. They never did." Stories of disingenuous humanitarian gestures abounded.

The empathic psychiatrist of Ward 3, Volodymyr Fedorovych, invited me into his office. His superior, a Russian-speaking neurologist, said that his presence on the ward constituted his "leisure work." His other work consisted of privately selling intravenous products from a German pharmaceutical company to local hospitals. I was later obliged to see the virtual palace he had built for himself on a tract of land belonging to a former collective farm; he had contracted collective farm workers and Chernobyl resettlers as carpenters, bricklayers, and electricians.

Fedorovych gave an overview of who comes to the ward: resettlers, people who work in shifts in the zones, husbands and wives, sometimes together—"people with various doses." All the resettlers "have psychogenic reactions," he said. "These reactions were seen right away. The sufferers, regardless of age, are the same in terms of symptomatology. They experience panic, anxiety, loss of attention, weakness, head spins. These symptoms tend to lead to organic pathologies: encephalopathy, brain atrophy, dementia." Fedorovych emphasized the branching structure of the "Chernobyl syndrome" at the same time he stressed organic changes. Ten years after the disaster, "the very structure of the brain was changing—aging and atrophy now happens in thirty-, forty-, fifty-year-olds."

These organic pathologies in the brain, in turn, lead to more bundles of pathologies. The person enters a virtual prism. The pace of ruin is specific to each individual. "One of our patients is crumbled (rozvalenyi), he drove heavy trucks and buses. He is only forty-two years old, and he has no memory, no attention span, he can lose consciousness when he drives." Fedorovych was referring to Kyryl, whose story is forthcoming.

Fedorovych was typical of Soviet-trained physicians in that he considered disability, like health, to originate to some degree in the character of socioeconomic relations. He told me, "The sick man should understand

133

the nature of his pathology, he should understand *what he is ill with in order to know what to do with it socially*." This mind-set, construing illness as a kind of social abacus, cannot be called Ukrainian per se but is part of a Soviet legacy that promoted full social membership of the disabled. The invalid, particularly persons disabled for "social reasons"—war or occupational disability—was a specific kind of agent within state production relations. When Fedorovych said that the patient should understand the nature of his pathology, he was implying that the patient's experience of pathology should already incorporate an awareness of his or her socially active role.

After our meeting, a nurse led me to a room full of male patients. Women, including a blind elderly World War II veteran, walked over from a nearby room. The smell of hair tonic suffused the atmosphere. Checkerboards. Prone bodies. People of many ethnic backgrounds: Russians, Ukrainians, a man from Bashkiriia, an Azerbaidzhani, and a Pole. Someone took a stool and placed it in the middle of the room for me.

"To the grave with nothing!" one man interjected. "Nobody wants to take him on as a worker anymore," another man commented about someone else. People complained about the cost of getting disability status and the necessity of paying a *vziatka*, a bribe; they confirmed each other's experiences. "I can't work, and I have a family to raise." There was talk of unfairness in the distribution of entitlements and arbitrariness of criteria, a reality I would later confirm in the offices of the Radiation Research Center. Some still worked at the plant but "didn't have disability," one man said, "while others who were in the Zone for only a few hours have disability." A woman with a child born in 1986 said that "the boy was born sick with an enlarged thyroid gland from radioactive iodine poisoning," to which another added, "Children of leaders go to Cuba and Italy for treatment, ours don't." Patients complained of joint and muscular pain and said that they were generally weak and tended to lose consciousness. "You lie, that's all, it's the illness," someone said, characterizing "the illness" as an autonomous and impersonal force. Everyone took sleeping pills.

Depression and disorientation over the loss of work were part of the illness as well. Some patients were restless and disoriented about what to do next. One man who had disability status said he was depressed because of his inability to work; economic conditions and physical disability prevented him from doing so: "My boss threw me out of work and the doctors won't let me work."

Lev and Kyryl, aged forty-eight and forty-two, respectively, began their odyssey through the system with the same diagnosis: vegetovascular dystonia. Both worked as cab drivers in Kyiv. Both had been divorced and remarried. Lev's first wife left him because of his impotence, which he attributed to radiation exposure. Kyryl's first wife left him for his excessive drinking, a habit he gave up once his health started to deteriorate. For both, the Pavlova was like a second home. Whenever they felt weak, experienced blood pressure difficulties, had family troubles, or felt for some reason that they were at risk of suddenly dying, as they put it (a fear that many had), they went to the Pavlova to get treatments or to get Fedorovych's advice on health or disability procedures. They stayed for one month, or two weeks, with the freedom to go home whenever they wished.

Both kept their "sick lives" separate from their domestic lives, but for different reasons. Kyryl, whose family I got to know over time, tried to hide his illnesses and medical documents from his two children and his second wife, though his disability was evident in his need to use a cane. Lev was less forthcoming about his domestic life. In fact, over the months when I was getting to know him, he said very little about who he was, other than an invalid. He said his grandfather had owned a famous candy factory in Kyiv that "Stalin stole," and that he took care of his ailing father with his Chernobyl pensions. His second wife irritated him and exacerbated his poor state of health, he said, because "she does not believe that I am sick."

Lev was an activist of sorts. He knew the system and claimed to have personally known all of the key players in it: former health minister, clinic administrators, public health officials. He surrounded himself with social and symbolic resources: empathic physicians like Fedorovych, powerful bureaucrats like Mudrak (the manager of the center), and anthropologists like myself. He later introduced me to a so-called *fond* (fund) in the city, a nongovernmental civic group, which mediated the interactions of sufferers and the disabled with the state and clinical institutions. (I will discuss these funds at the end of the chapter.)

Lev created a virtual world in which he lent his access to others and educated patients about how to work the system. He had just recently been admitted to the fund in exchange for his promise to contribute his social resources to it—the anthropologist was a key resource. He calculated how he would use the political influence of the fund to obtain lifelong disability status, and I became part of his strategy. That is why Lev insisted on becoming a subject of my research.

Lev had an excellent command of the Ukrainian language. This was not typical of the majority of Kyiv's inhabitants, who spoke, at best, a mix of Ukrainian and Russian (*surzhyk*). He seemed to know everything and was also ready to deliver stories on cue. The first sentence on the tape of an interview that he insisted on having is "Adriana, what do you want to hear?"

135

He was also literate in the psychiatric and neurological sciences that defined his current medical state. He said he compared his constellation of illnesses, kept watch for symptoms that might match those presented and compensated for in other patients. In one medical report, the ward psychiatrist Fedorovych wrote that Lev's personality was "perfectly intact. Patient is oriented in space and time. Does not show signs of psychotic illness [he does not require confinement]. During conversation, he displays a calm awareness of his illnesses and *keeps track of the state of his health* [my emphasis]."

Lev's pattern of illnesses correlated with the "Chernobyl syndrome." "Organic brain disorder, psycho-organic syndrome with astheno-neurotic manifestations" was the wording in his medical records. Lev made Fedorovych write in bold letters, "Not burdened by a history of hereditary mental illness" above his diagnoses. This important stipulation reflected Lev's ability to protect himself from a bureaucratic system that used the label of hereditary mental illness to delegitimate claims. In this way, he preserved his right to engage the state's science and sites of distribution as an autonomous agent, minimizing the surveillance and discrimination such a label might incite.

Lev had a distinct political history. He said he had connections to army generals as well as bureaucrats. He had worked in the Zone "for one month and five days," driving an army general who inspected sites where contaminated technical equipment was being buried. "They took me away and that was it, as they say, a volunteer. And now the general has the level one disability with the ARS diagnosis, and I only have level three. What kind of justice is that?"[16] During one meeting he explained to me the process by which he felt that injustice came about: "A person sat in our headquarters and read all the doses from a dosimeter. He sat there all day. In a day, I could have been at the burial sites, I could have been at the reactor. And when I arrived at night, he registered my dose on the basis of a reading from inside the headquarters. When I told him where I was, he would say, 'I don't know the radiation levels there,' and just wrote what he had measured inside. He gave me 9 rem, all in all." Lev spoke of the injustice of the selective use of medical categories: "How many people should have gotten the ARS diagnosis? There are many people who were there but who did not receive this diagnosis. There was a law then and everybody knew of it: if a person received 25 rem, then he would be entitled to ten times his average salary. Nine rem meant nothing. They say we have democracy. That is a fairy tale for the ignorant because many people who were there have already died."

In 1986, Lev was interned in the Radiation Research Center. He said that he had no desire to eat, and that he slept all the time. "When I got up to get something, I wobbled from left to right. My body temperature fluctuated. It measured 36.6, then after a half an hour, 37.5, then again, 36.9, then 37.2, then 36.0. A doctor told me that I had a thermo-regulatory disturbance. I had a sense of how much of a dose I absorbed based on these symptoms. Then I started to get heart pains."

VvD appeared on Lev's medical records immediately, but he knew it was "worthless." "At that time they wrote one diagnosis for everything, 'vegetovascular dystonia.' The minister of health told us that no doctor is withholding information about the actual condition of our health. He told me that everything that is happening to me was not connected to Chernobyl. The doctors said we have heritable genetic conditions; that my illness was passed from my grandfather, to my father, to me. Nobody connected our conditions with Chernobyl." He said he fought with doctors, particularly with the outspoken Dr. Khomaziuk, who would not diagnose his heart ailment and temperature fluctuations as part of a Chernobyl-related syndrome. She conducted a battery of tests on Lev; they failed to indicate significant morphological changes in his heart.

That same year, 1986, Lev began to organize strikes in Kyiv's main taxi service (its members worked in the zones and were in Chernobyl clinics). He worked with others to plan a hunger strike at the Radiation Research Center.[17]

"There was a person with whom I shared a room, who already had disability status, a young man, about thirty-five years old. That Khomaziuk entered the room and raised her head like a nasty goose. She demanded to know who had granted him disability status, as if to suggest that the man had bribed a physician to get the documents." Khomaziuk apparently wanted to distance herself from what she perceived as illicit trading in diagnoses and symptoms already happening then. She threatened to repeal the man's status because his cardiac condition was unverifiable. "He got very nervous and said to me, 'I will fight this, are you with me?'" Lev recounted. "We organized the sick, telling them about what had happened to the man. We started a hunger strike and had patients sign a petition attesting to what had taken place."

Lev acquired the identity of a clinical insurgent. "They said I was very aggressive toward them at the center. Well, I exercised my rights. I stopped relying on doctors, because I didn't believe they would be truthful enough. What's the point of going if the center, set up to handle this problem, if the doctors there wouldn't acknowledge a thing? I didn't turn to anyone anymore, I knew I was wasting my time. If I had not fended for myself, I would have gotten nowhere."

By 1992, when Ukraine and its radiation research establishment became independent, Lev's insurgency had paid off. "Something new had developed," he said. Authorities wanted to accommodate his demands. Ihor Demeshko, whose office we have already visited in the previous chapter, confirmed the general shift in the system's attitude toward its insurgents. He told me that he had personally received a command "to pacify [the Zone workers] with whatever means available." Medicalization was the available means. Lev continued with his account: "Suddenly, I was called to go to the center. What for?" An administrator asked Lev up-front what he wanted. Lev received a full medical evaluation, including an ultrasound that measured any changes in his internal organs. His VvD diagnosis was removed and replaced with stenocardia and arteriosclerosis of the aorta; he was registered in the system as a disabled person.

According to his medical records, he subsequently received diagnoses that were heart-related, brain-related, and stomach-related; his vestibular functions were said to have entered a mode of "decompensation." As I examined his records, he amplified his illnesses: "The doctors also discovered I have an illness of the vestibular apparatus. I'm thrown from side to side, I can't walk straight. I feel like a cloud, I don't feel the ground I am walking on. . . . Then I went to cardiologists. Now I am going to eye doctors, I am getting a cataract, they think it's glaucoma. Then there is the neurological." He said, "If I start to tell you about all of my current illnesses, you would grab your head in disbelief." Lev had acquired more than thirty diagnoses. *How could he even be alive?*

Like Rita, Lev became a cog in an emerging medical classification of Chernobyl's effects and an agent in the state distribution of disability entitlements. Rita experienced tangles and blockages in her pursuit of her biological truth. Lev knew, from a bureaucratic standpoint, that it was futile to pursue truth. Rather, he became literate in the sciences and symptomatologies that were available to him. In this environment, Lev engaged his symptoms like an abacus.

Law, Medicine, and Corruption

Lev's workplace, one could say, was the city of sufferers. He placed himself in the role of representative, revolutionary, mediator, and small-time *blatmeister*, a word denoting a person with *blat* resources within informal networks. Kyryl told me that while staying at the Pavlova, he had "first learned about his rights" from Lev; that Lev had motivated a number of patients to "organize their documents." Lev offered Kyryl access to a top-ranking cardiologist in the city "who would make the necessary documents for him." Lev wanted a few of Kyryl's elaborate homemade fishing traps in exchange.

Kyryl had worked as a driver since 1969. He had an eighteen-year-old daughter and a twenty-three-year-old son from a former marriage. Kyryl's mother had died several years earlier, and his father was a pensioner living in a village in the Chernihiv oblast. Both had been collective farmers. Kyryl had been expected to work in the local sugar factory or on the collective farm. At age fourteen, he left for the city, where he received a technical degree and went to work for a taxi service in Kyiv at age fifteen.

Kyryl's case shows how bureaucrats and mediators working in the Chernobyl apparatus remain unrestrained in terms of their hold over individuals' lives.

Though he had spent most of his life in the city, Kyryl retained the telltale signs of a village *khlop* ("primitive boy"). His hair resembled a thick brown mop. His blue eyes rarely blinked; he often struggled to remember his train of thought. I couldn't help but notice his almost folkloric portliness, set off by his long mustache and beard. On ten long shelves he stored herbs that he had collected himself. He picked "roots in the fall, and the buds in the spring" in special areas around Kyiv designated for such activity. He spoke a curt rural Ukrainian, rhyming many of his word endings, and a broken Russian to his wife Tania, who spoke Russian exclusively. Like other evacuees and Zone workers, he had been given an apartment on the newly built Chornobyl'ska Street, but he had a desire of leaving this eighteenth-floor concrete flat and moving back to his village to live near his father. He had recently gained more benefits than he had expected from his Chernobyl status—a free telephone, his first, and free installation. He relied on city clinics such as the Pavlova for treatments, and on the Ministry of Transport's Hospital for medical evaluation. He needed injections of a drug called Noshpa to improve his cerebral blood circulation. He needed Relanium to alleviate the pain in his legs. A friend with whom he had worked in the Zone lived in Kyryl's apartment block and was currently on pension, "near death." Together, they enacted a sociality of illness. "We are almost all the same, like mirrors, we see ourselves in the other."

Between May 4 and May 31, 1986, Kyryl transported bags of graphite and clay dumped over the reactor "right to the helicopter." He drove families, cows, and pigs out of the Exclusion Zone and into the "clean zones," "one family every other day." He said that he had "started to feel sick and lost his consciousness." The Russian word for losing consciousness is *perekliuchennia*, literally meaning "switching."

Kyryl said that every work enterprise had a designated dosimetrist who was responsible for monitoring workers' doses. According to Kyryl, "this monitoring rarely happened." He believed that "essential documents" registering the number of work days "were destroyed, burned or thrown out. They stole days and paid little." As a result, Kyryl could not even begin to calculate his dose. His medical papers indicated that his dose was "unknown." His work history was similar to Lev's.

We searched one day in his apartment through his medical documents to find evidence of his first symptoms. We found a document from May 3, 1986, the day before he was sent into the Zone. Apparently Kyryl received a quick medical evaluation before his recruitment. The diagnosis was largely illegible. We could make it out only partially. In the patients' complaints section of the document, Kyryl reported that the left side of his body "went numb." Kyryl had either somatized his fear of recruitment or feigned illness to avoid recruitment. The fact is that he was numb and was recruited anyway.

Upon returning to Kyiv one month later, he was placed in a hospital for a month-long internment. Thereafter Kyryl avoided hospitals because he feared losing his job. Kyryl's hospital internments began again in 1990, when he got into a car accident: "I lost consciousness and became paralyzed." He spent eight months in a body cast. The doctors immediately registered Kyryl as a disabled person, and the director of his enterprise dismissed Kyryl from work. Kyryl treated this expulsion as a primary betrayal: "My own director, after twenty years of work, didn't take me back." Under Soviet labor laws, the boss would have been required to place Kyryl in a less physically demanding job. But in the moment of economic and political turmoil, familiar norms of obligation were suspended. Kyryl lamented losing connection with his former work enterprise: "Everything is broken and I can't afford a lawyer to take him to court." He lacked such social resources as Lev had built up to ensure his protection by the state.

Kyryl's financial and family situation was quickly deteriorating. He was two months behind in rent because the Chernobyl Ministry hadn't paid out his monthly disability pension. For weeks, he had no idea where his eighteen-year-old daughter *propala*, "got lost." He had no idea how she survived on her own and feared she might have been engaging in prostitution. He was the object of much directed paternalism himself. By the time he left the Pavlova, Fedorovych and Lev had convinced Kyryl that he would never work again, and that he "needed to protect himself." "The doctors say I am incurable," he told me. Yet Kyryl never accepted the disaster and his participation in it as his primary emotional ballast; he was still upset over the fact that he could no longer work.

He expressed confusion over the need to consolidate documents that would make him eligible for a better disability pension. He had not "caught up with himself" to collect the right documents. "If I put them together I'd have a bigger pension. I'd have money for apples, for vitamins, for bread, for the apartment. They can't throw me out of the apartment. I waited for it for twenty years. I have to get those little papers (*bumazhky*) in order. They torture me." He characterized the control that

140

little papers, closed doors, and closed circles had over his life: "Drop off the *bumazhka* there to carry it somewhere else. Give the first *bumazhka*, take the second *bumazhka* so that with that *bumazhka* I can get a third. I don't have enough strength to run. Knock on one door, on a second, on a third, on the fifth, they send you somewhere else. It's a closed circle. It's clear to me. And I don't know what I say anymore." As we made our way out of the Pavlova one day, a nurse handed him a few pills and a packet of *sorbenty*, compressed charcoal tablets that bind radionuclides in the body and draw them out through excretion. He carried a brown vinyl bag. The word *aptechka* or "pharmacy" was stenciled in white on the bag "so that if I lose consciousness and fall on the street, people will not think I am a drunk and ignore me." His greatest fear, he said, was suddenness of change or movement. "When it's bad for me and I start to fall, I inject myself or I ask someone to do it for me." His kit contained the hypertensive drug Troxevasin, made by a Bulgarian pharmaceutical firm, the psychotropic Melleril (thioridazine), made by Novartis, and some other "humanitarian aid," for headaches, with an overdue expiration date.

Early one morning in the Kyiv metro, I was sitting on a bench along the path trodden by the morning multitudes: those descending the elevators into the tunnel to my right, those exiting the trains and ascending the elevators to my left. Suddenly I noticed Kyryl with his aluminum walking cane, struggling but running with the crowds. Frustrated and suffering from the pain in his leg, Kyryl noticed me and said, "I need to walk, walk, walk, walk. I need motion to live. I need this motion." He told me that he had decided to engage the bureaucratic process of procuring his disability with the little energy he had left. He was on his way to the Pavlova to pick up a CT scan to take to the Institute of Transport's own hospital serving Chernobyl invalids. There he hoped to have a meeting with the head of the hospital's medical-labor committee. Kyryl needed this man's approval for a medical examination at the hospital.

A few days later, Kyryl chose to record a meeting using a microcassette tape recorder I had loaned him to keep a diary of his symptoms at home. The head examiner's treatment of Kyryl was taunting and highlighted the everyday financial interests involved in this type of bureaucratic exchange. This exchange with the examiner, whose traditional role was to advocate for, rather than to abrogate, the rights of workers, symbolized further breakdowns of health responsibilities. Kyryl told the head examiner of his intention to be medically examined for his Chernobyl status. He had gathered supporting documents and asked that the examiner secure him a bed so that final medical-labor assessment could be carried out. The dialogue went as follows:

"Did you go to Pavlova to get a CT scan?" the examiner asks.

"Yes I was there," answers Kyryl.

"Were you there?" the examiner repeats himself as if to undermine Kyryl's credibility and certainty.

"I was there."

"Should I write the referral for you here?" the man asks.

This circularity and repetition leads Kyryl to throw himself at the mercy of the examiner, "Oh my God, my head is burning, and I can barely stand up, my back hurts."

"When were you interned at the Pavlova?" the examiner asks, unaffected by Kyryl's plea for mercy.

"I was there in February."

"That ward is for the dumb (*duraky*)!" the doctor cynically exclaims, as if to knock Kyryl off-center once again, labeling him a "dumb psychoneurological case" (something Lev had learned to protect himself against). The circularity of the dialogue indicated that money was at stake, though never explicitly so.

Kyryl continued his plea: "It's a Chernobyl ward [referring to the Pavlova], doesn't it suit you? I lay there for my head, I got a CT scan done—the evidence is there. Look at the papers you have sitting before you," Kyryl said.

The doctor began to recite the diagnoses written on Kyryl's medical records: "Vegetovascular dystonia, psychogenic tendency."

Kyryl was astonished. For the first time, I heard him express a basic awareness of the right diagnostic terms, "Didn't they indicate it, I mean the lesion for my head? Look, my leg is drying up, you can see that it is, can't you? Won't you write it, the diagnosis for the lesion?"

"Come back to me on Monday," the doctor responded.

The noise of the door opening and closing in the background is audible throughout the recording. At one point, the examiner asked a young girl who had walked into the room what her profession was. She said she worked where "the other girls work." As Kyryl played the recording to me, he was fascinated by the sounds of the social environment he had captured on tape. He rewound the tape and especially wanted me to hear "how the examiner talks to the patient" and how "the examiner asks for money," and to "listen to the prostitute." Indeed, the prostitute was a sad metaphor capturing all sorts of illicit exchanges in which the body is exposed, bartered with, sold, or given away.

A few weeks later, Kyryl was assigned a hospital bed. As he rested on it waiting to be called for a last exam, a physician approached him and said that she could "prepare the documents" to upgrade his disability from level three to level two at a cost of four hundred dollars. This physician, an intermediary for the medical examiner, would receive a percentage of Kyryl's money. The cost of upgrading his disability was ten times Kyryl's monthly pension.

Kyryl managed to extend his level three disability status for five more years. He continued to receive level three pension payments of $40.00 a month. Lev told me that his level three pension was worth $153.00 a month, and his status would soon be upgraded to level two. Levels of disability are broken down even further in terms of degrees of severity. The discrepancy between Kyryl's and Lev's pensions is explained by the fact that Lev had managed to buy more diagnoses for his medical records, making his medical condition appear much more severe than it was. This example illustrates the kinds of routine inequalities that occur in the distribution of entitlements. These inequalities persist in part because the operations of bureaucracies and corruption remain unsubordinated to any stable legal system (Kornai 1992:47).

Material Basis of Health

The extent of bureaucratic obstructionism and corruption is evident in the following text from a local newspaper article, signed by members of a consortium of nongovernmental civic organizations (funds). These funds advocate for the rights of Chernobyl invalids and sufferers in Ukraine, and in some cases they attempt to mitigate inequalities within the system. The article is entitled "Chernobyl Monies—For Those Who Are Eligible! For State Criminals—Jail!" The article appealed to Chernobyl sufferers to police their bureaucrats and civil servants.

> Good people, don't be patient, don't let yourself be fooled! Demand that your local civil servants make reports on distributions of funds public. Be wise, uncover their abuses. Ask, who was awarded a new resettler's home? Ask, were the recipients actual resettlers? Did you pay for their new home? Ask, are the children-sufferers the ones going to the health sanatoria or is it the children of our civil servants? Which fictitious "Zone worker" received social protections that should have been yours? (*Komunist* 1996:4)

Serhii was a thirty-eight-year-old active member of the International Chernobyl Disabled Persons Aid and Charity Fund and co-signed this document. He walked with a cane, complained of having a terrible memory, and said that his lungs were "Swiss cheese" from all the irradiated hot particles he had inhaled at Chernobyl. Yet he was always ready with facts exposing the corruption of civil servants. This readiness to expose in itself constituted a kind of democratic sport. "Twenty-eight tons of humanitarian food and medical shipments last year, 10 percent went to pad the pockets of our Parliamentary Cabinet," he once told me.

As an active member of the fund, Serhii kept track of hospital food menus to ensure that Chernobyl sufferers were still getting their daily nutritional norms of beets, milk, poultry, carrots, cabbage, and so forth. Members of the fund initiated petitions that were signed by patients in clinics and sent to the mayor's office, the Health Ministry, and Parliament. One such petition was signed by patients in a local city hospital: "Today, the state can no longer assist the sick cleanup workers. Specialized clinics can no longer provide medicines and food. We the invalids and sufferers of the catastrophe offer you the following facts: the clinics' cafeterias do not provide meat or bread. Many of the interned are forced to sign out of the clinic earlier because there are no medications and no food. On weekends, the heat is shut off, and medical personnel tell the sick to go home."

This fund was one of over five hundred such groups in Ukraine. These types of disabled persons' civic groups had an initial important role to play in Ukraine's democratization. Chernobyl funds, unlike typical nongovernmental organizations, were fostered by the state itself to supplement its weaknesses in terms of providing financial and medical resources to sufferers in the post-Soviet crisis context. The state allowed these funds to import goods from Western retail markets and to sell these goods in an unregulated manner. The orientation of these funds was initially state-cooperative and nonoppositional. Funds organized by village and by city district. Members were given a seat at local medical-labor committee meetings. They have their own lawyers and business partners, and they provide important social services to their members (such as distributing parcels of land for small-scale production and financial support for the disabled).

They also provide representation and advocacy for Chernobyl sufferers, and they influence the outcome of medical decision making. I noticed that members of funds received better treatment in wards than did individuals who were socially unrepresented or who lacked protection. During my work at the Radiation Research Center, I often came across letters of advocacy written and signed by the presidents of various funds, making sure their members were given hospital beds and received fair consideration at medical-labor committee meetings. These letters were included in patients' medical files and were addressed directly to administrators or to heads of specific wards. "Please show humanity and mercy, admit this man," read one letter. Another letter read, "Please admit this man, payment will follow shortly."

One of their most important functions is to facilitate the inflow of humanitarian resources from international relief organizations. Humanitarian shipments of medicines often ended up in the hands of the wrong people, who profited by selling these items on the streets. So many of these disabled persons' funds have proliferated that they own, according to one estimate, an astonishing 51.6 percent of the country's import operations (Samborski 1996:12). Informal economic activity such as this has become an essential component of the economy of Ukraine, a country that has one of the largest unofficial economies in Central and Eastern Europe. Disability, trading in diagnoses and symptoms, and market economics found compatibility in a country that has otherwise created a vastly unfavorable business climate.

This last section tells the story of how the fund that Serhii belonged to attempted to improve Ukraine's health care, using its own growing financial resources. It made a proposal to the Cabinet of Ministries, offering to pay for Chernobyl-related health care with money made through its domestic sales of tax-exempt foreign products. Further consideration of the plan was blocked, and new legal restrictions were placed on the sale of goods by persons categorized as disabled by Chernobyl.

The offices of the International Chernobyl Disabled Persons Aid and Charity Fund were located in a partially abandoned building in downtown Kyiv, a few blocks from the parliamentary building. The fund's membership in 1996 consisted of six hundred people in the city of Kyiv alone, professionals and nonprofessionals, resettlers, and Chernobyl workers. The fund had over twenty urban-based affiliates across Ukraine and had established bank accounts in the United States and in Western Europe. It had the support of the Socialist Party, which depended on operations like these for financial support. The fund's members attended Socialist Party meetings and voted.

Serhii pointed out to me that Chernobyl invalids, together with pensioners and war veterans, made up an entire quarter (fourteen million people) of the Ukrainian population. This population constitutes a large voting bloc for socialists who campaign on promises to raise pensions and workers' salaries. On my first visit to the fund, I noticed a tall stack of cardboard-colored booklets entitled *The Socialist Party Program* in a wall cove near the entrance to the main office. "They need us for now," Serhii sarcastically remarked, suggesting a relationship based on convenience rather than on long-term ideological commitment.

The fund's president, Mr. Repkin ran an operation that looked like a cross between an NGO and a business. He was particularly proud of the fact that he employed disabled people. Their special Chernobyl status allowed them to "shuttle" goods from Western Europe to Ukraine and pass through Ukrainian customs with relative ease. These young men transported anything from cigarettes and alcohol; to Italian-made parkas, bought for fifteen dollars and resold on Ukrainian streets for fifty dollars; to crates of frozen chicken and hot dogs from Germany, which had originally been imported from the United States. The virtual halt of domestic forms of production made these imported wares desirable, if not indispensable.[18] Repkin affiliated himself with businessmen—for example, young entrepreneurs who were interested in establishing American-style supermarkets. He routinely gave money to needy mothers who had lost their spouses to Chernobyl.

But the word "Chernobyl" became a magnet for another set of discourses and activities that left the group feeling marginalized. For example, an exhibition of biomedical products called Chernobyl Expo had opened in a luxury exhibition center near the fund's office. The exhibition showcased state-of-the-art sonographic machines, magnetic resonance imaging, new pharmaceuticals, and hospital supplies.

Fund members understood these Chernobyl-inspired capitalist ventures as signs of their further political exclusion and economic powerlessness. Their claims to inclusion implied the need for a strong state. At the same time, the state lacked resources and actively promoted trade from which it could profit. In this context, fund members made their claim for inclusion on the basis of the nation's threatened biological existence—their rhetoric of extinction intensified in the globalizing political economy, in which they felt that their fates counted less and less (Sassen 1998).

In press releases, they characterized radiation as a "demographic scissors." They invoked terms from population genetics, making arguments for the improvement of the radiation medical system on the basis that "radiation is pulverizing the gene pool (*genofond*)." The biological existence of a nation, they claimed, was contingent upon the state's willingness to become a "gene pool steward," rather than a facilitator of private foreign capital and technology that only a few could benefit from.

As in other areas in the former Soviet Union, the death rate has skyrocketed in the period of transition.[19] Sudden deaths accounted for the majority of new deaths, particularly among males. In 1989, the country's Ministry of Statistics reported a population growth of 90,391. By 1994, the population had declined by 243,124.[20]

Edvard Katz, an engineer and cofounder of the fund, kept an independent record of Chernobyl workers' deaths. He estimated that by 1996, 125,000 persons had died as a result of Chernobyl, and that 105,000 had died in the previous three years.[21] He also reported that deaths among workers between the ages of twenty-seven and forty-seven were 6.8 times higher than the average for this age group. Katz found that these workers were dying suddenly and in greater numbers as the years

146

passed. His research conclusions were circulated as press reports and reports to Parliament.

As Repkin told me repeatedly, there was "no more time." In the summer of 1996, Repkin and Katz developed a proposal to "rehabilitate" the Ukrainian system of radiation medicine. They felt that much of the bureaucratic corruption and obstruction (such as that to which Kyryl was subjected, for example) had a deleterious effect on people's lives; they also knew that much of that corruption could be mitigated if doctors' salaries were regularly paid.

They proposed a system of "genetic protection" modeled on a program developed for populations affected by the 1957 Kyshtym nuclear disaster. The fund intended this system—the "SOS system," as members called it—to provide access to "geno-protective" foods, ecologically clean seeds, fruits, meats, milk products, diagnostics, and "medico-genetic passports" for every Chernobyl sufferer of Ukraine. They proposed to donate 80 percent of their overall income to funding this program, substantially cutting their reliance on state health care. They intended to pay doctors' salaries on their own, purchase new hospital equipment to replace aging Soviet equipment, and buy necessary medicines and foods— in short, to medically insure themselves as a group.

Before a crucial meeting with its regional affiliates, Repkin's fund obtained approval for the plan from key health administrators in the state's Chernobyl apparatus. He invited me to join him at a meeting with the deputy director of the Radiation Research Center.[22] As the director reviewed the proposal, he insisted that suicide "had to be included in the list" of Chernobyl's health effects, as if enumerating suicides among Chernobyl workers added weight to the moral claim that "the state is killing us." There seemed to be consensus on that point.

The proposal to rehabilitate radiation medicine received support from over one thousand people who attended a meeting held in June in a large auditorium near the fund's office. It was impressive, attended by the then Socialist speaker of the house, who was planning a run for the presidency. The deputy director of the Radiation Research Center spoke passionately in support of the invalids' proposal.

By gathering such a large number of delegates, the funds revealed their political solidarity. Yet the plan did not go much further. That month, new amendments were passed to curtail the financial and entrepreneurial autonomy of funds. The amendment placed limits on the types of products funds could import and made many products that had been tax-free subject to new taxes. The state reaffirmed its paternalism and eroded the funds' economic base. Repkin took this defeat personally and felt that the window of opportunity was closed.

By the end of that summer, Repkin's fund's orientation toward state authority shifted from cooperation to opposition. Members continued to exercise moral authority by keeping checks on corrupt officials and informing key legislators about the "decline of the material basis of health."

Chapter 6
Local Science and Organic Processes

Social Rebuilding

To reach the Radiation Research Center, I hailed taxis in the morning from the Boulevard of Lesia Ukrainka to the metro stop near Kyiv's opera house. I moved along perimeter streets lining the grand Bassarabskyi market where the construction of new casinos, imported food shops, and kiosks overtook the last of the state-operated restaurants and food stores. Villagers from the city's surrounding areas stood along the market's outer wall, behind stands made of cardboard boxes displaying eggs, herbs, flowers, salt, and fruits. Some had just one product to sell—a loaf of bread, a jar of homemade milk, or dried fish. The market is located at the eastern end of the stately Khreshchatyk Street, rebuilt from rubble after World War II and exhibiting eclectic combinations of Stalinist socialist realist architectural motifs. A red granite statue of Lenin stands across the street from the market. Its commanding elegance prompted the city's architectural league to lobby city administrators in the early nineties to protect it from being torn down. The monument serves as a point of origin for a street running perpendicular to Khreshchatyk. A tree-lined walking path splits the street's traffic, running uphill past the university and the celebrated Volodymyrskyi Cathedral, up to the metro stop. After a lengthy descent on the metro's escalator, I took the subway line to its last stop, beyond the city limits. One hour into my morning commute, I pushed my way into a crowded bus or hailed rides from more unregistered taxis.

149

During those numerous taxi rides, I heard stories of the drudgery and promises of everyday life, mostly from otherwise unemployed middle-aged men who had children, wives, or ailing parents to take care of. One man drove to make up for the terrible expense of his father's recent funeral. Another drove so that he could afford to send his young son to a private school to learn English. Another spoke of how lucky he was to have a car, and compared himself to some of his friends who were caught up in bureaucratic struggles having to do with Chernobyl. Other drivers sold over-the-counter drugs and herbal remedies. An African man from Burkina Faso who had moved to Kyiv to receive a technical education in the early 1990s now peddled French cognac to street vendors; he was refreshingly detached from all the crises of his adopted land. He said he would have been much worse off in his native land. One man wept about the fate of his mother, who had been resettled from the Chernobyl zones. He then told me a joke about an encounter between two friends, one an academic and the other a "new Ukrainian" (*biznesmen*). The joke highlighted the everyday violence of rapid class stratification and crime. Under such conditions, what was once a friendship now becomes a broken social tie.

ACADEMIC: How are you?

BUSINESSMAN: Well, you know, the customs agents gave me a hard time at the border again. They held up my truck and gave me a fine. I'm in the second year of hiding my wife and children from the mafia (*reket*). And how are you?

ACADEMIC: Well, I don't have any work and I haven't eaten in two weeks. This new period of social rebuilding (*perebudova*) has really put me in a vise.

BUSINESSMAN: You shouldn't make light of that fact, *make* yourself eat!

The pressures and paradoxes of adjusting to a new world are captured in the perverse metaphor of the vise, a device made of two jaws moved by the turning of a screw and used to clamp an object. By encouraging his friend to eat, the businessman highlighted his friend's inability to eat: economic circumstances were the vise, and bodies were the objects "clamped down." What was being sawn or filed here were new class-based moral orders based on limited engagement with the needs and desperations of others.

Sometimes these illegal drivers were tailgated by registered taxi drivers protesting their excessive numbers on the road. We drove past young and old women who lined up every morning outside the gates of a cemetery to sell flowers; men loitered without renewed contracts outside an airplane factory (which has since landed a contract with a Western firm).

We then passed a rotary with a raised police platform and a folkloric wooden signpost pointing the way into Kyiv's leisure park area.

Radiation Research

The center was located approximately thirty kilometers north of Kyiv; and from there it was a thirty-kilometer drive northeast to the nearest border patrol of the Exclusion Zone. The reader has accompanied me to this center before, first to consider the work of its authoritative medical-labor committee and to place the expansion of disability claims in their economic and social context (chapter 4); and then to consider the details of individuals' legal plights in their pursuit of compensation (chapter 5). This chapter draws from fieldwork in the center's Division of Nervous Pathologies and among members of the neurological subcommittee of this institution's medical-labor committee. The role of the center's scientists and physicians is to clinically observe the symptoms of patients, most of whom do not know their actual dose, and to devise medical classifications, diagnostics, and forms of treatment for Chernobyl-related illnesses. In the Division of Nervous Pathologies, I was allowed to observe interactions among physicians, nurses, and patients, to sit in on decision-making meetings related to compensation claims, and to look into current forms of clinical research. Researchers claimed that the majority of disability claims were being made in neurological wards on account of a variety of nervous system disorders. Yet it was unclear whether these disorders were related to social stresses brought on by the country's dire economic situation or to radiation exposure due to Chernobyl, or to some combination of the two.

These medical ambiguities strained relations between clinicians and research subjects. The process of clinical observation and research reflected the social paradoxes of that contemporary society; it was an intervention into people's lives that would have consequences for the way their futures would unfold. The decision to become a human research subject here is mired in particular socioeconomic pressures and demands, as it is all over the world.[1] On the one hand, researchers and physicians know that human participation in their research is fueled by economic and social needs. On the other hand, they are testing ways of accounting for the biological effects of radiation in arguably the largest cohort of living radiation-exposed populations—research they see as critical but that is sorely undervalued in the international arena. They are consequently pulled in two directions: they need to create research cohorts and legitimate science at the same time that they need to treat sickness in all of its physical, social, and economic aspects. For those subjects participating

151

in it, particularly children, research amounts to a double-edged sword: it makes stepping out of a symbolic order of sickness more difficult at the same time that it guarantees a place in that order. This dilemma is clear in the case study presented at the end of this chapter. In it, we follow the plight of a boy conceived in the Zone of Exclusion and his parents, who were determined to gain formal confirmation of a medical link between radiation and their son's ailments.

The Radiation Research Center functions under the auspices of the Ukrainian Academy of Medical Sciences and the Ministry of Health; it comprises three subdivisions. The epidemiological division operates a registry with names of people who sustained "even an insignificant dose" of radiation (Marples 1988:38). The clinical radiological division, whose activities I will discuss shortly, is referred to here as the Clinic, or *Klinika*. The experimental radiological division analyzes the effects of low-dose radiation on the behavior of rodents collected in the Exclusion Zone; the staff of this division works with members of medical-labor committees to ascertain levels of work capacity, stress, motivation, and behavioral changes among Chernobyl-affected populations, particularly among the Zone cleanup workers.

Professor Symon Lavrov, a leading Ukrainian dosimetrist and radiation hygiene specialist, developed computerized local fallout models and models for calculating internal doses from radiocesium and other radionuclides in all territories and populations affected by the Chernobyl accident. Data from these models are used clinically to estimate individual doses. Based on his experience in the laboratory and in the field, Lavrov told me that doses of ionizing radiation affect rodents and humans in different ways. "In rats, the effects are 95 percent biological, maybe 5 percent other, such as experimental stress. In humans, it is the opposite, 20 percent biological, the rest is other." Transformed into experimental objects, animals manifest precise quantities and repeatable patterns of observable radiation-induced behavioral effects. On the basis of data derived from these experiments, Lavrov believes that the biological significance of common clinical complaints such as fatigue, loss of consciousness, or a general inability to work is grossly overstated and more closely correlates with depression and anxiety related to socioeconomic conditions.

Yet he admitted that he was not immune from the forces constructing the biological dependencies of these states of mind and gave me an example of his "vulnerability." He said, "When a crying mother comes to my laboratory and asks me, 'Professor Lavrov, tell me what's wrong with my child,' I assign her a dose and say nothing more. I double it, as much as I can." The dosimetrist's "gift" of a higher dose, I concluded, increases the probability that the mother will be able to obtain social protection on account of her "sick" child. Lavrov supported this interpretation and simply responded, "There is a red dose, a green dose, and a blue and yellow dose [the colors of Ukraine's flag]." The colors of flags—be they that of the Soviets, of the environmentalists, or of the Ukrainians—sanction specific truths, interpretations of dose, and courses of suffering and illness. The critical issue is the political context in which knowledge is placed and the values that data are used to support. Lavrov's constructionist approach was anthropologically gratifying; yet, given the fact that there are some things known with relative certainty about the effects of ionizing radiation (see chapter 1), even this observer had to question the dosimetrist's "it's all in our heads" account. His comment illustrates the extent to which government and scientific interventions not only contribute to a lack of resolution in the Chernobyl aftermath, but are entangled with and to some extent create new social tensions. For Lavrov, the Chernobyl aftermath conveyed a lesson: "We have learned that tragedy is not defined by the numbers who have died"; he suggested that the truth of Chernobyl was much more somber than what numbers can tell.[2] Indeed, his mode of work placed constraints on what he and those whose dose levels he specified could legitimately aim for in the quest for truth.

This chapter explores the ethical positions that local scientists and clinicians take with respect to their scientific work and the social context in which they practice. It examines these positions from the perspective of Soviet and post-Soviet scientific trajectories as well as in relation to international scientific influences. Scientific and political pressures at the international level restrict local discourses on the health effects of radiation from Chernobyl. They also influence the processes through which the biology of such effects becomes an object of contested scientific understanding and research. In clinics, such biological effects are colloquially referred to in the singular by the term *organika*. The concept of *organika* captures the commingling of biomedical definitions and measurements and social context in the assessment of biological effects of radiation. The biological facts, discourses, practices, and technologies subsumed in references to the *organika* form part of the history of rational-technical interventions that have framed the course of illness experiences in the Chernobyl aftermath.

This history is objectified in the clinical research process, where individual experiences and family and social dramas fuse with research protocols to transform illness into disease. "Illness" refers to the subjective meanings and experiences of symptoms; "disease" refers to pathology, biomedically defined (Kleinman 1988, Turner 1987). In order to have their experiences transformed from the status of illness to the status of disease (with a confirmed radiation-related etiology), Chernobyl patients must subject themselves to clinical observation and scrutiny with congeries of assessment tools and technologies. Such interventions not only

153

objectify disease; they remake the very basis through which suffering is expressed and codified. The clinical research process makes connections between ailments and the disaster real, that is, organic. In doing so, it demonstrates how interventions can shape and intensify the physicality and lived experience of tragedy. Research is an objective and an intersubjective intervention. It becomes part of a social and moral enterprise that redefines the scope of the disaster and transforms symptoms, individual narratives, and collective histories of error into legitimate tools in the exercise of a biological citizenship.

■ ■ ■

The center's clinical radiological division (the Clinic) admits four categories of patients. Medical records are marked accordingly: "Π" for sufferers (*poterpili*), "E" for evacuees (*evakuyovanni*), "Y" for participant in the Chernobyl cleanup (*uchasnyky likvidatsii*), and "C" for inhabitants of Slavutych, a town located twenty kilometers east of the Chernobyl plant and housing nuclear plant workers. Through an agreement with Zone administrators and the administration of the Chernobyl plant, Slavutych inhabitants and current Chernobyl workers are entitled to receive short-term (five-day) medical care and monitoring at the Clinic.[3] Others are required to stay for a three-week period during which they are clinically observed, and their disability status is confirmed or reconfirmed. These patients are obligated to undergo screenings by a variety of medical specialists. If patients fail to show up for their hospitalization period, they risk losing their benefits. There is no room for personal miscalculation.

The Clinic's compound comprises four concrete slab multistoried blocks surrounded by wooded areas. The compound occupies what used to be a health sanatorium. Corridors connecting blocks had green carpet liners, typical of Soviet hotels. Interior walls were partially covered by wooden paneling. Exposed areas were painted an institutional light blue. One block consisted of administrative offices, auditorium space, and a basement cafeteria. Another block contained laboratories and a gym, the latter typically unused. The facility had no ambulances or emergency wards. Stepping inside the courtyard, I could always see a few ARS patients sitting on the balconies smoking cigarettes. They were housed in a block that also contained diagnostics facilities (including equipment for genetic typing, cytogenetics, bronchoscopies, and ultrasounds), a laboratory of medical cybernetics, a demographics and archival section, and the offices of the medical-labor committee representatives. The block to the right contained other patient wards distributed over five levels.

As of July 1996, 242 people were interned according to the following medical categories: gastroenterology—24, cardiology—34, therapeutic—35, endocrinology—49, neurology—46, hematology—19, acute radiation sickness—35. The center has a total of 250 beds, with almost twice as many beds available in the neurological and endocrinological wards as in the others. Each room (*palata*) contained four to six people. Patients walked around in robes and slippers or sweatsuits on their way to medical appointments, as if they were in the privacy of their own apartments. They carried their own cups, plates, and spoons to the cafeteria during meals. In general, they brought their own treatments to the Clinic. Corridors were not normally a place for conversation. Geared toward their own purposes, people appeared to carry on without interfering in each other's business. When in the corridor I bumped into one evacuee who had not shown up for a meeting I had scheduled with her, she told me, "Friends and I don't talk about illness. Why traumatize each other? Medicines? Too many to list." And she walked away. Trauma was this group's personal terrain. The fact that it varied little from one member to the next made it even more private.

In this public space, patients were also careful not to reveal themselves, or to reveal themselves only in the right way. Dr. Nina Dragan, the deputy director of the ARS ward with whom I spoke often, described this kind of self-vigilance as characteristic behavior of what she called the *seredniak* ("middle person"). Dragan bucked trends in her unapologetic refusal to speak Russian while all the other scientists and most clinicians unapologetically refused to speak Ukrainian. Tracing her roots to a Ukrainian village in the Zone (which she had visited once), Dragan saw herself as both an insider to and a critic of the Ukrainian psyche as it has been shaped by Soviet influence. She compared the behavior of the *seredniak* to prison life, "where the disciplining technique included inculcating the ability of persons not to be singled out or noticed."[4] She used an agricultural metaphor to describe how Soviet Ukrainians related to the system both as anonymous and passive subjects and as participants in the productive fabric, which she likened to a wheat field:

> It was better to be a *seredniak*, as in a wheat field—not the shortest or the tallest wheat, but somewhere in the middle. Because when the combine passed over you, it mangled the tall wheat with its blade, missed the short wheat, and cut the wheat in the middle. Such was our society. Cut wheat: *all in the middle and ready to be cut.*

Dragan's observation did not imply a simple lack of resistance as much as it signified her and others' familiarity with paradox. To be in the middle was to be both invisible and part of the productive fabric. The readiness to be cut also suggested a readiness to merge one's identity into the system as a form of self-preservation. One had to disappear.[5]

Patients in a variety of passive and aggressive ways marked and resisted these paradoxical arrangements. While sitting in a nurse's office, I overheard a conversation between two men on the other side of the door, in the corridor. The men were talking about their efforts to be assigned a hospital bed in the center. One asked the other which ward he would be assigned to. "Wherever they shove me in (*Kudy mene vsunut'*)," he said, giving the door a solid punch. The man's aggressive gesture bespoke his frustration over the fact that disability had forced him into capricious exchanges with the state and its new disciplinary grids. Having to rely on his illness as the only sure means of economic survival made him anxious and aggressive. By choosing the word *vsunuty* (to shove), he also evoked a Ukrainian phrase referring to bribery, *vsunyty hroshi* (shoving money).

In the war of wills between patients and institutions, voice itself became part of a complex cost-benefit analysis.[6] I learned about this process while sitting in corridors with other patients who were waiting to settle their social welfare matters with the center's medical-labor expert, Ihor Demeshko. One rural woman with a second-grade education told me that she thought it was necessary, as she put it, "to stay silent and to act aggressively" in these bureaucratic encounters. Silent aggression shielded her from potentially fatal deficiencies in her level of knowledge and self-presentation. Another patient, a man, provided further insights. When I asked him whether he thought hypochondria (*khandra*, as it was sometimes called) had any legal bearing, he thought about the term for a moment and then told me that it revealed "the patient's own work in the illness." He said that *khandra* gave evidence of "self-placement" (*samoulozhennia*) of the illness, and "*that's when you have to act aggressively.*" The way to success, he explained, was to describe one's ailments in ways "that do not put the blame on you." His observation highlights the behavioral changes some patients consciously undertook in order to be "cut" into the productive fabric of that society.

Between the Lesional and the Psychosocial

The Division of Nervous Pathologies is located on the second floor, one floor below the leukemia ward and one floor above the gastroenterological ward. During my work at the psychoneurological hospital (the Pavlova), I encountered many patients who said that they wanted to get a bed *v nevrolohii*. Dr. Angelina Ceanu, the sixty-year-old ward director and neuropathologist, called me the "unprecedented visitor" when she granted my request to conduct ethnographic fieldwork in her ward. She headed the neurological subcommittee of the center's medical-labor committee and had also served as the chief medical-labor examiner for neurological diseases during the Soviet administration. Through her experience one can come to appreciate how bioscientific and clinical criteria expressed in compensation laws for Chernobyl sufferers changed. One can also gauge the tensions that arise when Western biomedical categories are exported to the East and suggest how, in the context of a disaster, such categories are integrated, adapted, or rejected at the level of local knowledge.

Ceanu's presence was striking, threatening, and warm all at the same time. Her distinctive bearing made her stand out in the poorly lit hospital environment. Prior to her Chernobyl work, Ceanu had worked as a medical doctor and researcher in the Soviet Academy of Medical Sciences in Kishinev, Moldavia, her native country. She researched open brain injuries, the clinical and psychological mechanisms of compensation for brain activity disorders among patients with traumatic lesions, and "lacunar states" of the brain in the atherosclerotic phase of hypertension. After Chernobyl, she was recruited to the center, where she turned to the study of nervous system changes and changes in the functional state of human brain and autonomic nervous disorders due to long-term exposure to ionizing radiation.

Since 1987, her team has been mapping the pathologies of the four major affected populations: resettlers, current Zone workers, inhabitants of the contaminated city of Slavutych, and Zone workers who worked at the accident site within a period of three months after the disaster. In 1990, she reorganized the work and diagnostic standards of the national medical-labor committees and established a "domestic neurology" with the then acting minister of health. She embarked on a general inventory of symptoms presented by patients and began to assess the "forces of influence" on nervous disorders in cases where doses were not registered or were unknown.

Ceanu's collaborator, Artem Borovsky, aged thirty-one, had recently been awarded a prestigious state prize for excellence in scientific work. The prize is intended to stem the country's brain drain, to keep researchers recognized to be doing valuable scientific work in Ukraine. Borovsky has been instrumental in broadening the center's diagnostic capabilities by integrating brain-imaging technologies he acquires through research trips abroad. These technologies include nuclear magnetic resonance and positron emission tomography, in addition to the standard Soviet computerized tomographic scanner.

Ceanu and Borovsky see their work as being in tension with two other approaches to how the effects of Chernobyl fallout on the nervous system should be interpreted. These other approaches can be called the "lesional" and the "psychosocial." They differ in terms of how they define populations at risk and interpret the causality of symptoms; they also rely on different diagnostic criteria. With respect to the lesional approach, Ceanu was critical of a group of Ukrainian neurosurgeons headed by A. P. Romodanov of the Institute of Neurosurgery in Kyiv. She felt this group's interpretations of radiation's cerebral effects were extreme (Romodanov et al. 1994). She told me that Romodanov had visited her neurological ward in 1988 at a time when Chernobyl workers were on a hunger strike in the Clinic, protesting unfair medical treatment. In what became a familiar state tactic, appeasing the workers meant giving some of them more critical diagnoses, ones these workers believed they deserved. According to Ceanu, "These neurosurgeons had a political project to do, to appease the workers. They wanted to say that anybody who got a dose is subject to lesions. They wanted to interpret the trauma in lesional terms."[7]

Rejecting internationally accepted standards, these neurosurgeons claim that "exposures to ionizing radiation [even at low doses] can produce neurological signs" (Romodanov et al. 1994:61). Based on long-term screening of three hundred living Chernobyl cleanup workers and on the autopsies of deceased workers, these researchers concluded that organic damage to the central nervous system manifests itself in the form of "progressing lesions" in the cortex, the subcortex, and the brain stem.[8] In their monograph, *Post-Radiation Encephalopathy: Experimental Research and Clinical Observations* (1994), the researchers state, "The Chernobyl disaster gave birth to the Chernobyl illness" in "various forms that seized hundreds of thousands of people." Using Ukrainian (rather than Russian, the former official scientific language still predominantly in use), they maintain that long-term low-dose exposure results in a "genuinely mass illness" that is "already visible today and showing itself as not being of one type" (24). They express particular concern with populations experiencing chronic exposure in contaminated areas and advocate incorporating new diagnostic criteria into the state's existing set of specifications for compensation.

At our second meeting, Ceanu elaborated her opinions about what she simply called "the West." Soviet models of clinical research had long suffered from an absence of an epidemiological approach that includes strict exclusion and inclusion criteria, randomized sampling, and the use of controls.[9] While she perceived such approaches to be useful (and indeed her younger coworkers were actively integrating them), she also perceived them to be influenced by "American standards of judgment" that diluted the uniqueness of her patients' experiences. She viewed the imposition of these standards as another means through which a dominant international radiation research establishment appropriated the Chernobyl situation for political aims. This battle-fatigued champion of the truth advocated a clinical science that remained committed to discerning the destructive effects of Chernobyl in a nonabstracted manner: in the clinic and on a long-term, per person, per symptom basis. She insisted that many times, "humanitarian aid groups and foreign experts go to the Zone and arouse fear in populations living there. Today it's the Germans, tomorrow it's the Japanese," she said. "The foreigners come to the Zone, look at the inhabitants and measure their thyroids, tell them nothing, and return home. They are medical practitioners, but they don't understand the complex interdependencies between the thyroid and other physiological systems." Her research indicated, for example, that radiation-induced malfunctions of the thyroid system form an important biological mechanism in the genesis of mental disorders, particularly in prenatally exposed children. For Ceanu, medical competence also implied social competence. She singled out the Japanese Sasakawa Fund as exemplary in this regard. "They paid the local doctors some money, so we let them go." She said her own research team must provide humanitarian assistance to Zone inhabitants to get research done. "We make sure the bread truck arrives once a week. We bring people German clothes, they're good even if they are used."

In contrast to the locally derived lesional approach, the psychosocial position is rooted in transnational expert discourse. The incommensurability of the two positions has engendered further sites of local research and scientific interaction. When I asked Ceanu how she would characterize her view with respect to the lesional and psychosocial positions, she answered, "We work between the trauma of the lesion and the nonexistence of scars."

Ceanu's presence commanded respect; she displayed undeniable empathy toward guests. Her Russian was pure and unassimilable to her emergent Ukrainian surroundings. She often joked about her linguistic shortfall as a form of personal maladaptation, not necessarily indicative of an anti-Ukrainian attitude. She left the writing of Ministry of Health reports (which were now mandatorily written in Ukrainian) to her collaborator, Borovsky, a Russian-speaker whose parents were ethnically Ukrainian. Ceanu traveled regularly to scientific research institutions in the Zone to personally collect overdue payments and salaries for her staff's medical services. She found the new times exciting if one was willing to "look for money" and felt free enough institutionally to do "what's important." In spite of the economic hardships, Ceanu once told me of the enthusiasm she had felt, in some small village in Moldavia several decades earlier, for the socialist system. She described how she "ran, not walked," to the new school that appeared in her village.

159

Her first name, Angelina, exposed a certain irony that was occasionally remarked upon. She and Dr. Angelina Guskova, who had managed the Soviet administration, were associates. Both were ranking officers in the military and received training in the Soviet school of neuropathology. The Angelina/Angelina doublet captured the doublespeak surrounding Chernobyl's human effects. "She reduces all the problems of Chernobyl to the psychosocial," said Ceanu. It was not 237, but "tens of thousands of people who experienced acute radiation sickness." Both Angelinas, as I learned through my encounters with them, were respectful of each other's scientific work in spite of the fact that their views were so far apart.

In a plenary session of the international conference on Chernobyl's mental health consequences, Ceanu referred to a "psychoneurological tendency" in the Chernobyl disaster consequences. She stated the necessity of research that should focus on cleanup workers, persons who returned to the Zone after being resettled, and children who had been in utero at the time of the accident, and their mothers. She believes that "psychoneurological disorders show a non-linear relationship of dose to the effect of the dose in the body" (31). By contrast, Guskova refers to new claims of radiation-related illnesses, especially among adults, as "psychosomatic realizations." At the same conference, Guskova stated that populations (mainly resettled persons) are suffering social and psychological discomfort of a nonradiation origin. She incensed the local Ukrainian medical community by asserting, "Specific unfavorable factors especially significant for children include the irrational behaviors of parents, teachers, and some medical workers" (23).

Guskova's view largely coincides with that of international experts who have rejected a causal relationship between ionizing radiation and nervous system effects. First evaluations of the psychosocial dimensions of nuclear power plant disasters were based on studies of the Three Mile Island disaster. Drawing from this literature, Sergeev, in 1988, attributed stress to a "lack of information" and to "wrong interpretations of truthful information" among members of affected populations. Borrowing from Robert Jay Lifton's analysis of "atomic neurosis" among Japanese *hibakusha* (Lifton 1967), minister of health Romanenko coined the word "radiophobia" to describe unwarranted fear and panic among populations, again, due to "chronic informational stress." Guskova's Soviet superior, L. A. Ilyin, clarified in a later publication that radiophobia "is not an illness, but a condition, namely the fear of the biological influence of radiation" (Marples 1988:49).[10]

Later proponents of the psychosocial position include American, Russian, Dutch, and Swedish psychologists, risk behavior analysts, sociologists, psychiatrists, and physicians. Havenaar suggests that "everyday symptoms have become potential heralds of serious radiation induced disease" (Havenaar et al. 1996: 435).[11] The psychosocial/chronic informational stress model has recently been invoked in the summary of conclusions section of a World Health Organization report on Chernobyl's aftermath:

> By far the greatest impact on the population living in the contaminated territories was the mental stress caused by fear of the possible future radiation-induced health effects. . . . much fear and mistrust had occurred because of the lack of information provided immediately after the accident. It is apparent that many psychosomatic health disorders have resulted from these concerns. (WHO 1996:429)

As defined by the terms of Soviet-American and European cooperations, the basis of this psychosocial research has been strategically limited to the study of rural populations living in contaminated regions and excludes Zone workers.[12] Psychosocial interpretations do not offer an adequate account of the ways state interventions influenced lived experiences in the aftermath of the catastrophe. In the previous chapter, I showed how official structures of accountability were made in the Soviet administration. Causal explanations of radiation's biological effects were framed in psychosocial and psychological terms, which had the effect of foreclosing rights of compensation to the many populations who had sustained injuries from radiation exposure or might in the future discover that they had done so. Such interventions, in turn, precipitated new forms of suffering and political struggle. Given this political history, it is partial and inaccurate to reduce experiences of this aftermath exclusively to matters of irrationality, improper perceptions of risk, or fear. A focus on these pathological effects alone not only fixes blame on the sufferer but also creates an illusion that these effects should be the sole and legitimate targets of professional and government intervention. Moreover, such a focus sidesteps fundamental and practical questions left behind by the history of interventions, namely, of how to monitor and respond to biological change among populations living in conditions of heightened radiological risk.

In light of predominant international opinions, Ceanu took up her work as a matter of social justice and moral urgency "to get the story straight." A part of her local science involved isolating radiation dose as an independent contributor to the etiology of illness and developing methods of dose attribution. Her team drew support for its views from the fields of neuroradiobiology and neurophysiology, and from ongoing animal research in the center's experimental radiological division. As early as the 1890s, specific human neurological reactions to radiation were noted. Early reactions included behavioral changes, paralysis and numbness, developmental delays, nervous fiber sensitivity, autonomic nervous system disturbances, retinal reactions, brain stem excitation, cerebral arterial effects, morphological changes in the neurons, and radiation-induced hypotonia and neurotic states. From the mid-1950s to the 1980s, during the nuclear arms race, the neurophysiological aspects of low-dose irradiation became subjects of international collaboration and research. Countries such as the United States and the Soviet Union were concerned with designing treatments that could extend the life and work capacity of a soldier fighting in a radiation-contaminated field (Hunt 1987). According to Ukrainian radiation biologist Varets'kyi, this research was "formulated in a totally different framework: it was about how to extend the life of a soldier so that he could continue to shoot, or whatever he needed to do. The question of what will happen to him later, well, this question was of little significance."

Ukrainian radiobiologists and clinicians were acutely aware of the political contingencies and interests that framed the production of knowledge in radiation science and particularly in neurophysiology. The works of American researchers Kimeldorf and Hunt (1965) described the influence of radiation, even at low doses, on the central nervous system and were translated into Russian, yet the significance of their data is not accounted for in current international standards (UNSCEAR 2000).

Numerous studies and local collaborations helped to further illuminate the human aftereffects of nuclear exposure. Ceanu told me that "it is inconceivable that an organism of any kind is passive to its own destruction." Ceanu wasn't being philosophical. She was quoting yet another scientific source, the Soviet radiation biologist Komarov, who observed in one of his experiments in the late 1950s that sleeping rats, without prodding, wake up when exposed to minute doses of ionizing radiation. This example reflected the specificity of Ceanu's Soviet-trained approach inasmuch as it illustrated biological activity, not as an independent function, but as something "awakening" at the interface of organism and environment. Not radiation or stress alone, but some combination of the two particularizes a degree of biological sensitivity. Though she conceded "nonradiation origins" as contributory to neurophysiological effects, Ceanu considered stress, for example, a factor that "strengthened the biological negativity of radiation." In short, and following radiobiological experiments at low doses in animals, clinical observations and diagnostic practices were focused not solely on differentiating the radiation- or nonradiation-relatedness of neurophysiological effects in humans, but on establishing the biological dependence of those effects. Thus at stake was the differentiation of a particular biology. Radiation-related or not, this biology arose from new challenges and adaptations occurring at the interface of organism and environment.

This view of biology as an active agent of adaptation has implications for approaches to clinical diagnosis. Uncertainty, contingency, and probability become valued in the diagnostic process. Diagnoses take on a specific written form to express these values. Typically, they indicate the name of the ailment and its stage, accompanied by a phrase indicating its probable origins and future tendencies. For example, a diagnosis may read "organic brain syndrome, stage 2" with a "neuro-asthenic" or "hypochondriacal" tendency. Inasmuch as the patient's own capacities are seen to carry the ultimate cure, these diagnoses resist reduction biologically or otherwise. Rather, they reinforce the fluidity of relations among biological states, environmental conditions, and human responses.[13]

According to Soviet definitions, an organism's health-oriented activity always occurs with reference to an "optimum" where the success or failure of adaptive responses can be clinically observed and thus treated (*Bol'shaia Meditsinskaia Entsiklopediia* 1956:356). Radiobiologists in the center's experimental radiological division spoke of a *diapazon* of biological activity, a range in which such an optimum could be observed. The radiobiologist Varets'kyi worked in neurophysiological animal experiments at the local Institute of General and Communal Hygiene prior to his recruitment to the Radiation Research Center. He explained the logic of this *diapazon* in this way: "You understand, we can always go to lower and lower levels, to individual cells, to individual molecules, but then we lose the pure biological aspects. The effects at lower levels might not have any consequence for the higher levels, and vice versa. We look for an optimum, a golden center, where the data will be understandable."

■ ■ ■

If Ceanu sets the research direction, Borovsky, a neuropsychiatrist, is the expert on the technologies by which these directions are realized. He analyzes "radiation pathogenesis" of "organic personality development" at dose ranges that Guskova would consider far too low to be of any biological significance.[14] He states that persons irradiated above a very low 0.3 gray (see chapter 1, n. 33) exhibit "disturbances in brain information processing that are traceable back to an organic structure." In working out a logic of pathological responses, he often used the word *zakonomernyi*, which means "in conformity with law," "regular," or "natural." Though his logic was poorly reflected in the numerous and often complicated flow charts he published,[15] it found strong support in previous work done by researchers from the Nagasaki University Scientific Data Center of the Atomic Bombing. These researchers have shown a correlation between radiation and the brain (mental retardation, epilepsy and "endogenous psychosis") through a study of children exposed prenatally at the time of the American atomic bombings.

Today, Ceanu directs an internationally funded pilot project, "Brain Damage *In Utero*," in Ukraine. The aim of the project is to identify cases of mental retardation and other brain dysfunctions in children irradiated *in utero*. Children born between April 26, 1986, and February 25, 1987, along with their mothers and teachers in contaminated regions are under investigation. She points to a trend of mental retardation and borderline emotional-behavioral disorders among prenatally irradiated children. This trend in her opinion points to the need for follow-up of these children, and for other investigations such as individual fetal dose reconstructions. This work will be important to the analysis of a clinical case presented at the end of this chapter.

In short, Ceanu and Borovsky are replacing the psychosocial model with an approach that emphasizes the heterogenous nature of radiation and its effects on the nervous system. They claim this open-endedness as their scientific turf. Their nosography is evolving, blending new Western diagnostics such as posttraumatic stress disorder with existing Soviet-derived diagnostics. They are refining their diagnostic instruments to capture larger cohorts of Chernobyl sufferers (even those not officially designated). They are defining the technological terms of the *organika* at low doses.

Such work has attracted critics on account of its "pro-radiation" stance. One administrator in the compensation bureaucracy called Ceanu an "idealist" because she transforms mental experiences into legitimate responses to Chernobyl—because she "Chernobylizes" her patients. Ceanu told me that she has resisted pressure from her Russian and Western European colleagues to give up diagnostic methods that do not correlate with categories found in the International Classification of Diseases.

By pointing out these tensions, I aim to draw attention to the ways in which international classification systems influence the construction of local diagnostic practices and to explore the epistemological and political grounds that provide the basis for resisting these influences. I also want to point out that the work of these local scientists is situated in worlds that carry "particular rules of inclusion and exclusion" and recognition (Asad 1993:8). These "local" scientists recognize their work as having a certain "practical reach" within national, postsocialist, and capitalist contexts. The immediate objective of their limited agency "is to change aggregate human conditions (distribution, trends, etc.) towards profitability and utility" (ibid.).[16]

Much as is the rest of the population, Ceanu's team is concerned with systematizing the *probability* of relations between the disaster and the Ukrainian population. In so doing, the team forms its own pool of potential research subjects; team members are engaged in a strategy of intellectual ownership that does not forfeit scientific resources or future scientific potential. Ceanu and Borovsky were planning to "open up" the orphanages in Kyiv to find ten-year-olds born around the time of the disaster who might be showing signs of schizophrenia today (this work would link up with research carried out by Japanese psychiatrists on the Hiroshima bomb victims). Ceanu's team used Afghani war veterans as controls to test for "posttraumatic stress" among Chernobyl workers (this work is in keeping with international interest in and use of the posttraumatic stress disorder diagnostic).[17] Although they lacked resources, notably money and state-of-the-art equipment, the team conveyed a sense of satisfaction with owning the unknown, a pleasure that compensated for the fact of its brute inescapability.

New Sociality

One day a man walked into Ceanu's office wearing a black leather coat and carrying a black briefcase. He identified himself as the vice-director of a large construction enterprise in the city. "Here is a perfect Ukrainian," Ceanu told me, somewhat facetiously. "He has a perfectly Ukrainian surname, Mykhail*ychko*." By emphasizing *ychko*, she drew attention to the man's diminutive-sounding surname, a humorous taunt about Ukraine's historical subordination to neighboring masters, and about her own inability to get used to the idea that she was now a Ukrainian citizen.[18] "*Ychko*," she continued, "built the Sarcophagus from the ground up."

The man tactfully interrupted. He said that he needed to be examined "because of some problems that came up regarding his disability status." He was vague but said he wanted to make the formal request for disability (*oformyty hrupu*, literally to "make the group"). After Ceanu reviewed his medical dossier, she said to him, "You know we have a deficit of medicines and basic supplies here." The man looked as if he understood that he would have to provide some humanitarian assistance in exchange for a diagnosis. "How's it at work, have you been paid?" Ceanu asked. "Not in the last five months, a major scandal," he replied. Ceanu and the man struck a note of complicity when they recognized one another's work as "charity." "All right," she said, "we'll take a look at you, you're in our databank already, it'll be quicker here than anywhere else." The meeting concluded with the standard presentation of a box of chocolates.

After he left, Ceanu said, "He's registered as having absorbed 50 rem. We multiply that number routinely by five. He should be an acute radiation sickness case, right? Like those in the initial Soviet cohort. But

165

because the pathophysiological processes didn't show up in his blood right away . . . those who showed immediate changes got the diagnosis. The system missed the others. Their *organizm* was compensating." Ceanu used a standard Soviet biomedical term for adaptation. "His illnesses were masked at this stage. But now he is showing all the signs of pathology. He is decompensating. He has the head spins, the pains, and so on. But he wants to work and has every reason to work." Apparently receiving the diagnosis he needed, the man did not return to the ward for a formal examination.

Borovsky entered the office and announced the arrival of a new patient, a woman who had been working at the Chernobyl plant since 1971 and a first-time visitor to the Clinic. She had not sought medical care or been under any medical surveillance or treatment since the accident. Borovsky explained that she showed all the signs of chronic radiation sickness to the point that her "eyes were rolling around." Petrovskaia worked as an engineer at the Chernobyl plant. Her registered dose was 70 rem, on the order of 350 rem according to the clinicians' revised estimates. Borovsky referred to her as a "pure case" of chronic radiation sickness. He told me that she was a well-trained professional, and pointed out that "there was no social component to her disease. It's pure radiation." Borovsky diagnosed her with organic brain damage and *senestopathia*, a medical term designating painful damage to the afferent nerve system. Her electroencephalogram showed "slow delta waves" possibly indicating an organic brain disorder.

Petrovska wanted to say very little when I interviewed her, only that she had avoided mandatory clinical monitoring and diagnosis from the moment that she was evacuated from the city of Prypiat' in 1986: "I left the hospital then because I knew I'd become a worthless worker. Where would I go?" She knew that her blood indicators were depressed, but she had "lost those medical documents." In the meantime, she took care of herself with herbs, citrus fruit, and berries: "Eat them together and their acidity flushes radiation out of the body." She applied paraffin-soaked gauze, "like hot plastic," on her spine.

She had adjusted her work routine to hide her symptoms and to avoid the medical surveillance system. She took on more drafting duties so that she could be seated, in case she was struck by a sudden loss of consciousness. Petrovska waited until the last possible moment to be hospitalized and was not invested in recovery. By her reasoning, she had come to the clinic exactly on time, when her illnesses were so overwhelmingly realized that she would have little chance of being denied full compensation.

The arrival of Petrovska upset Borovsky. He expressed ire toward the "international experts" affiliated with the IAEA, who he believed have underestimated the health effects of Chernobyl (this view was a common one). Indeed, the "regimes of truth" these experts have constructed (more often than not based on short-term surveys) can cost them little as they can enter into and leave this context relatively unscathed. On the other hand, such regimes can have devastating moral effects for those scientists and clinicians continuing to be involved in the inventory of the disaster. These expert regimes embed and restrict local scientific action. They use their authority and control of technological resources to categorize scientific knowledge into "official" versus "unofficial" discourses and "legitimate" versus "illegitimate" science.

Borovsky said, "If I say there are more than 237 cases of acute radiation sickness, these experts will say I am crazy. They will not even consider supporting our work. Call me paranoid." Borovsky also pointed out what he considers to be experts' abuse of the word "social": "According to the experts, every health problem should be called social in origin." For him, the social was everything that contradicts a Western nosological approach; it was a kind of epistemological dump site. "The West doesn't believe our data," he said. In Borovsky's view, such processes indirectly legitimated a state system that in his view encouraged citizens to hide their illnesses until it was physically impossible to do so anymore, while it simultaneously exploited their physical resources. This was precisely Petrovska's situation. Borovsky's patients were not typical human subjects. They were people trapped within a system—that is, living the social paradox until it literally killed them. That was his feeling, at least. It was morally and scientifically incumbent on him and others to do good science while assisting patients in their struggles for social health.

These commitments, however, did not mean that clinicians were blindly appeasing the demands of patients for social compensation. Ceanu routinely expressed dismay over the fact that so many ready and willing human subjects were coming to her ward. Such collective readiness was indeed novel. Clinicians recalled how difficult it had been to recruit patients for their research in the early nineties, difficulties they ascribed to inhibitions related to socialist work regimes (see chapter 4), which discouraged people from seeking medical help, particularly if their illnesses could be interpreted as psychologically related.

According to Ceanu, these new patients were primarily of a "low-dose" nature. And while she maintained that there was a connection between low doses and neurological effects, she also maintained that patients' demands for clinical treatment and disability status were driven by a "social infantilism" (something she urged me to explore in my interviews with patients). She stereotyped Ukrainians as possessing a "slave" nature that made them overly dependent on hospitalization to resolve social problems—an observation that Western researchers have made in the context of the Soviet health care system as a whole (Field 1967). She agreed with Angelina Guskova when she attributed this dependence to "pathological personality developments." In Soviet classification, these developments are referred to as "behavioral weaknesses and deficits." They are most commonly expressed in the form of depressions, asthenias, obsessions, and hypochondriacal syndromes—what in the West would typically be recognized as neurotic states (*Bol'shaia Meditsinskaia Entsiklopediia* 1956:416). In Soviet fashion, social environments serve as the basis for the normalization of individual character and clinical arbitrations of its weaknesses.

These "innate" human weaknesses, according to Ceanu, became more pronounced in the new economic environment. Forms of dependence were embodied in the commonly invoked stereotype of the *rentnyk*. The word means "one who rents," referring to a person who has an overly dependent and hence pathological relationship with the state. Among clinicians, the *rentnyk* type was the basest and most "infantile" of characters, possessed of a persistence of demands that made clinicians "wilt into subjection." Those most adept at calling forth from clinicians an almost automatic submission were sometimes called *vovky* (wolves). One patient indeed suggested that it was individuals who had taken on an animal nature who survived the system. "Those who survived were wolves, not slaves." Human nature, even when reduced to its "lowest" form (slave), was no match for the system.

Every Monday, and as part of her pedagogical work, Ceanu made rounds through the patient rooms; a fleet of young neurologists-in-training trailed behind her. Each physician had an assigned set of patients. These assignments were, as a rule, not based on preferences. Attending physicians reported on individual patients, including the medical reasons for the individual's entry to the ward, the type of labor he or she performed at Chernobyl, the patient's probable dose, and therapeutic progress. Ceanu's routine was to make personal contact with each patient, engaging them with what struck me as a random mixture of compassion and disaffection, intimacy and threat. This unpredictability of affect was deliberate, as it provoked behavior among patients allowing the clinician to gauge their psychological strengths or weaknesses. She could better discern the veracity of people's claims and the forces influencing their illnesses based on their reactions and defenses.

We met three middle-aged women in the first rounds I participated in. One said that she was waiting for a financial sponsor to obtain treatment for her hyperactive thyroid; thyroid problems were common among adult patients. She also reported that she had "already seen the psychiatrist," suggesting a confidence in her disorder's having been "cleared" of any mental components. A second woman was sitting in her bed, leaning back against a wall; she had tied a blue scarf around her head. She appeared to be depressed and spoke in monotonous and muffled tones. She said she was a telephone operator, and that the pains in her head began in 1986, "but there weren't any medicines around." She stared through a window while listlessly itemizing her ailments. Ceanu observed her for a little while and said to the ward doctor, "Give her [a diagnosis of] posttraumatic stress disorder (PTSD). It is less organic and more neurotic." I was surprised by Ceanu's almost painterly use of a popular Western psychiatric diagnostic. The "neurotic" diagnosis meant that the woman could go no further with her claims without seeing the resident medical-legal psychiatrist, but it also made her a possible candidate for the ward's PTSD study.

On another round, we met a man who reported having skin rashes and an autonomic nervous disorder. He referred to the second condition as a "recent gain" of somatic illness. Another middle-aged man lay in an adjacent bed. His physician said, "This is a Zone recruit from 1986." When Ceanu asked him to explain his work, he said that he was a biologist from the Institute of Zoology. He worked in the Zone monitoring disease outbreaks and physiological changes in rodents (considered to be sentinels of radiation-related disease), and the relationship between sudden human evacuations and epidemics. Ceanu wanted to know more about the biological changes he had observed in the Zone. "After people had been resettled, it was just like after a war," he explained. The man emphasized his direct exposure to radiation. "A hoard of small animals appeared, we worked without protection, we were completely exposed . . . We didn't see major changes in the first year, only that animals reproduced in greater numbers. The next year we started to notice the physiological changes. The animals started to age much faster. They used to live for one year, maximum. Now they live for only three or four months. They reproduce much younger and die off much faster." When the man finished, Ceanu commented, "We do the same work." Her statement underscored the ironic identification physician and patient had with experimental animals, but also suggested that just as the biologist had observed animals, now the clinician was observing him, like an animal.

Next to the biologist lay a tall, lanky, and somewhat agitated eighteen-year-old, evacuated from the city of Prypiat'. The young man listened in on the conversation. His doctor reported his symptoms and said he had been eight when he was evacuated. He lived with his parents, both of whom, he said, had Chernobyl-related disability status. His mother worked as a nurse, and his father was a cleanup worker. The attending physician reported that he had an autonomic nervous disorder. Trained in Western biological psychiatric imaging techniques, she added that his electroencephalogram indicated abnormally large "delta curves" and normal "alpha rhythms." Ceanu, seemingly ignoring the data, leaned over his bed and asked him in an almost confrontational manner, "What do you want to say about yourself?" Anxiously, and with apparent guilt, he responded that this was his first time in a clinic. He said that his memory was poor, and that he couldn't do his mathematics assignments. He said he had difficulty learning English in school. "It seemed like I was learning it, but I really wasn't. I didn't take well to the book, and later, the learning didn't last long enough to give me something. Everyone in school went ahead, and I stayed in the same place." "All you students pity yourselves!" Ceanu snapped. She then turned to the consulting doctor and told her to add "hypochondriacal syndrome" to the boy's cluster of diagnoses. Ceanu, who knew the patient's mother, intimidated the young man, knowing his objective desire: he was desperately afraid of military recruitment. Ceanu's threats were more like moral reprimands. Enduring them was a small price to pay for the promise she would give him next, "You will not go into the army." Ceanu's promise reassured him that he would be guaranteed a place in a communitas of ill people instead.

A part of my field research involved carrying out interviews with patients in the ward. I was assigned a room where I conducted these interviews in private. The room was two floors below the neurological ward and located along a well-trafficked corridor. The sign on the office door read "Office of the Psychotherapist" (*kabinet psikhoterapevta*). But Dr. Morozov, the psychotherapist, had left two years earlier.[19] Patients had regarded the psychotherapist's therapeutic "séances" and meditation sessions as effective, yet there were no efforts to hire a replacement. Nurses spoke of their physical attraction to the psychotherapist and regretted his absence. The office was filled with unused or worn-out equipment and cables (a television monitor, biofeedback machines, electric stimulation devices). Chairs with cushioned headrests lined the walls of the room, as did some commemorative images of Morozov extending his arms in trancelike positions over his subjects. He was a neuropathologist and hypnotist by training and worked with Borovsky to introduce "psychic categories into the accident's registry of risk." He conducted studies on the bioelectrical activity of the brains of workers in the Zone, and he researched the onset and treatment of anorgasm among women evacuated from the Zone, and of sexual impotence among men. With Ceanu, he researched the effects of psychological factors on the functional state of the nervous system. His absence underscored the fact that, given the massive social and political demands upon the state, there was no more room for the psyche in that ward.

Every few days I reviewed the patients' charts and tried to assemble a representative sample. I gave lists of names and meeting times to the nurse on duty. Patients typically received notes from the nurses telling them to "see the psychologist" at a given time. I didn't know that nurses were identifying me in this way until one day when a patient showed me a nurse's note.

Male patients struggled with the system, voiced anxiety about being a part of it, and justified their illness as imperative to social and economic survival. Becoming objects of a paternalistic relationship with the state also caused many of them to reflect on who they were in the context of their most intimate roles as fathers and sons. In their reflections, I understood that many of them were attempting to find a mode of symbolizing themselves in ways *other than* those associated with illness. "A person needs to extract the slave from himself. This process takes generations," I was told by one patient. These men identified strongly with their fathers. At the same time, they could not be fathers—that is, providers and protectors—themselves. These men lacked formal employment and lost their attachment to their Soviet labor collectivities. It was upon these forms of collectivities that strong ideas of manhood and fatherhood were once built. Given such instabilities across generations, what could they pass on to their children?

Yurii Tabor's medical records identified him as a "mixed" (psycho-organic) case with "hypochondriacal syndrome." When I knocked on his door, he was lying on his hospital bed, scanning a newspaper article that was circulating among the patients about the curtailment of Chernobyl invalids' rights. He was thirty-eight years old and came from the coal-mining region of Ukraine; his parents were collective farmers. He gestured toward another patient, who was lying on a bed nearby. Tabor started to speak on behalf of his forty-six-year-old neighbor: "See this man? He is like any other man. Pylypko has a family and wife. And look at him. Look how the man prostrates himself here. He wants disability so that he can get a little more pension money, so that he doesn't have to rely on food from his father in village." To this comment, Pylypko himself responded. Momentarily lifting his head from the pillow, he asked, "Is there such a thing where one's father provides food, money, and clothing to his son at my age? My father gets a $22.00 pension—and he divides it among us." Tabor commiserated, noting, "I live that way, too." Pylypko complained of back problems and said that he couldn't work. "He will have to experience further humiliation to be rightfully acknowledged and compensated for," said Tabor.

In the middle of the conversation, Nina Dragan, the physician who has given us the instructive metaphor of the combine, knocked on the door and asked me to step outside. She said she had been looking for me to introduce me to more patients whom she believed were "truly cured." She regretted that she hadn't found me earlier that day: "We signed out a very healthy man, a part of the original acute radiation sickness cohort." She divided patients into two groups, those "wanting to work" and those who "survive by being sick," a group for whom she had little tolerance. For her, the *organika* was a morally indefensible means of resolving social problems. From the corridor, she had overheard Tabor's impassioned consolation of his ward mate and told me the patients were classic *rentnyky* and suggested that I take a hard line with this "mass type":

> If they say they can't work, ask them why, ask them what hurts. If they don't work, if they are disabled, ask them if they have a car. Ask them how they spend their day. Ask them if they just sit in front of the television and whether their wife works. If they say they can't get medicines, then ask if they have sick grandparents. And if they say they are going to the parents' retreat house (*dacha*), how is it that they can be invalids? Living at a *dacha* requires work! Then ask them how much land they have. If they have a *soroksotok*, they must be working!![20]

Sighing, Dragan concluded, "Nowhere else in the world is there a situation where it is better to be sick than healthy."

Pylypko, like most patients, had three weeks to make the rounds to the various doctors, including the neurologists and psychiatrist. Two weeks had already expired, and no doctor had entered his room to examine him. Tabor interpreted this inactivity as a bad sign for his neighbor's clinicosocial fate. Also working against him was the fact that Pylypko did not know how to use the system of *blat*; nor did he have any connections to a disabled persons support fund to advocate for him politically. He was just passively lying there, expecting to be examined as in any other hospital situation. The morning of the day Tabor and I were scheduled to meet in my office, Pylypko encountered a bureaucratic obstacle: a nurse informed him that he needed to retrieve some additional documents (evidencing that he had worked in the Zone) at home before he could be examined. The round-trip would have taken four days, which would have left Pylypko with one working day at the center. He left the ward and didn't return, forced to forfeit his long-awaited twenty-one days for medical-legal examination.[21]

Tabor, on the other hand, was combative and verbally aggressive. He and his wife had started their married life in a communal apartment with one other married couple. The couples shared a three-square-meter room. After his Zone work, he "received his diagnosis" in 1990 at a clinic in Kharkiv known to have had many hunger strikes, "which precipitated official actions." In 1994, he joined a Chernobyl fund in his hometown, which gave him a small private plot where he grew vegetables and fruits.

In another interview, he conveyed a detailed inventory of his symptoms, knowledge of their progression, and an account of how he responded to them. He spoke of the capriciousness of radiation's effects on the body, his powerlessness over them, and their pervasive nature. "My arms get numb and when the blood flows finally, then the little needles come. The arms get numb again, totally numb. I can't feel them. You can prick them and I can't feel them." At other points he described losses of consciousness: "Those who were there know them. The impact is so sudden you can fall. It gets dark in the eyes. You can't do anything. You switch off (*perekliuchennia*) for some time. Not only are my nerves weak from this radiation, everyone's nervous system is susceptible. It acts in other ways on others. It happens in a variety of ways." Tabor was critically engaged with the new social reality in which his own inadequacies were revealed. He referred to his ailments as diffuse "little illnesses." He spoke of his symptoms as a "mistress." This ironic term conveyed his sense of impotence.

"What are you losing?" I asked him. Tabor shifted from an involved description of his symptoms and engaged my question in very literal terms.

My son is sixteen years old. He's going into the eleventh grade. My wife hasn't gotten anything from the state since April. I work as I did before. I began as a foreman. But I had to stop. I couldn't work after Chernobyl. I couldn't. I had to refrain from physical pressures at work and became a metal worker instead. I had to change jobs because of my physical state and once again, I was losing. I was on my way to becoming a director of a shop floor. I was bound to make $190.00 a month. And now, anywhere I went to find a job as a metal worker, they pay $140.00 a month. As a metal worker, I am losing $50.00 a month. Now, because of my health I am working at a job that is of lower rank and pay. It pays only $97.00 a month. I am losing my salary. And I won't last in my current position for too long. You adapt to your *organizm*, but you are losing your salary.

The new capitalist work environment made his efforts to adapt even more obsolete.

And how do people work now? They do everything quickly, to get more pay. I can't make it that way either. And now I have to send my son to school. Buy him boots, that's $35.00. There aren't cheaper ones. Sneakers, $10.00. Sportswear? $24.00. And so it goes."

"What's the way out?" I asked Tabor.

"To trade petty goods, to buy and resell things. My wife and I garden. We plant potatoes and cabbage. This work is an additional burden on my wife because I can't do the physical work. I try to turn it into a joke."

173

These "father-patients" had thought a lot about what they could and could not pass along to their children in that society. When asked what he could teach his thirteen-year-old, another patient reasoned that social conditions were changing so quickly that "he didn't have time to adapt. Children must become adults, our age, and older than us. I cannot teach my son how to act, I don't have the capacity." If these men were teaching their children anything, it was to recognize how a system of power contributes to their social incapacity. Through such awareness children can be "freed" and taught to act on their own.

Such stories reveal how aggregate human conditions run parallel to the reconfigurations of the most intimate familial relations. They convey a self-awareness of the limits and possibilities of life in a context where, as Dragan put it, one had to disappear in order to become part of a social fabric.

Doctor-Patient Relations

Clinical monitoring, however, was anything but an anonymous and impersonal experience. Long hospital stays, a Soviet legacy, altered doctor-patient relations in the sense that doctors could get to know patients very intimately. In the pages that follow, a psychiatrist reflects on the relationship between intimacy and social control, how it structured mutual perceptions among doctors and patients, and how both groups manipulated medical power in order to adhere to or to secure good relations with the state.

Oleksandr Tolkach was a rotund thirty-eight-year-old forensic psychiatrist occupying an office in the basement of the Radiation Research Center's complex, two floors beneath the offices of the medical-labor committee. He worked with patients (referred to him by other doctors), determining whether the basis of their illnesses was psychogenic or organic. The depressions and other psychological ailments he diagnosed became the bottom-line basis for discharging patients. Until 1993, Tolkach served on the forensic psychiatric committee at Ward 1 of the Kyiv Psychoneurological Hospital, confining the city's severely mentally ill. The psychiatrist's work included determining whether criminals could plead not guilty by reason of insanity.

Tolkach was a down-to-earth and amicable member of Ceanu's collective and worked closely with his friend and colleague, Borovsky. Tolkach deferred to Borovsky's machine-based assessments, which Tolkach considered to be superior to his own "face-to-face" assessments. Whenever he arrived from his basement office on the neurological ward, he conveyed a down-in-the-trenches approach and an intimacy, certainty, and even lightness with patients that no other clinician had. "The patients turn us into kiosk workers!" he once joked, invoking an image of a patient purchasing a diagnosis from a street merchant.

In his opinion, psychiatry in the Soviet period had served two purposes: treatment and surveillance (*ukhod*, or "looking after"). "When a patient was readmitted to a clinic, the same doctor looked after him, as a rule." The role of the psychiatrist was to ensure "that the sick person does not fall out of society, his surroundings, or his collective." Many asylums were open-door. "Our task was to maintain the social ties of the sick person—with his work, his family, and his neighbors." According to Tolkach, "No one at work necessarily knew whether a sick person was being treated at a psychiatric asylum. He'd be working, and no one in his collective (*kollektiv*) would know this." In the effort to maintain social ties, a contract (a mutual dependency) formed between psychiatrist and patient to preserve the social anonymity of the mentally ill.

Micronegotiations between doctors and patients helped to sustain the particular portrait of mental health mandated by socialist society, but these bonds also had a positive dimension. Systemic nonacknowledgment of mental illness meant that normal citizens were not predisposed to judging deviance in the same way their Western counterparts were. During my work at the center, there was a debate over the proposed admission of a man simultaneously diagnosed with schizophrenia and a blood disorder allegedly related to his Chernobyl experience. Hematologists one floor above the neurological ward refused to admit him, claiming that he would upset the well-being of other patients. They even threatened to quit their jobs. The deputy director, himself a well-known hematologist and radiation specialist, refused to give in to general demands that Eshevsky be denied a hospital bed. As far as this administrator was concerned, Eshevsky was a Chernobyl patient. Doctors in the neurological ward privately mocked their chief, a socialist with a portrait of Lenin still hanging prominently in his office. According to Tolkach, the deputy director was so socialist that he "can't even recognize mental illness."

No one was quite sure, however, what Eshevsky's Chernobyl experience consisted of, or whether he had ever been in the Zone. He told Tolkach that he had worked as a journalist in the Zone, but no one could confirm his claim. Borovsky said, "We live in a democracy now. Patients with extreme conditions have the right to choose whether they want to be put into a mental hospital or not. Here, Eshevsky is free." In chapter 7, I examine the impact that this newfound freedom "to be publicly ill" has on domestic life.

Tolkach suggested that Eshevsky capitalized on his social role and, in a sense, had the upper hand: "The patient knew that he could always come for medical care, he could lie down in a clinic, settle his/her social and material matters, get some treatment. Nobody was going to chase him away. It was *his* space. He could lie there for two months and then get a two-month pension on top of his regular salary. He could buy himself extra clothes. When he was in the hospital, he didn't need a pension. He got fed, dressed, and treated here."[22]

Soviet psychiatrists often disagreed over when to assign a diagnosis of mental illness. They typically engaged in a practice of *hypodiagnostika* or underdiagnosis: "We didn't even write this diagnosis, we wrote something else." This lessened the social blow of the diagnosis and fostered the anonymity of mental illness. A schizophrenic could work and function normally in society. Because the socialist system emphasized universal employment, psychiatric acknowledgment of the "defect" was synonymous with a form of real defection, an unsanctioned withdrawal from society and escape from a duty to be employed. There was discomfort and anxiety over this sort of labeling because it potentially exposed both patient and doctor to social sanctions.

Tolkach felt that colleagues "didn't want to take responsibility for mental illness." Psychiatrists even disagreed as to the kinds of behaviors that would warrant the label of "defect." Thus there were rules guiding practices of labeling, and we can see some of these being redeployed in the context of Chernobyl's aftermath. "Patients debuted their illness," Tolkach said, using a theater term, "but this didn't mean they were defective yet." He believed that staging was a practice inherent in the system; people had learned how to do it. A new set of medical-legal interventions and a new contract between psychiatrist and patient had to be formed once the defect was authorized (or successfully enacted).

No One Is Hiding Anything Anymore

Tolkach felt that most cases referred to him for evaluation "were neurotic in nature." During another of my visits to his office, he grabbed a 1960 Russian translation of a German psychiatric textbook. Pointing to the table of contents of the original text, which he also had, he compared the two. "Soviet psychiatry threw out Freud. Look, all the chapters were retained in the translation except for the ones on the theoretical writings of Freud on the development of neuroses. Everything was translated, except those parts."

In the void left by those untranslated texts, the mechanistic neurophysiology of Ivan Pavlov came to dominate Soviet understandings of the unconscious and nervous system changes and thus supplanted Freud's theory of neurosis. Pavlov was interested in the study of the unconscious from the standpoint of an experimentalist and, in his laboratory, generated what he called "experimental neuroses." In his study of dogs, Pavlov circumvented the problem of resistance, key to neurosis, by surgically implanting an "artificial fistula" into his subjects' stomachs. This device provided a "window" into the functioning of the unconscious activity of the nervous system (Wells 1960:40).[23] He attached this fistula to a duct and then to a tube. Pavlov activated digestive glands by an external stimulus and measured quantities of gastric secretions flowing in the tube. The point of this hideous experiment was to reveal the facts and laws of unconscious activity. In the meantime, Pavlov created an "animal" physiology: research subjects' resistance could be literally removed by design. Interior life was made to be completely visible, measurable, always exposed and subject to experimental control. Pavlov and his secreting dogs "became a symbol of the power of experimental biology to explain, and perhaps even control, human behavior" (Todes 1997:947).

Tolkach seemed to suggest that this experiment of totalizing power was no longer in existence. Yet in his view Pavlov's status as an experimentalist and as a cultural icon remained: "No one has gone further than Pavlov in the science of human behavior," he said.[24] While Tolkach described the banishment of Freud from Soviet psychiatry, the ear, nose, and throat specialist who shared the office with him, and who typically sat quietly through my discussions with Tolkach, burst out with, "We lived like dogs but we weren't repressed!"

Tolkach reflected further on neurosis, this time keeping the management of the Chernobyl aftermath in mind. Pavlov's theories, he said, "did not account for actual neurosis. Under socialism, there was no social premise for the development of neurosis. Neurosis manifested itself exclusively in capitalist lands. Therefore, to speak of social premises for alcoholism, neuroses, drug addiction, even prostitution—we never had such a thing! Well, we had neurosis, but its social reason was never taken into account. . . . We had the *organika*, pure *organika*, without any social twists."

He then explained how the Soviet state management of radiation and its effects fit into this arrangement. He began by giving a description of the situation in the Pavlova in 1986. "After the explosion, the authorities of course hid information about the high levels of radiation. They said that radiation did not exist. A new term was implemented; it wasn't in any of the textbooks that I showed you. It was called radiophobia. If a person came in and claimed that she was exposed to radiation, and asked me what she should do. Well, nothing! She had radiophobia. Radiophobia was used to solve all emerging social problems. . . . No one wanted to take public responsibility for saying there were illnesses resulting from Chernobyl." In an ironic paradox, the system actively condoned using a social (neurotic) condition as a way of containing the spread of potential

177

(organic) disease. "In the last years we've had two international congresses on this here, and there were papers on the psychoneurological course of illness of patients. . . . Today, *no one is hiding anything anymore.*" Tolkach's remarks highlight the importance of the Soviet legacy to the construction of mental illness. In his logic, people were "granted" and could learn how to deploy "their neuroses" through a range of tactics; at the same time the interpretive apparatus that regulates those tactics is changing.

The ensuing pages are based on observations of routine engagements Tolkach had with patients. I then turn to a specific clinical case to show how the process of "staging" informs a research process and authorizes illness.

The blue-scarfed woman who had spoken in a monotonous, muffled tone during Ceanu's Monday rounds visited Tolkach as part of her mandatory screening. She was a resident of Zone Four. That summer (July 1996) the government was phasing out compensations to inhabitants of Zone Four; the woman needed to get into the system and start her pilgrimage. She complained of depression and said she had been diagnosed with organic ailments, "encephalopathy, spasms, other vestibulary disorders," in 1991. Tolkach asked her to have another encephalogram done to confirm the presence or absence of an organic component. She insisted that she had already had the necessary tests. "I don't see the results," Tolkach said. She attempted to divert his attention, saying that her small child was in the hospital: "When my little child is in the sun, he turns white and his lips turn black." She said she took tranquilizers and sleeping pills, but "nothing helps." The night before, "I couldn't sleep until the morning." She said she heard "knocking sounds on the doors and windows all night." These digressions made Tolkach even more skeptical: "What are you afraid of?" he asked. The woman kept up her story of fear. "Why be afraid if no one is there? Just go to sleep," Tolkach said. Fear, as he saw it, did not constitute the defining center of the Chernobyl sufferer's social experience. In a last-ditch effort to convince Tolkach that her condition was Chernobyl-related, the woman said, "This never happened before."

Patients like this woman reported a variety of sensations and symptoms. They included head pains, vertigo, vomiting, loss of memory, high blood pressure, insomnia, pains in the heart and stomach, hypochondria, anxious states, loss of hearing and vision, auditory hallucinations, anxiety understood as a "chronic internal alert," and numbness in the arms, face, and legs. Conversations typically centered on drugs. Tolkach prescribed antidepressants and antianxiety agents, and treatments and self-injections aimed at improving cerebral circulation.

178

Tolkach then asked the woman which medicines she used, and she said a doctor provided her with a local antianxiety agent as well as samples of one produced in Germany; "it works best, but it's not available here." She listed several more drugs, mostly tranquilizers, and wanted a prescription from Tolkach. After she left, Tolkach told me that she was addicted to tranquilizers. "But what about the fact that she's afraid?" I asked him. "I think that she sleeps very well at night. Of course some things bother her, her future." His next sentence surprised me. He talked about the woman's "defect" as if it were a separate entity but said that he would have nothing to do with its sustenance. "The defect will come out of her or it will not come out of her. She will not get herself to crawl out of those clinics. She describes the defect very well." Tolkach's comment about "active description" suggested that the patient first had to know the illness in order to get it. "She'll qualify sooner or later. It's only a matter of time. . . . Next it will be the psycho-organic syndrome, organic damage, with delusions of all kinds. What does she need all of this for?" The woman's defect, the one she "wished" for, indicated how far she was willing to go to break relations of social control, and to form new ones around the illness she took pains to claim as so real.

After this Zone Four inhabitant left, an evacuee entered the room. She had been evacuated from the city of Prypiat' and had the familiar U-shaped scar on her neck, a sign indicating that she had had her thyroid surgically removed. I found such procedures to be common not only in children who contracted thyroid cancer as a result of exposure to radioactive iodine-131 but among adults as well. Tolkach immediately asked what her problems were. "Head pains, dizziness." She looked to be about sixty years old. "Are you a pensioner?" Tolkach asked. "No, I am here because of Chernobyl, I am forty years old." Tolkach said that she too must go to Borovsky and have an encephalogram done before he could assess her case. Tolkach then tried to determine her economic state by asking what her husband did. "I don't know," she said. "What do you mean you do not know what your husband does for a living?" he countered. "I know he works for a firm, I know he brings home some money." She divulged as few facts as she possibly could about her life. By saying "half-things," she made herself look half-crazy, ill.

A man with a cane walked into the office—a 1986 cleanup worker with an official registered dose of 39 rem. He threw his medical records on Tolkach's wooden desk. He had driven a bus, evacuating people from the Zone, and had been an invalid since 1989. Tolkach asked him on what basis he'd been registered as disabled. "I don't remember. It's all written in there," he said, pointing to his records. Tolkach asked, "Why the stick?" "Gangrene and amputation," the man answered. Tolkach then asked him, "Do you have the results of your encephalogram?" "They did it yesterday."

"What bothers you?" Tolkach asked. "Where do I start?" the man responded. "Considering your particular line of work," he went on, "I sweat, I don't sleep. When I lie down, everything spins. The balcony attracts me. I want to jump. I'm on the fifth floor and the ground looks like it's half a meter away. I walk and walk." Then Tolkach asked, "Do you have the Chernobyl disability tie? How long is it valid for? Is it effective for your lifetime?"

Tolkach asked, "On what basis did you get your disability?" The man then spoke as if he hadn't heard Tolkach's questions: "They buried my bus in the Zone because it was so contaminated." Tolkach continued, "Do you see a psychiatrist?" The man answered, "We don't have one at home in the village. Here there are many. I drink herbal teas, and take Nootropil and Kaventon. There's always a scandal at home. I'm hurting my family with my illness." He started to weep and said, "I am not weeping, it weeps by itself." Something autonomic was expressing itself. Tolkach prescribed more medication for sleeping and anxiety. The man seemed unaffected by Tolkach's professional gesture. He grabbed his cane, stood up from his chair, and said, "I'll continue seeking my health elsewhere, thank you," and with that he left the room.

Tolkach made no response. As he left the room, the man's gestures indicated that he had suffered much pain, family conflict, and bureaucratic mistreatment. Not a father, a husband, or a man. Depressed and alone, he was seeking the impossible: health.

While returning home a few days later by bus, I noticed the blue-scarfed woman from Zone Four talking loudly to a fellow patient, giving advice about how to get documents to establish disability. She was enraged about the arbitrariness with which disability status was handed out. She called the process a "swindle." Her tactics hadn't worked.

I stood at the front of the packed bus. Suddenly, apples spilled all over the bus floor from a rural woman's burlap bag. She desperately collected them as the bus drove on. While collecting, she asked the driver to drop her off at the next stop. She had even shined an apple and a plum for him on her cotton sleeve. He grabbed the plum and said, "It's a little hard," in Russian, and gave her back the fruit. Then he said, "That stop doesn't exist anymore," as he sailed past the bus stop. People waiting for the bus waved their hands in protest and berated the driver, something he seemed perversely to enjoy. "I thought you said this stop doesn't exist!" I yelled. "It exists!" he said. "But you told that old woman that it doesn't exist," I said. "It exists, it doesn't exist. So what. It was a joke. Our people are so agreeable."

As we maneuvered toward a public square where a giant bronze statue of Lenin once stood, I thought about how power and aggression are resources at every level of society. Lawlessness seemed to have become the order of the day. At every turn, opportunities to subject were seized upon like bits of unclaimed property; each seizure produced one more slave. Little lives were doomed in little ways. Dr. Dragan diagnosed the moral fabric of her society in these terms: "Here, one can't criticize too much. Where there is an opening, one must be willing to seize it. One must be cunning. We are all sinners in that regard."

From the blue-scarfed woman whose sick role tactics sorely failed, to the men in the neurological ward who tried desperately in their own ways to obtain or to maintain their status of disability or face the prospect of joblessness, to the boy who much preferred joining a community of sick people to joining the army, to the engineer who continued to work in the Zone in spite of her disastrous health status—these citizens' politics illustrate a complex web of relations among injury, biomedicine, policy making, and the framing of the future in terms of disability. Personal experiences of illness, whether physical or mental, were retooled by all parties to correspond to a more general framework of scientific and bureaucratic classifications. Biologies, along with mediated forms of personal suffering, institutional savvy, and biomedical knowledge, became instruments in a play of probability: all in search of an opening.

In the Middle of the Experiment

A boy, aged nine, is seated in a chair in the brain-mapping room of the neurological ward. The child's head is covered with electrodes connected to a nineteen-channel analyzer, the "Brain Surveyor." The pediatric neurologist, Lena Brasova, conducts a spectral analysis of the somato-sensory evoked potentials (SSEP) of the child's brain. To the left of his head, Brasova examines a computer screen that registers the amplitudes and latent periods of cerebral biopotentials.[25]

The pediatric neurologist tells Ivan to move to another chair facing the electroencephalogram (EEG). In this second examination she places black rubber straps, sewn together as if to form a soft helmet, very tightly over his scalp. The brain's abnormal energy densities are registered by the electrodes (from the occipital to the central lobe). During the examination Brasova asks the boy to open his eyes, then to close them and to be "relaxed." Abnormal activity in the delta and beta ranges appearing on the screen is alleged to reflect an organic brain disorder. One objection to the neurophysiological results gained by the EEG is that they are impossible to evaluate "because the contributions from muscle artifacts are unknown." The "myogenic signal" would constitute an "interference" in the data.[26]

Ivan drags his left foot, and, in his parents' words, "he cries and complains all the time about headaches. He is very nervous, a light sleeper, and very active. We cannot stop him. He is difficult to manage. He walks normally, then he forgets and drags his foot again."[27] He is the child of Oleg and Elena, scientific workers from Prypiat', the so-called Dead City in the Exclusion Zone. She works as a pediatric orthopedist in the local hospital, and he works in public relations in a research institute that monitors the structural stability of the *Sarkofag*. Elena and Oleg moved from different places in search of jobs and met in the Zone in 1988.[28] Following the evacuation of Zone inhabitants, Soviet policy makers made opportunities for internal migration available to any technically or medically qualified Soviet citizen seeking better pay and desiring to work in the Zone. Soviet newspapers lauded the altruism of Elena and others in their decision to work in the Zone. In 1989, the state established an official threshold of safe doses of radiation: 35 rem.[29] Persons living in territories exceeding this lifetime threshold dose qualified to receive health and housing benefits elsewhere. Oleg and Elena remained in the Zone, receiving three times their average salaries for increased occupational risk. That same year, they conceived a child.

Before the Chernobyl accident, Elena lived in Krasnoyarsk, in the eastern reaches of Siberia.[30] She explained to me why she had moved to Ukraine. Her Ukrainian paternal grandfather was demobilized as a soldier after World War II. Limited housing quotas following the war prevented him from returning to his native Kharkiv. Authorities assigned him a house and work in a local brick factory. Elena spoke of the family's longing to live in Ukraine. "Things came together in such a way that— many years—we dreamed about living in Ukraine, because all of our ancestors lived here—everyone—in Ukraine. Mother, grandmother, great-grandmother, and from the father's side the same. After the accident we had a chance to move here." She used ethnicity to anchor her individual identity and birthright.

Oleg and Elena brought their son to the center's neurological ward to obtain a diagnosis linking what his parents alleged to be a neurological disability caused by prenatal radiation exposure. A Chernobyl tie on account of his dragging foot would allow the parents to receive compensation for Ivan's condition, as well as guarantee the boy's access to ongoing medical treatment, financial benefits, and educational resources. They were all already receiving additional benefits as legally designated sufferers.

Both the researchers and I were not entirely convinced of the validity of this case; it was unusual for a ward that mainly monitored adults. Researchers were aware of the fact that the boy's case had been expedited because his father had connections to a high-ranking administrator of the center. They acknowledged that Ivan's case was probably a "*blat* case" and hence "more political," and that they were "doing the work for the administrator." Indeed, Ivan's biosocial status was about to be determined by some powerful triangulations. Ivan had potential scientific research value given the circumstances of his conception. Researchers were interested in exploring associations between his presumed prenatal exposure and his neuropsychiatric state. Ivan's parents wanted to increase their son's value as a research subject and, in order to "assist" in the research process, provided a carefully scripted account of the circumstances of their son's birth. Their narrative became essential research data. Just as a human research cohort was being made, so was a destiny, one that the parents, the clinicians, and administrators—all from multiple positions and interests—would pass on to this child. By way of their not-so-incidental detours through Ukraine, the Zone, bureaucracy, and science, Ivan's parents used all means available to transform Ivan's illness into a disease. In doing so, they foreclosed the child's sense of health while giving him a permanent place in the state's system of compensation.

The parents told me that they had already taken Ivan to the Institute of Biophysics in Moscow, where they encountered Angelina Guskova. Guskova's diagnosis was insufficient to support their legal claims. During my work at the center, I had heard of adult patients who said that they traveled to Russia and had experienced similar rejections. I had to wonder whether this narrative of rejection was in itself used as a resource to tilt assessments of disability claims in favorable directions. Having been denied at Guskova's institute could well increase the chances of automatic acceptance in Ukraine. In the words of the Ukrainian dosimetrist, Lavrov, there is a red dose and there is a blue and yellow dose. Oleg and Elena returned to Kyiv, where their claims were more advantageously legitimated.

Ivan was overdetermined as a research subject from the perspective of radiation research, state epidemiology, and patient history. In a scientific article, "Perinatal Loss and Neurological Abnormalities among Children of the Atomic Bomb: Nagasaki and Hiroshima Revisited, 1949 to 1989," Japanese and American authors Yamazaki and Schull compared the early evaluation of the effects on unborn infants of the atomic bombs dropped on Hiroshima and Nagasaki in 1945, which indicated that the mother's distance from the bomb's hypocenter was a critical factor, to more recent studies which have found that some consequences, such as severe mental retardation, are more highly associated with the gestational age of the fetus at the time of the bomb (ATB). According to the authors, observation of fetuses at different gestational ages ATB has provided important data about the vulnerability of the developing brain to ionizing radiation. Later studies helped establish the period of maximum vulnerability to be between the eighth and fifteenth weeks of gestation. This is the time when neurons (brain cells) proliferate the most and when they migrate to take up their proper positions in the fetal brain (Yamazaki and Schull 1990).

According to the Ukrainian Ministry of Health's Center for Medical Statistics, the prevalence of diseases of the nervous system and sensory organs among children of the Exclusion Zone doubled between 1988 (two years after the accident) and 1995.[31] In the area of the Exclusion Zone that belongs to the *oblast* of Kyiv,[32] prevalences of these illnesses jumped from 66 out of 1,000 children in 1988 to 122 out of 1,000 in 1995. For the same area, prevalences of psychiatric disorders were much smaller but also doubled during this period, from 12 out of 1,000 children in 1988 to 24 out of 1,000 in 1995. For adults in the same area, the prevalence of nervous and sensory organ disorders remained stable, around 120 out of 1,000, between 1988 and 1995.[33] The prevalence of psychiatric disorders among adults slightly decreased, from 59, in 1993, to 54.5 out of 1,000 in 1995 (*Indicators of Health* 1995:173). Higher prevalences of nervous, sensory organ, and psychiatric disorders among Zone children (as compared to adults) allegedly reflect in the Ukrainian population what has already been confirmed in other studies, such as those on the *hibakusha* of Hiroshima and Nagasaki and in radiobiological experiments—that human and animal fetuses exhibit an increased radiation vulnerability.

The prenatal stage has thus become a locus of scientific inquiry about neurological and neuropsychiatric disturbances of children born in and evacuated from the Exclusion Zone.[34] Yet such research is complex. Maternal and fetal biologies are interdependent. The research process must first "purify" the prenatal anatomy as a distinct scientific object and designate it as an autonomous locus of research.[35] This is a difficult task, as researchers must rely on the mother's narrative to determine whether the fetus was exposed to radiation before, during, or after the period of maximum vulnerability of the developing brain. On the basis of such information, radiation can be confirmed or disregarded as a significant etiological factor in a child's state. Indeed, Elena said that she stayed in the Zone until the twentieth week of fetal gestation.

IN UTERO RESEARCH

Researchers Brasova and Borovsky coordinated Ivan's examination. Both had been trained at a Canadian laboratory of biological psychiatry where they refined their techniques of brain mapping and carried on their research programs. The brain-mapping room was adjacent to an office where the boy's parents waited. While his wife conducted the brain mapping, Borovsky explained to me the utility of the diagnostic machines. "According to local psychiatrists, measuring EEGs is very useful for diagnostics of many disorders, not only for neurological ones, but for psychogenic [mental] ones as well. The localization of abnormal activities indicating schizophrenia and schizophrenic spectrum disorders is related to the left brain. Depression and affective disorders can be related to the right brain." The organic and psychogenic are also distinct in terms of the different social values assigned to them, of which Borovsky is acutely aware.

The boy's examination was supplemented with an examination of the mother. Researchers administered a verbal subscale of the Wechsler intelligence test to determine Elena's intelligence quotient (IQ). The father's IQ was not assessed. (In fact, Oleg remained quiet much of the time.) Researchers used the data derived from Elena's examination to make further determinations as to the significance of radiation in the etiology of Ivan's alleged disorder. Elena's IQ was normal. A chromosomal aberration assay and an estimation of her thyroid dose indicated that her radiation dose was a very low 3.7 rem (.037 gray; see chapter 1, n. 33). The results suggested that the mother's contribution to her son's state of health was minimal, thus increasing the probability that "the responsibility is on the government or on the radiation factor," to use Borovsky's phrasing—that is, if indeed the boy's diagnostic tests indicated evidence of a brain disorder. Since the mother alleged that she had worked in the Zone until the twentieth week of her pregnancy, the radiation factor continued to be strongly considered. The results, together with the maternal narrative, served as pretexts for further research into the possible link between Ivan's neurological disorders and an in utero exposure to radiation. The results of research would not be framed in terms of a distinction between the radiation- and nonradiation-related effects, but rather in terms of a probability that would factor in the contribution of all effects to the production of a "biological negativity," and from which "the contribution of prenatal irradiation to this overall negativity cannot be excluded." The establishment of such a probability would be enough to grant the boy Chernobyl-related disability status on the medical determination that he would most likely fail to adapt. Within this still Soviet biosocial logic, state compensation offsets individual incapacities to adapt, provided that those incapacities are shown to be social in origin.

The researchers were careful to remind me that their sponsors had proposed the use of another questionnaire in the "Brain Damage *In Utero*" program. This questionnaire was designed to facilitate an assessment of

185

the mother's mental health status and the discovery of any evidence that might exist of its damaging influence upon the child's mental health in cases of suspected brain damage in utero.[36] "Unfortunately, this type of psychological assessment is unusual in our routine clinical practice." Borovsky's remark highlighted the continued undesirability of psychological indices in that research context.

I examined the records of similar examinations involving other children. I found that clinicians routinely declined to acknowledge the operative role of the mother. Yet the mother's statements were central to establishing the time of prenatal exposure and identifying the child's specific ailments. The fathers were not interviewed; neither were the children. The maternal proxy in the scientific research remains unexplored but is fundamental to it.

American psychiatrist Evelyn Bromet and colleagues compared three hundred ten- to twelve-year-old children in Kyiv who had been in utero or infants at the time of the disaster, or living in contaminated areas, and children who had never lived in contaminated areas (Bromet et al. 2000:563). Based on a battery of standardized questionnaires and physical examinations, they found insignificant differences between the two groups in terms of levels of psychological impairment. Bromet et al. identified maternal somatization and stress as the most important risk factors in the children's self-rating.[37] This work was significantly biased in that it ignored dosimetric data as well as data from Hiroshima and Nagasaki on the biological effects of in utero radiation, among other things. Where Bromet et al. disregard important biological data, Borovsky disregards maternal psychology in the estimation of radiation-related effects. Both positions avoid addressing the intermediating nature of social contexts in the construction of illness. Moreover, they illustrate the risks of simplification in this area of postdisaster research, risks that are of a medical as well as ethical nature.

After the brain mapping, holding a nurse's hand and dragging his foot, Ivan walked past the room where Elena was being tested. The nurse directed him into another room, where he would undergo an intelligence test (based on the "Drawing as Measures of Intellectual Maturity" test).[38] When the nurse asked Ivan to draw a man, he drew a figure of a man standing straight, with his hands clutching his body. The man wore a protective helmet with an attached lamp like those coal miners use. His neck was elongated and tilting away to the left. His smile was off-center. As the nurse told me, what mattered was the logic of how the boy connected parts of the figure's body and facial features (such as the mouth to the nose, and the nose to the eyes).

After Ivan had taken this nonverbal intelligence test, I asked him some questions.

"Where are you from?"

"Vorsel."

"Why are you here?"

"Treating myself (*likuius'*)."

"Why?"

"This leg walks poorly." He referred to his leg as autonomous and separate from him.

"Which one, this one or that one?"

"This one."

"What games do you like to play?"

"I don't know . . . With the boys, machines."

"And with the girls?"

"Hide-and-seek."

"You drew a man for the nurse—who is he?

"What I drew? A coal miner. He works there, in the mine."

"What do they see there?"

"They see the ground and they walk beneath it."

"What do you want to do when you get older?"

"Be a policeman."

"What does a policeman do?"

"When someone kills someone else, he arrests them. He catches the killer."

"Who would you arrest?"

"Those who kill children."

Though it would be inappropriate to read too much into the boy's statements, I sensed that something was at stake for him in the research process as well. When I asked him why he was there, he didn't respond, "Because of my leg" or "I can't walk well" or "Because my parents brought me here." He was there because he was, as he put it, "treating himself." He sensed and expressed his dependency on his leg "for treatment" as a means of personal satisfaction. Perhaps he understood that accepting and even enacting his disability is a prerequisite for being reunited with his parents after his examination. The boy embodies his defect, yet he still speaks about "it" as being separate (or walking separately) from him. It is his double, so to speak, put into motion through the research process, along with maternal narratives and scientific proofs that organize his new role and new social intimacies (between the boy and clinicians, the parents and the researchers, the parents and the state).

After he took the drawing test, a nurse brought Ivan to another room, where his brain's functional capacity was checked with a rheoencephalogram. As the nurse examined him, she said, "Close your eyes, don't open them, quietly, put your hands here. Don't open your eyes! Breathe deep and don't breathe. . . . Breathe! And now, breathe deep, and breathe out!

Breathe! And now quietly, don't move your eyes around too much, make as if you fell asleep. . . ." His compliance with these instructions suggested a sense of abdication in a world of rules that didn't make sense.

IVAN'S CONCEPTION

Traces of the disaster's political and rational-technical administrations appear, disappear, and reappear in Elena's narrative of her son's birth and her account of Ivan as an apparently sick child. Asked whether she had been aware during her pregnancy of the risk associated with working in the Zone, Elena responded in a typical terse fashion: "In principle, yes, we knew about this. But life is life. We needed the work." Material concerns overrode concerns for her fetus. "That's how things came together," she said, adding, "A child was needed, and that is all. I expected a better life." She suggested, rather explicitly, that the desire for material improvement influenced her choice to have a child.

Remaining in the Zone for "about twenty weeks," Elena subsequently left to take another job in Kyiv. She described the conditions of Ivan's delivery. "The birth was difficult. It was premature. I gave birth to him at thirty-five weeks." The implication was that something internal to the gestational process induced the birth to happen ahead of normal delivery time. Elena described her first impressions of a strangely symptomatic newborn. "He was very small, two kilos altogether. He practically didn't breathe, he didn't scream. He was not a normal child." Elena's description of Ivan's birth conveyed her ambivalence toward the attending physicians. She initially referred to them as sympathetic allies, protecting her from feelings of disturbance but justifying her fright. "The medics were bringing him back to life, stimulating him. I didn't see him right away. The medics did not show him to me. No. They do not show the mothers such children. He was terrifying, blue. Everything there was not as it should be." But at other times she cast the physicians as her enemies, who withheld information about the cause of Ivan's symptoms. "They understood everything but wrote some other diagnosis," she said, referencing the practice of *hypodiagnostika* Tolkach had detailed earlier.

After two months, Ivan experienced seizures. Elena complained that the Soviet clinical networks, established after the accident, refused to address the complex situation of prenatal exposure from Chernobyl. "They didn't want to seriously monitor him," she said. The child never received a definite diagnosis but was put on a course of healthful supplements. "This isn't treatment which removes the cause," Elena noted. "I know the reason. It is some pathology of the brain. Now he walks poorly. He drags his foot a little. This happened after three years of life. There is a lot of atrophy in his lower muscles. His left leg is thinner. His left arm is weaker. But slowly, the attacks became less frequent." Elena marshaled representations so as to lay blame on the Soviet medical system for her son's apparently sick state and to bolster her ability to make a claim (*skarha*). She connected her experience to a broader political and bureaucratic history of error, mismanagement, and risk.

Elena's husband, Oleg, who had been sitting quietly, had apparently heard enough of his wife's pathologizing of the boy. He insisted that illness was not a stumbling block in Ivan's life. Oleg saw his role as "making sure" that his son sees himself as normal. "We are raising him like a normal child. He doesn't have any particular limitations. He runs, he skips, he falls, everything, like normal people do. If I have some kind of goal, it is to make a psychologically normal person out of him, so that he doesn't have complexes from his illness, and so that he sees himself as normal."

In the following week, the researchers summarized the findings from Ivan's examination. The possibility that the boy had endured cerebral damage owing to a traumatic birth did not receive further consideration. The description of Ivan's etiology was similar to that of the entire cohort of prenatally exposed children. The precise dose these children received is secondary to the final assessment. The diagnosis identified a mild form of cerebral palsy resulting from prenatal damage to the central nervous system; left-side hemiparesis; seizure syndrome; hyperkinetic disorder. The prognosis pointed to the sequelae of a persistent but not progressive organic brain damage. His IQ was normal, but he was "neurologically deficient." The boy's condition was hereafter regarded as most likely incurable. "His behavioral and emotional disorders could result in social limitations." The medical conclusion supported the father's goal.

In tracing Ivan's clinical examination, one sees how individual histories and family dramas fuse with a clinical research program to shape an experience and interpretation of disease. Clinical research involved not only observation or identification of disease; it also bore an "inductive" property. Through clinical, scientific, and intersubjective processes, researchers identified the biological effectiveness of radiation in a prenatal anatomy—all the while they were assembling it. The research process purified the prenatal anatomy as a scientific object and designated it as an independent site of research. Through this research, one also sees the ways a biological destiny was produced and assigned. The child's individuality was foreclosed, and his social future was medically guaranteed.

Four years later, in August 2000, I went back to see how Ivan's social future had unfolded. Researchers told me that they had not seen him since his 1996 examination. They complained that with so much migration, they could rarely conduct follow-up studies. Based on an address they had given me, I hired a taxi and rode an hour out of Kyiv to a rural location. I found a small empty brick house. The neighbor, who called herself Baba Hania, told me that the family had moved to another country a few months earlier. When I asked Baba Hania about the boy's state, she dismissed any suggestion of disability and instead recollected how Elena had chain-smoked all through her pregnancy. She said that the boy never had any health problems, or at least none that she could discern. Maybe, in another country, Ivan is healthy.

Chapter 7
Self and Social Identity in Transition

Anton and Halia

What I observed at the Radiation Research Center was a painful determinacy of illness claims, reconfiguring the relationship between family and the state, parents and children, and the present and the future. The research process shaped the "truth" of illnesses and facilitated its transfer into other bodies. Technical, political, and subjective processes combined in the research setting and shaped the biosocial circumstances of individuals and their future. Ivan left Ukraine, thus perhaps leaving behind the illness script his parents had prepared for him, and which his social and political environment endorsed. There were many more, however, whose bodies and futures remained trapped in an unfolding and remorseless social logic of Chernobyl.

What effects do changes in the conditions of self-recognition have on domestic life and on marriage contracts formed prior to the breakup of the Soviet Union? My patient-informants introduced me one man who they felt represented their future. Anton had been cast out of his social and cultural role as a breadwinner. His life became a spectacle in a changing moral order: a subject of an unstoppable course of radiation-related illness whose causes one administrator attributed to the "discoordination" among the state, the enterprise, and the family (see chapter 4). Anton's life was an illustration of the kinds of smaller tragedies that were generated within the bureaucratic and legal contours and pitfalls of the Chernobyl aftermath, and by the social dead ends of a harsh market transition. Anton was unique in that he could speak—albeit in a broken manner—about the price that the "unstoppable course" of illness, corruption, and economic and moral decline exacted from his life, his voice, and his "soul" (*dusha*). When I first met him, he told me, "My soul is out of place." His narrative brought together individual and collective realities and the way they were organized, contested, and lived as social trajectories.

As a military recruit, Anton had worked for six months at the Chernobyl reactor site. He drove bags of lead oxide, sand, and gravel right up to the reactor; the bags were airlifted and dumped over the burning reactor by men in helicopters (many of whom died soon after their work). He doesn't know how much radiation he absorbed. Anton was routinely passed through the clinical system, and like any prospective invalid, he was monitored. Over time, his symptoms progressed. His medical records indicated that he experienced chronic headaches; that he had lost his short-term memory, exhibited "antisocial behavior," developed a speech disorder, and experienced seizures and impotence, among many other symptoms. But for a long time, his diagnoses had not progressed. His condition cannot be characterized as anomalous. At our first meeting, he expressed his financial and emotional bankruptcy in this speech-disordered way: "The state took my life away. Ripped me off, gone. What to be happy about? An honorable man cannot survive now. For what? For what? There was life. There was butter. There was milk. I can't buy an iron. Before I could buy fifty irons. The money was there. My wife's salary is less than the cost of one iron."

Anton's vocation as a truck driver, which he took pains to describe to me as a job he loved, terminated abruptly one day when he lost consciousness while driving and caused an accident. This first real accident of his life cost him his driver's license. His wife, Halia, was a civil servant. Like many civil servants, she hadn't been paid her meager salary in the previous six months. Anton, Halia, and their granddaughter (Little Halia) were living in a small, one-room apartment; they were trying to manage on the $52.00 monthly pension Anton received from his work, a pension that had been slightly increased because of his status as "sufferer." He repeatedly told me that he "didn't know how to trade goods," that is, to engage in selling petty goods on the market. This inability or unwillingness, together with his low pension, left Anton with few options. He faced the demeaning choice of either breadwinning with his illness in the Chernobyl compensation system or shunning such exposure and facing a life of poverty. At first, it seemed to me as though his wife was pressuring him to choose the former option—that is, to be ill.

The political and bureaucratic aspects of Chernobyl pervaded the intimate details of the couple's life. Their story demonstrates the complexity of life's disruption by unstable parental and marital relations, unpredictable physical symptoms and emotional stress, patterns of hospitalization, unemployment, and bureaucratic transactions.

As an ethnographer, and out of respect for the difficult unknowns they faced, my initial stance was to limit engagement with the Nimovs and to offer help in terms of referring them to clinicians at the Radiation Research Center, if and when they wanted it. Yet Anton and Halia seemed to have no difficulty in inviting me into their apartment and leading me straight into their predicament. Observing them in their daily life, I realized that the institutions and actors I was investigating—such as state bureaucracy, disabled collectivities, Chernobyl-related sciences, and the clinical monitoring system—were to be found in one form or another in their apartment. I joined Halia and Anton as they moved between the apartment, hospitals, state institutions, activist organizations, and later, in a difficult turn of events, the police. Their troubled and confused existence was but a small piece of a larger jumbled puzzle of massive societal change. The couple's routine, their management and failure to manage emotions and distress, represented a trend in the way they and others evolved as individuals in a formerly collectively based society.

The concept of *lichnost'* sheds light on some of the social and personal dynamics that influenced the couple's life. Kharkhordin (1999) demonstrates how Soviet practices related to *lichnost'*, or a sense of individual self, were important to the everyday constitution of *Homo Sovieticus*. Following the brutal "collectivization-of-life drive" of Stalin's first Five-Year Plan, which led to the dual phenomena of rapid industrialization and famine, Soviet work collectives (*kollektivi*) fostered *lichnost'* as a mass social psychological trait of the Soviet citizen. Local leaders purveyed elaborate pedagogies, inculcating a relationship between newly Sovietized subjects and their collectives that was strengthened by disciplinary techniques, public confessions, methods of self-analysis and self-accounting, and "mutual horizontal surveillance." While such practices ensured the dominance of the *kollektiv* and suppressed public unfaithfulness, they also reminded Soviet citizens of how and why they needed to keep certain behaviors hidden. Taught in "official life," these practices were applied to "mend the split between official and intimate spheres" (278). Dissimulative behavior became part and parcel of a social repertoire and a characteristic of Soviet personhood. "Switching of faces becomes an embodied skill" (ibid.).

These totalizing cultural masks and human natures were no longer abiding as conditions, for new collectives were in the making. Halia and Anton helped me to understand how the familiar idea of *lichnost'* was being forced out by "superimposed masks" (Mauss 1985:12); and how new techniques and forms of self-accounting were evolving through symptoms, moral choices, and individual struggles to adjust to and not capitulate in a new market-oriented world. In a world of competition for scarce state resources, the central question was how long Anton could afford to "pretend" to be someone else. His task was to renew his chances for political and social membership: to "know what he is ill with in order to know what to do with it socially." These practices and the material conditions supporting them were shaping a different personhood. Anton's pains, truths, instincts, and acts became key components in the realization of his biological citizenship.

My meetings with Halia and Anton happened over a five-month period. In that time, the relationship between the two and their senses of bodily integrity and moral values were rapidly reconfiguring. Anton's self was being taxed and transformed within the legal and medical context of claiming radiation illness, a pervasive lack of money, and uncertainty. Halia told me that Anton "never got sick before Chernobyl, he had plans for the future, he had desire to do something. . . . He is not the same person anymore."

Beyond the Family: *Kvartyra* and Public Voice

I first heard of Anton through Lev, who became a member of the International Chernobyl Disabled Persons Aid and Charity Fund. During one of my visits to the fund, Lev asked members and me to sit around a table. He had recorded the voices and stories of several disabled persons with a tape recorder I had loaned him; he wanted his audience of ten to hear one particular interview. Members did not know Anton personally, but they could certainly identify with him: "Anton, tell me what year you were involved with Chernobyl?" Anton could barely speak: "In a-a-a-eighty six." Lev asked, "How long were you there?" Anton tried to answer: "Ta-ta-take the document, ta-ta-take a look at it."

Anton's voice was broken. He spoke in disconnected words and sentences but appeared to answer Lev's questions faithfully. Anton spoke of himself as a "driver of the first class" who now suffered from "sudden attacks" (*prystupy*). There was some hesitancy in his voice; he didn't seem at ease at first with telling his story, perhaps knowing that it would circulate and be heard by strangers. When Lev asked him why he was crying, Anton said it wasn't him; it was "his soul that was crying." Anton continued, "Some thoughts come." "What kind?" Lev asked. "Say it. When you feel your soul is crying, what do you want to do?" With a sigh of resignation, Anton replied, "I want to end my life."

In a quasi-pedagogical mode, Lev paused the tape and asked us to acknowledge how serious this case was. Lev's questioning of Anton moved directly and without hesitation from topics such as disability and a broken sense of self to the most intimate aspects of Anton's life. Anton appeared ready to answer Lev's questions, regardless of the angle from which his questions were coming. Lev probed further in his elicitation of Anton's self-account. "You'll excuse my question, but what's happening at home?" There was a long silence. "Tell me, when your wife sent you to the mental asylum, did she at all trouble herself over you?" In his relentless questioning, Lev attempted to demonstrate the objective social conditions that had accumulated in Anton's life, and that made his changing nature into a spectacle of things to come. Lev seemed to suggest that Anton's wife was an unwitting accomplice of a new immoral order that seemed to have made Anton go mad.

In February of that year, I learned that Anton had beaten his wife, Halia, who in turn had had the police lock him into Ward 1 of the Pavlova, the psychoneurological hospital near Kyiv. He was confined there for one week. During the period of her husband's confinement, Halia had hoped to collect the legal and medical evidence she needed to file for divorce. Just five months later, Halia would look back at her desperate act as having imperiled her husband's chances of getting disability status. His identification as a mentally ill person could only do more legal damage by corroborating his psychogenic diagnosis of hysteria.

Anton continued to answer Lev's questions regarding his wife: "No, she left me, she went to live another life. My health got worse. She doesn't understand." He attributed his violent actions to his "illness." Lev stopped the tape and made his mission statement clear: "We have to get Anton's diagnosis [of hysteria] removed. His illness is not self-inflicted. The diagnosis is humiliating." At stake in this diagnostic politics was nothing less than a restoration of a man's familial, socioeconomic, and civic dignity.

Quite often issues that related to what were presumably the most private realm, such as complaints of impotence, bad marital relations, and domestic abuse, became public discourse among these invalids. They understood pathology to be their common bond; this sense of pathology crosscut more familiar male solidarities. When I listened to this tape again at home, it was clear that Lev had projected his own feelings of humiliation over his first wife's having left him. With the exception of the fund's director, Mr. Repkin, and the engineer and statistician, Mr. Katz, the eight other members present at the meeting were either divorced or experiencing marital difficulties. One member told me that his wife had left him because of his impotence. She blamed him for being "too dutiful to the state." He quoted her as saying, "You threw yourself at Chernobyl and now you are worthless to me as a man!" On account of such humiliating experiences, many said that they would never send their own sons into the army unless "they knew what they were defending."

The interview, specially produced for me, continued. "Any children?" Lev asked. "Two daughters and a granddaughter." "State?" "It doesn't help." "Drugs?" "They don't give them." "Pension?" "9,600,000 a month [$50.00]." "What do you take?" "Pills that make me weak and pills that put me to sleep [Valium]." "How much do they cost a month?" "3,500,000." Lev then spoke into the tape: "Adriana, the man has no wife, no land, no health, no money, and no state. He doesn't want to live."

Anton's plight drew an empathic response from these men who had found relative success in their pursuit of compensation. Mr. Katz, who sat across the table, commented that Anton was a "typical case." Serhii, a communications expert and assistant at the fund, said, "There are many more like him." On the tape, one could hear Lev trying to talk Anton out of suicide. "Yes, the doctors told me already," Anton sighed. The conversation ended with Lev educating Anton about his rights and urging him to take up a more politically active role.

A week later Lev took me to meet the man. The apartment was located about five kilometers from the capital's center and near the last stop of a main urban tram and bus route. The unit was typical of the many mass-produced socialist-style housing districts (*microraiony*). A local hospital and covered market, serving area residents, were located within walking distance of the station. There was a police station on the ground floor of a nearby housing block. The baroque-style belfry of the Monastery of the Caves was visible from the bus stop and through columns of housing units. Anton would often stand on his eighth-floor apartment balcony with a cigarette in one hand and binoculars in the other, staring at the monastery's vibrant golden domes. Near the bus stop there was a lush park where Halia and I would go to talk in the subsequent months.

The interior of the housing unit was run-down. Sometimes mothers sat outside watching their children play in a small parking lot. The glass doors separating the communal elevator core from corridors leading to the apartment units were shattered. The photo of a truck Anton had driven for much of his adult life hung on the wall directly across from the apartment's entry door. "I lost it," he said, as he noticed me looking at it. I soon discovered the truck's rearview mirror hung on the bathroom door, facing the toilet stall at an amusing eye level.

The kitchen was dominated by a small wooden table covered with chipped formica, large enough for four people. The bedroom held a small bed, a shelf full of books, and a reading and work table. I noticed that the popular book by Soviet author Sholokhov, *One Man's Destiny* (*Sud'ba Cheloveka*), was lying facedown on Anton's pillow. He slept on this bed, while Little Halia and Halia slept on the sofa (*divan*) in the living room next door. There, I couldn't help but notice the photo of Halia's deceased mother perched on the main wooden wall cabinet. A black ribbon had been placed over the image. "She lived through famine, war, and more famine after the war," Halia said. The face of this female collective farmer looked shocked, perhaps in reaction to something as mundane as the camera flash. Dolls and other gifts that Anton had brought back to his family after long surveying trips with the Oil Institute were stored or displayed. These were objects from a time when the family seemed harmoniously intact, and when its members were proud of their cultured manners and their possessions. Anton said that he hated the television set.

Anton was born in 1952, the eldest of five children, in a village in the Ural Mountains in Russia. He had been expected to become a tractor driver, his father's profession, but he left his family in 1968 and moved to Turkmenistan. His mother was alive in 1996 and still working as a collective farmer. Between 1970 and 1972, Anton served in the army in East Germany and also in Ukraine. Anton met Halia while transporting sugar beets from her village of Horlytsia in the central province of Vynnytsia. Asked how they met, Anton said that he first saw Halia in a photograph that her sister had shown him. Halia in turn said that she had dreamed of a man "in silhouette" the day before she met him. They were proud of the fact that their wedding celebration had lasted a full week. "That was then," Halia said, noting that such celebrations were no longer affordable in terms of time and money.

Halia had also been born to collective farmers. Her background was more important to her than Anton's was to him. She said that her maternal grandfather and his five brothers and one sister had died of hunger during the famine of 1932–1933. Her mother, the woman in the photograph, had died of a cerebral stroke. "She didn't have one living organ left from the hard labor on the collective farms," Halia said. She conveyed no resentment about the past. Rather, she associated the hardship of her rural past with the need to cultivate strong communal bonds, bonds that she continued to rely upon in her life in the city.

She happily recalled participating in the *toloka*, a communal event in which neighbors gathered to help build a villager's house. "After working on the collective farm in the day, I helped my mother cut trees in the forest at night to help Grandmother build a house." Halia said that her father "did very little" because he was too traumatized by having been persecuted as a member of a *kulak* family. "He typically just sat on a bench and broke stones used for the home's foundation." She used the Ukrainian term for breaking stones, *molotaty kaminniamy*. *Molotaty* is also a local derogatory term that means to "talk nonsense." In Halia's reconstruction

197

of her past, her father, much like her husband now, "talked nonsense." Her attitude conveyed traces of a stereotypic rural matriarchal rule. Wives found ways of compensating for the inactivity of their weakened or demoralized husbands. They derived their moral strength from the values of hard work and cultivation of communal ties. Halia kept cultivating these values and ties in order to ensure her family's security when her husband no longer could.

In her later years and when health problems arose, Halia's mother traveled to the Pavlova to receive neurological care. She was treated there for three years by the neurologist Ivana who came from the same village of Horlytsia. Halia referred to Ivana as her *rodychka*, which means "person from the same soil." This soil connection became a resource that Halia attempted (fruitlessly) to deploy as she tried to craft a legal and medical basis for divorcing Anton.

In Kyiv, Halia received a higher technical education and worked as a site surveyor. Anton transported Halia's work collective around the republic to survey and photograph historic old towns and factory and school sites. Halia spoke proudly of herself as a *subbotnyk* (Saturday volunteer). With a red ribbon tied around her arm, she joined other *subbotnyky* raking leaves around apartment blocks, picking up garbage on the main streets of the city, painting walls, and planting flowers in public gardens. Being a *subbotnyk* made Halia feel socially well regarded. The voluntary activity also provided vital time away from the domestic pressures of the *kvartyra*. "No one has time to work in a public garden anymore," she said. The other life that socialist society created and enforced disappeared. Individuals like Halia had to find new spaces beyond the *kvartyra* to rekindle the old values of *lichnost'* or to replace them with other modes of collective life. The hospital and civic charity funds became those key alternative spaces.

The couple married in 1973, and until 1980 they lived in an urban communal apartment. In 1981, and after waiting on a housing list, they obtained a one-bedroom apartment. They had two girls, Sasha and Iryna (the mother of Little Halia), and steadily began to furnish their home. Anton expressed his desire to furnish the house: "In a year, we got the couch. In two years, we got the wooden cabinet. Every Saturday I would go to the store and the attendant would ask me, 'Do you still want it?' I said yes."

Sixteen-year-old Sasha lived with her fiancé's mother. Twenty-year-old Iryna lived in one small room in her husband's parents' apartment. Iryna entrusted Little Halia to Halia and Anton's care. Little Halia called her grandmother "Mother." She called Anton "*D'ed*," or Grandfather. This disassembly of family roles, names, and identities reflected broader disassemblies created by a precarious economic situation; they have exacerbated young adults' dependence on their parents. Anton and Halia, for example, still had a minimum pension and owned an apartment; through social ties, they had access to private plots for small-scale farming. Halia divided Anton's pension among Little Halia, her young and unemployed daughter and son-in-law, and herself and her husband. As she and Anton became locked into a situation of parenting their grandchild, Anton's symptoms and erratic behavior became more aggravated.

The couple began the process of converting the pains of that private life into a new public resource of illness. They organized several dinners. As Halia, Lev, and I sat one day in the dining room eating a lavish feast, Anton kept anxiously wandering in and out. He behaved erratically, rarely engaging in conversation yet talking loudly about his pains, as if he couldn't hear himself speaking. "He had plans for the future," Halia said to Lev, "to buy a car and a summer house near Kyiv, and then there is illness. Doctors and psychiatrists avoid him, because they are afraid of him," Halia said. "He's threatened to kill his family and himself." Lev concurred that Anton's illnesses had "progressed very quickly since February." There was agreement between Lev and Halia that Anton was desperately ill.

Yet in private (away from Lev), Halia told me what a good personality Anton had, as if to lament the passing of a world in which such a being could thrive and could earn an honest living. "Anton was reliable, his driving record was flawless. In twenty-five years of driving he had not had one accident. He received awards from his transportation collective. The director of the Oil Institute wanted to promote Anton to the position of director of the institute's *avtobaza* (motor pool)." Halia said that at the time she advised her husband not to take the job. She argued that the promotion would not result in a better salary, and that he would be exposed to other people's constant demands for favors; she warned him, "It will make you sick." Anton told me a similar story later. A powerful minister once asked him to chauffeur him around the city at the institute's expense. "I told him there is no gas."

Honesty, hard work, *lichnost'*, and a sense of duty—Anton's attributes—helped to bring this generation of a Soviet family to experience new civilized heights. The Nimov apartment, like everyone's apartment, had a kitsch quality. Medallions, certificates, photographs, plastic-covered furniture, red decorative carpets on the concrete walls, dark inner spaces, and an infinite quantity of souvenirs from vacations were proudly accumulated and formed a living museum of sorts. The concept of *kul'turnost'*, or "culturedness," the relative level of personal and cultural education, illuminates the significance of this bricolage way of life. Anton inhabited his *kvartyra* as if forced to inhabit a landmass cut adrift. It was no longer the intimate cultural tinkerdom he made it to be.

Kul'turnost', argued literary scholar Vera Dunham, exemplified the everyday social and individual effects of the Stalinist civilizing process. It was a concept that peasants who were moving into cities in the 1930s learned about, as they were expected to become cultured middle-class urban dwellers and Soviet citizens (1976). Dunham argued that the Soviet system owed its regenerative power and stability to a contract implemented between the Stalinist regime and its middle class, whose values were accommodated by the regime in exchange for loyalty and efficiency. By the late 1940s there had been a clear transition from "militant revolutionary asceticism and selfless devotion to public deeds, to individual consumption, prosperous private life and civilized conduct" (Volkov 2000:214). Through official and popular texts, urbanites learned how to improve their dress and personal hygiene while becoming efficient workers. "Culturedness as self-discipline and as self-monitoring was integrated into the industrial system: the cultured individual was identified with the efficient worker and the middle-class consumer of goods and activities associated with administrative elites" (ibid.: 291). As Soviet apartments became cherished private zones, they became populated with signs of *kul'turnost'*. The objects and images associated with *kul'turnost'* permeated not only the shared public world but also the individual's inner world and sense of domestic cultivation.

The concepts of *lichnost'* and *kul'turnost'* informed the Soviet version of what Marcel Mauss called "a category of mind" (1985). Each Soviet person found these concepts to be "natural, clearly determined in the depths of his consciousness, completely furnished with the fundaments of the morality which flows from it" (1). The passing of these fundaments was a painful thing to accept, as they had grounded Anton's and Halia's senses of pleasure, aspirations, and forms of mutual recognition. They no longer had sufficient funds to maintain their culturedness; the former world and the social mechanisms it contained to keep things, people, and emotions in check were disrupted. Anton lamented: "My daughter has been married twice. Her husband doesn't work. He doesn't make money. Little Halia cries. We take care of her here. I am honest. My soul is like that. I don't have anything to feed them with. I have no money. I cannot finish living my life. I don't want to live like this."

For the Nimovs, civic morality and the sense of obligation no longer counted for much either. "Let's put it this way," Anton told me once, "Thieves and dishonorable people have everything: a Mercedes, a country house, and dollars. But the honest people don't have anything now. I am ashamed. I won't sell at the bazaar. I don't trust what will be tomorrow. Will I buy meat or not? I have to think about tomorrow, what will be tomorrow? I detest being on this side of the world."

Halia also did not see a way over to the other side. She endured the that her social insurance pension was rarely paid, rather than using her time to buy and resell goods at higher prices. She was very proud of herself and her manners, and wanted to give her granddaughter the best possible education. But sending Little Halia to a special school for motivated children meant that Anton had to increase his pension by $25.00 a month.

Whereas she had once sent her husband into psychiatric confinement to protect herself, Halia was now engaged in helping him to increase his pension and, in a sense, to get even sicker. In this regard, the couple's private space was open to admitting the values and moralities of their postsocialist environment. Yet both were convinced that a part of Anton's "weakness" was the fact that he *hadn't* changed. I construe his resistance to change not as dissent or malingering, but rather as a confusion that expressed itself in ways that were intimately connected with and even authorized by his social surroundings. Not changing made life, if not impossible, then possible through illness. For Anton, becoming medicalized meant becoming "cunning and cheating"—he later characterized Lev in this way—and hence less of a man and less the person that Anton thought he himself still was. Yet that moralistic self-perception was modifying, too, as he engaged new structures of common sense (Geertz 1983).

On the balcony once, Anton told me that he thought "his psyche was disrupted." This psychological claim afforded him the means to begin to test a new social identity. But what kind? Anton wasn't quite leaning toward mental illness; he had been too inculcated in Soviet models of sociality to accept that self-definition. In the same conversation, he admitted that he had beaten up Halia in February, but then followed up on his statement: "I am a *Chernobylets* [of Chernobyl]." For the first time I heard Anton justifying, if not attempting to cover up, his violent actions on the basis of a "sufferer" status, a status he had previously rejected.

Medicalized Selves

Anton's initiation into a new collectivity of sufferers actually began the year the Soviet Union ceased to exist as an administrative entity in his life. After his truck accident in 1990, Ukrainian doctors, freed of government dictates and constraints on their medical interpretations, related his loss of consciousness to his Chernobyl exposure. Anton recalled the doctors drawing his blood and informing him that "they found Chernobyl blood." As a cleanup worker exposed to radiation, but with an unknown dose and an unexplained loss of consciousness, he fit the profile of someone with an "ill-defined state." Statistics show that registrations of ill-defined states soared in 1990 (see chapter 1). In a sense, Anton was an originary biomedical subject of the new Ukraine—a country whose government forged its legitimacy, in part, with respect to a tragedy and an expanding legal and medical bureaucracy. It is difficult to know whether Anton was medically targeted or simply psychologically predisposed to demanding his place in the state apparatus, but his story resonates with those of so many others who were medically "recruited" into the state's collectivity of sufferers.

I asked Anton several times to show me a computerized tomographic image that he said had been made during that time, an image that might show evidence of radiation-induced organic brain damage. My requests were made in vain. "Later," he always used to say. Halia told me that many workers did not want to be medically screened because "they were afraid" of how their diagnoses might be used against them in the context of work (see chapter 4). Researchers in the Radiation Research Center's neurology ward confirmed this initial resistance among workers to be diagnosed.

After his accident and medical treatment, Anton was seen as a liability and no longer hirable as a driver. As a sufferer, he received a minimum income from the state. Yet this short-term stability was disrupted in 1994, when his newly divorced daughter Iryna returned from Siberia with a two-year-old daughter. Soon Anton realized that he couldn't support this new family; it was up to him to fight for his disability to obtain an additional pension. Right then, Anton underwent new medical examinations, but by that time the system had become much more closed and selective. He had not learned to be an efficient administrator of his suffering. As a result, he lacked a medicalized specificity or role.

By February 1996, as Halia told me, Anton became despairing and preoccupied with his own death. He had visited the Oil Institute, where he learned that some of his coworkers, also sent to Chernobyl, had already died. This knowledge had a harrowing psychological effect on him. He became delusional and told Halia to do things like "take his clothes out of the apartment and stuff them into a hearse." He called his mother and other relatives whom he had not seen since 1968 "to say goodbye." He even picked out the suit that he would wear for his funeral and burial. He told his wife that he didn't "want others profiting at his expense or taking advantage of him while he was dead." Anton even instructed Halia to slit the back of his suit with scissors, "so that when the grave robbers come they only take my clothes and leave my body alone."

How can we approach Anton's delusional behavior and imagery (which the couple recollected with cautious humor)? First, the organic etiology of his illness remained unproven, but it was also not disproven. A psychological approach might consider Anton's delusion in terms of his relations to the many women in his life and to his troubled fatherhood, his impotence, and his loss of work. The content of the delusional imagery also suggests that Anton was mourning a death—the death of a social world in which he once recognized himself as being human. He was also exposing a moral and medicalized system that had come to prevail and that haunted him, leaving him exposed and physically vulnerable. Anton's delusion was indicative of a new illness, produced in the interstices of a nuclear tragedy, lost social supports, and familial uncertainties. It was at this moment that years of Soviet psychological training gave way to violent instincts. At the same time, through his delusion, Anton voiced his resolve to regain his life at all costs.

Anton fell into a fit and physically abused Halia in February 1996. After one week's stay in the Pavlova's Ward 1, orderlies noticed his identity documents and transferred him into the hospital's Chernobyl ward, where he met Lev and began to recognize his rights as a sufferer. He learned that he had, comparatively speaking, more rights as a sufferer than as a mentally ill person. He was discharged from the Pavlova's Ward 3 with a diagnosis that read, "Organic brain injury of a vascular origin, depression and lowered intellectual capacity." Lev helped Anton make his way into the Radiation Research Center to undergo several specialized medical evaluations. He reported these bodily complaints upon his entry: "Headaches increase with emotional pressure, more on the left side of the head; head spins, poor memory, irritability, pains in the heart, pains all over the body." But now Anton's confusion set in. At the center, he was diagnosed by the neurologists with "hypertonia, gastroduodenitis, and ischemia." Tolkach, the tough-minded medical-legal psychiatrist, added, "with hypochondriacal syndrome and hysteria" (*vnushenni reaktsii* or induced reactions). Anton suffered a legal blow. The psychiatrist's diagnoses suggested that the origin of his illness was related to psychological "self-placement" rather than to a bona fide organic cause.

It was during this period that I was introduced to the Nimovs. Having put himself under the scrutiny of the Radiation Research Center, Anton worried that he would lose his Chernobyl status altogether in the next round of annual examinations. Members of the fund adopted Anton's situation as an exemplary case of the increased marginalization of the Chernobyl sufferers. These social dynamics shaped what Nancy Scheper-Hughes calls a "political economy of emotions" and a "travesty of interaction," where the situation of a marginalized person is locked into an intimate and personal relationship with authority figures (1992:126). Anton, once a dutiful worker, came to be dependent on and even penalized by the system and its representations of him. His psychological profile was generated within the legal contours of the state; he was both passive and at war with its mechanisms of benevolence. In the process, "the man was left with the task of reclaiming, little by little, the former human content of his life" (Scheper-Hughes 1992:127).

I went to talk with Tolkach at the center about the Nimov matter. Along with his other diagnoses, Tolkach also indicated "logoneurosis" in Anton's medical records. He explained it as a form of "traumatic, broken speech" but added that "he can speak normally," implying that Anton was engaged in dissimulation. "He'll make theater and then stop and seek a quiet place. Real mania just keeps going, without stopping." "What about his suicidal thoughts?" I asked the psychiatrist. "He won't kill himself, he says he's wanted to kill himself for two years now. He really won't. He'll keep creating theater instead." Tolkach insisted that Anton had a personality disorder, and admonished me "to never pity these people. They will draw you into their concerns like a dark force. They will cheat you just as they cheat the doctor." I understood his concerns. Yet it seemed there was no medical classification that could rightfully account for the new disorder Anton was experiencing. Though his symptoms correlated with a general Chernobyl syndrome, he initially lacked the bureaucratic acumen to be accorded a higher disability status. What Tolkach didn't realize is the extent to which Anton himself despised the social role he was beginning to master.

In July, Anton and Halia arranged a second lavish dinner. This time the couple invited Vadim Nezdorov, a neurologist and staff member of the neurological ward of the local hospital in the *microraion*. Anton introduced me to Nezdorov as "the one who is writing a book about me" to increase his symbolic capital with the neurologist. Anton and Halia hoped that as a result of their inviting him to dinner, Nezdorov would be motivated to write diagnoses and letters supporting Anton's claim of disability. Soon we were joined by Lev, a key link in what I saw evolving into a kind of medical potlatch: "total services of an agonistic type" (Mauss 1990:7). Anton reciprocated Lev's earlier help by giving Lev access to his private neurologist. Lev was eager to know this specialist, for whose knowledge he would find good use (Nezdorov subsequently promised him Prozac).

I was never able to fathom the exact quantities of goods or services being exchanged here. There seemed to be little hope that the agitation in this room could ever be fully appeased by such exchanges. Those services are better understood as promises, connections, knowledge, and social ties that functioned like advances of credit, to be used in the future when needed. This institution of exchange was part of an informal economy operating in parallel with the state, where diagnoses, symptoms, and

204

medical access were traded. The outcome of these exchanges was a changed, medicalized self.

While Halia was in the kitchen preparing dinner, Anton spoke about how he had a difficult time sleeping. He said he was "tortured" at night. He said, "My legs don't walk," referring to them as autonomous and separate from him, and claimed that his "arms were paralyzed." My sense was that Anton was learning to perform the role that had come to be expected of him as a sick person. Like his autonomous limbs, his sick self seemed almost a separate being with whom Anton struggled and attempted to come to terms. Arguably, he never did. His way of being with the illness was both confused and normal. People were complicitous with this normal confusion; it relentlessly foreclosed other modes of social engagement.

The conversation turned to the topic of medication. "I will not turn away from tablets anymore," Anton said. "Only pills, no shots. I hate shots." He went to the medicine cabinet. "We can't afford this anymore but this helps the most," he said, as he pointed to some ampules used to help cerebral vascular dilation (Nootropil). "They don't give it to us at the drugstore anymore, we have to pay for it now, even if we show them our documents." Anton then invited me to a smaller table near the television while the others talked. He pulled out family albums and started to pore over the photographs inside. He pointed to photos from the times when he and Halia had traveled, wearing sleek clothing, and exchanging loving and wistful gazes. Anton then skipped to a photo taken in 1986 after his return from the Chernobyl Zone. Dressed in a suit, he is seated at the dinner table, with his right hand holding a fork spearing a piece of meat. A sign in the background reads, "This year was a black year for us, and in 1987, we will see." Halia overheard our conversation. Opening what had once been used as a liquor cabinet, she said, "Anton's drugs have replaced Stalin's finest liquor."

Where there had once been a family, now there was a new kind of collectivity forming around the dinner table. The dinner was elaborate. The feast was beyond budget. Nezdorov had taken up much of the attention at the table by recollecting the trauma he had experienced in seeing nuclear explosions at a secret Siberian nuclear installation where he had served as a soldier. He had brought to this dinner a book on magnetic energy healing and tried to convince me, based on the color of my tongue, that I had a kidney problem. The neurologist had made it his business to ensnare people within fanciful medical diagnoses. Later, Nezdorov told everyone that Anton's personality change was due to an organic brain disorder.

Halia placed a roasted pig shank, spiced with dill and parsley and trussed with strings, in the middle of the table. She said she had prepared

205

it following a traditional recipe from her village. I found it startling that no one ate the meat. People were drinking, sampling appetizers here and there. Words, knowledge, potential favors, symptoms, and drugs were being consumed instead. At one point, Anton played with Little Halia. He pulled a white tablet out of the liquor cabinet. He tantalizingly asked the girl if she wanted it. Everyone thought it was a pill. The girl took it and put it in her mouth. She had learned how to play along with her grandfather. (The "tablet" was a Tic Tac.)

In fact the little girl became quite adept at "pretend treatment" herself. On a different occasion, I watched how she jumped into the living room and announced to her grandfather that it was "time for his treatment." This was a signal for Halia to search for a glass pipette or a small needle in the medicine cabinet and for Anton to lie down on the couch. He feigned agony as he decided which body part to expose to his granddaughter's ministrations. His arm, his knee, this time it was the bottom of his foot. After she rubbed the foot with a cotton ball and right before her reckless poke, she made sure that Halia was watching approvingly: "Mama, I'm giving *D'ed* a shot!" I was told that the girl commanded paramedics around when they came to the apartment to pick up Anton; she addressed them in the derogatory form *vrachikha* (*vrach* means doctor in Russian; *vrachikha* means witch). The little girl had begun to internalize and make a game of her medicalized surroundings.

In the kitchen and while talking with Halia, I discovered that she too had health problems. Every day at a certain time she walked to the local hospital to get treatment and massages for her chronic back pain—the pain was also a pretext to leave the *kvartyra*, to find some peace away from her restless husband and to meet new friends. "The stranger is our best friend," she told me. Chance relationships were now an important part of her life and survival strategy. She told me of a woman she had met who invited the couple to do small-scale farming on a private plot of land, four hours outside of the city. Anton and Halia annually traveled there with Little Halia to pick vegetables and fruits for the winter.

After dinner and as the neurologist Nezdorov stepped through the door, thanking Halia for the meal, Anton waved his right hand. He made his left arm look stiff and paralyzed.

Everyday Violence

Who was Anton becoming? In mid-August, he called me, extremely upset. He said that Halia's father had been "lying on the floor for three days, paralyzed," before a neighbor in his village had discovered him.

Halia and her daughter Sasha immediately took the next train to Hor-lytsia. Anton worried that he would not be able to pay the "impossible expense" of the funeral (though the father had not died). He said he was going to take sleeping pills that night, and that he "could not stand the thought of attending the father-in-law's funeral." His identification with that death was strong—some of his anxiety had to do with trying to re-claim his own role as a father in that world.

Two weeks later, Halia called and invited me to join Anton and her for an afternoon boat cruise. The Oil Institute Anton had worked for was celebrating its annual holiday on the Oil, Gas, and Oil Refinery Workers' Day. Anton had recently received a slight increase of pension worth $25.00 a month as a gesture of charity from the Oil Institute's director (who in turn received tax exemptions).

I met the couple at the boarding dock near the Dnieper River. Halia told me that Iryna and her husband had set off that morning with a bor-rowed car to the grandfather's village to deliver a winter's supply of food. Halia and Anton had just returned from Volyn', where they harvested vegetables with friends Halia had met in the hospital. She told me that she was now also concerned about Little Halia, who had developed an irreg-ular heartbeat. On several occasions the girl had complained about chest pain. Halia believed that the couple's difficult life was taking a toll on the girl's health. "She feels everything."

Separately, that day, both Halia and Anton recounted a story to me about an incident involving Little Halia and a dead bird that had taken place during their trip. Their interpretations conveyed preoccupations with deeply personal concerns of death, both real and imaginary. As Anton perambulated around the boat's deck, Halia recounted how Little Halia saw a dead sparrow that had fallen from a tree. "She asked me why the bird had died, I responded, 'Some birds die and other birds live, see how the others in the tree live?'" The girl asked her grandmother to bury the bird. They searched for a small container and found one of Anton's empty cigarette boxes. They placed the dead bird in it and buried it. "I told her," said Halia, "that at night the bird will fly away and it will not come back." Halia thought her granddaughter would forget about the bird thereafter. But instead, for the next three days, the girl woke up at five in the morning to exhume the box and check on whether the bird had flown away. Later, Anton told me fragments of the same story, but he emphasized Little Halia's sorrow over finding the dead bird: "She was crying all the time." To my surprise, he attributed the girl's crying not to the dead animal that she repeatedly found but to the fact that "she doesn't have a father. Her father left her—she was only eight months old. She doesn't have a father." He held his throat and added, "but she cannot say

207

it." As on other occasions, Anton invoked the painful conjuncture in his life involving his daughter Iryna's divorce and his new role as a weak foster parent.

■ ■ ■

The workers on the cruise were well dressed and cheerful. Oil was big business in Ukraine; new global fights were being waged over access to Central Asian pipelines, the routing of pipelines, and port building in Ukraine. Felix Davydovych the charismatic and much adored director of the institute, had paid for the cruise. I learned that he had recently promised Anton an additional monthly pension at his own expense. Halia and I sat at a table along the perimeter of the top deck. Everyone drank. Anton intelligently abstained, knowing that alcohol would have interfered with his medication. He mingled with coworkers on the deck, making a point of his acquaintance with everyone. Former coworkers seemed sympathetic to him at first, but, a little later, simply tolerant of his histrionics. He grabbed my camera and began photographing everyone; he broke up and rearranged dance partners as if he were a master puppeteer.

Nobody came to our table. It seemed to me that Halia and Anton had been invited as a matter of courtesy, and that I had been brought along as a participant-observer. Halia confided as we heard the sound of his loud voice drifting through the air, "They treat him like an ill person and he doesn't know it. He gets very violent when someone tells him he is sick."

Halia explained her ways of calming her husband down and keeping his drives in check. When he complained of pain, she convinced him that the cause of his pain was environmental. She said things like, "Anton, it's not illness that you are experiencing. When the atmospheric pressure increases, you get headaches. When the weather gets hot, you feel pressure in your heart. It is not illness exactly." Anton rarely spoke of himself as being sick or in pain. Rather, he made more graphic pronouncements like "I will hang myself," and people seemed just to nod. In a way, Halia and the others treated him as an ill and infantilized person who had no control over his fate.

A bleak film made in Kyiv, *Friend of the Deceased* (1997), precisely portrays this loss of control and the "disappearance" of Soviet men as they become part of a violent new moral and economic world. The film starkly details what I have already described throughout this book (and particularly in Anton's case) as the human cost of this transition and as the intractability of the new social logics. Anatolii, the film's protagonist, is having a difficult time making money as a translator and philologist. His wife, on the other hand, has made a successful career transition from philologist to advertising executive and has been cheating on her husband. She dates a man who owns a Ford, a symbol of new middle-class wealth. Dejected, a penniless Anatolii contacts a former academic colleague turned kiosk owner who has ties with the criminal underworld. In an elaborate scheme, Anatolii contracts with a hit man to kill his wife's new boyfriend, but then changes his mind and directs the hit man to kill him instead. Anatolii sends the hit man a photograph of himself, some money, and the address of a public space where Anatolii can be found and killed. As the day of his planned death approaches, Anatolii meets a prostitute, and a love interest ensues, making Anatolii rethink his plans. Yet the only way he can undo his deadly contract is to hire another hit man to kill the first while he in the act of ambushing Anatolii. The plan succeeds, and Anatolii survives his own contract killing. In the meantime, his prostitute friend is beaten up by a rich client. The mafia blows up his friend's kiosk.

The protagonist is restless and anguish-ridden once again. At the end of the film, he contacts the wife of the first hit man, the one whose murder he had arranged. Anatolii introduces himself as a "friend of the deceased." This ending has a chilling effect—there is an unspoken complicity binding the new couple, in that they "knew" all along what had been happening. They legitimate the new order of existence by simply staying together. Their choice is both terrible and redeeming. In the final scene Anatolii is leaning over a cradle where an infant, the dead assassin's son, stares back at him and calls him Papa. This last scene depicts the troubled if improbable course of the protagonist's paternity. In this scene of somber misrecognition, he accepts his fate. Tragedy finds reconciliation, but one that exposes rather than forecloses the violence that was required in pursuit of such reconciliations. Such were the terms by which the Nimovs, in their own separate ways, tried to reconcile themselves to each other and to their new social world.

■　■　■

The boat approached the island where it would be docked for a few hours. The island, lapped by industrially polluted water, was dotted with young pine trees and carpeted with long soft grass; a Ukrainian folk ensemble was waiting for the crowd. The director of the institute flirted with several women. Anton returned to the table and told Halia that he "needed aspirin." As Halia rummaged through her purse, Anton picked up a glass bottle and pitched it into the river. I asked him, "What for?" He replied, "I threw out my memory."

Two days after the boat trip Anton telephoned me and sounded extremely disoriented: "It's bad for me." His thoughts skipped back to the month of February. "Halia called the police. The police dragged me into a special car and took me to the ward for the insane" (*otdelennia duraka*, as he called it). He detailed the living conditions there. "The insane grab bread from each other. The faucets are shut off. The orderlies take men, put them up against a wall, and hit them. The insane walk without pants. The orderlies beat them until they bleed. The insane die there for wanting one cigarette." Then he admitted that he had battered Halia again.

Later that day, I spoke with Sasha. She told me about a seemingly mundane incident that had set off Anton's brutal attack. On her return from her grandfather's house, Iryna (Little Halia's mother) had not returned a car she had borrowed from a good friend of the family. Halia made the mistake of informing her husband of this incident while he was drinking. He exploded, berating his daughter as having a "bad character." Sasha said that he had beaten Halia not just over the head and in the face, as Anton had told me, but that "her kidneys were beaten too."

The next day I visited Halia on the third floor of the neurological ward of the local hospital; it was the same ward where she underwent daily treatment for her back pain. Halia had suffered contusions and spinal and kidney injuries. Her left eye was black-and-blue. She had a bottle of ami-triptyline (an antianxiety medication) by her side. She avoided talking about the incident at first and said how much she would like to have "visited my mother's grave today. It is her birthday."

Frustrated, she began talking about her situation. "I have no rights. Anton has all the rights." Wife battery was on the rise in Ukraine; a first women's shelter had just opened up in Kyiv in 1996. She said that it would be very difficult to leave Anton, mainly for economic reasons. Moreover, the police were now involved in mediating the couple's shattered marital relationship. But the police were as corrupt as any other official institution—Halia knew that there was no real protection for her: "Anton can pay off the militia with a few dollars and they will not touch him." She said that it would be even more difficult than before to get the police to lock him up. Getting a forensic report describing her battered body was also not easy. In February, Ivana (the neurologist and friend from Halia's home village) had written such a report, forcing the police to act. This time around Ivana was not willing to do the same. She was afraid for her own job and did not want to get involved in the Nimov matter any further. Everybody at the Pavlova knew that Anton was no longer "just" a psychiatric case; he was a socially legitimated victim.

From the *kvartyra* to the hospital—the characters of this illness narrative came together around Halia's beaten body. The callous neurologist Nezdorov worked in the hospital and had heard from Anton that Halia was hospitalized. When I visited Halia a few days later, she was in the middle of an argument with Nezdorov. She said she needed a forensic report from him. Yet concerns about institutional survival, enduring gender domination, and an entire medical balance of power shifted in Anton's favor. Nezdorov made it clear that he had no interest in writing a forensic report compromising Anton's social status. Halia pleaded with him, "Vadim, look at my body, I ask you to do the right thing." She said that every night at home she slept in fear, "with clothes on and keys in my hands. I cannot stay with Anton anymore. I cannot bear hearing him refer to my father as a worthless, old, decrepit man (*kalika*). He says he wants to bury the *kalika* himself." Halia continued making her case, drawing on the moral authority of family and combining it with a dreadful evocation of her confinement in it: "He curses my mother's photograph. . . . He goes to the institute and gives the impression that everything is normal in the house, but in the meantime he tells me, 'I will kill you morally and physically.'" Nezdorov listened and said, "It's the organic brain damage." Halia wept: "He seeks pity from everyone about his state, that life is bad for him." She said, "My nerves are shot, my soul is sick, it's pouring out of me. The sedatives don't help. I said to Anton as he was beating me, 'Was there ever a time where there wasn't food on the table or an unclean house?'"

Daughter Sasha entered the hospital room, this time with a bag full of syringes and pills. (The hospital no longer provided basic medical supplies.) Halia demonstrated to all of us how Anton beat her. "He knows how to hit," she said, looking at Nezdorov, "on the side of the palm where it hurts him the least." She showed us where he had hit her—over the head, the temples, the face, the kidneys." Nezdorov listened and told Halia that she needed to get a computerized tomographic brain scan. Nezdorov said he could refer her to a private diagnostic firm that would charge about sixty dollars—an unreasonable cost, given her lack of money.

Two days later, I met the doctor over some sandwiches at a local café. He bragged about his connections with the boss of the local medical-labor committee. I asked him whether he could clarify Anton's medical condition. He refused. He preferred to talk about Anton's relationship with Lev. Anton had promised Lev that Nezdorov would help in arranging a higher disability status for him (level two). Quite openly, he implied that he was profiting from those interactions. When I asked how Lev could have had so many diagnoses, Nezdorov said that he had paid the doctors. But he insisted that both men have the "brain organic syndrome."

In mid-September, Anton called again. This time he accused his daughter Iryna of stealing money from him. He asked me where Halia was. I didn't tell him, but I was sure he knew. Anton offered further justification for beating her. This time he related his violence to money, to "being robbed" by his daughter and son-in-law. According to him, the young

211

couple had come over to the apartment the day Anton beat Halia. "It was their fault," he said. "They took our savings and a leather coat that Halia and I had been saving for months to give to Iryna on her birthday." Anton started to weep. He said, "Halia is the insane one." He said he'd "kill [him]self," that there was "nothing to hold on to," and that he had not "found a place for [him]self." His shifted from the present tense, where there was no fixed place for him, and said that even his unconscious was now populated by the insane: "I dream about insane people. They invade my dreams."

Two weeks later, Halia called me from the hospital's public telephone. She said she needed some amitriptyline, but that her daughter couldn't find it in the state drugstores. I found some readily available for over-the-counter sale at a commercial drugstore. She reiterated her difficulties in leaving Anton. She said that "someone with experience" had told her that she had little chance of divorcing Anton because "I have to prove that Anton is mentally ill." But that was nearly impossible at this point.

Anton called again. He asked whether I had Sasha's telephone number. He then asked me whether I knew if there was a bed available in the Radiation Research Center. He wanted to go there to get reexamined, he said. He also asked whether I had seen Lev at the center. Anton seemed to know that the institution's medical-labor committee was about to begin a new session of medical reviews—this meant that cases would be assessed and dismissed, extended, or upgraded. I checked the hospital records that day; they indicated that Lev was residing in hospital room 502, but the nurses told me that there was no one in that room by that name.

I had not seen Lev for a month and a half. He seemed to have just disappeared. I learned that members of the fund were furious with him because "he represented the fund in an unauthorized way" in order to procure a level two disability. One member caustically said that Lev had promised the center's manager, Mudrak, gas and other resources in exchange for a guarantee of lifetime disability. The last time I saw Lev was in a corridor as he was leaving the office of Ihor Demeshko (the medical-labor committee's representative). He had a distinct look of triumph on his face and said he was off to a health sanitorium. Anton had to work the system one more time and try again the following year.

Lifetime

Halia stayed in the hospital for a month and a half. During this period, not once did she or her daughter Sasha step into the *kvartyra* to get Halia's things. Little Halia stayed with Iryna, who had not contacted her mother at all during this trying period. One day Halia asked me to accompany her on a walk to the apartment to get some of her things. I agreed to, with some hesitation, and met her the next day at the hospital. We first went to the militia station near the apartment block. The policeman on duty agreed to come with us. He was short and burly, sympathetic, but cautious. He changed out of his uniform into civilian dress. As we walked, Halia began to tell the policeman what had happened, but he said he was already familiar with the Nimov case. He told Halia quite plainly, "There's no way we could just take him this time," and advised her thus: "Anton should never know that we have no power over him." The balance of power had apparently shifted in his favor again.

Fortunately, Anton was not in the apartment. Yet signs of his shattered existence were everywhere. A large mirror to the right of the entrance door had been broken. There was blood on the floor mixed with pieces of shattered glass. The policeman sat down on the couch, and I stood near the door. Halia rummaged through piles of clothing, throwing items she needed into a plastic garbage bag. Suddenly, her hand touched a metal object in the pile. It was an iron with a heavy metal base. The object was wrapped in a cloth that formed a kind of a handle. Halia lifted it up to show the policeman and said, "He wrapped it so that there wouldn't be any fingerprints on it. This would have been me." The policeman told Halia to take the object with her. She decided to put it back into the pile. The iron reminded me of a desperate comment Anton had made several months back: "There was life. There was butter. There was milk. I can't buy an iron. Before I could buy fifty irons. The money was there. My wife's salary is less than the cost of one iron."

Signs of ruin and disintegration abounded. Anton had bundled up items that belonged to Iryna and her husband, making it clear that their things no longer belonged in the house. Once the bag was filled, Halia spent what seemed an interminable time searching for a white envelope containing her identity card and medical book, necessary for the registration of the number of days she spent in the hospital. Her attending physician would register that number so that she would be eligible to receive her salary for those days (the book could also show proof of Halia's battered condition). To her shock, the envelope she found was empty. She held it up and said, "See how smart he is."

As we left, Halia asked the policeman to help her carry the heavy bag. He apologetically refused. He couldn't carry it because "if your husband saw me carrying your bags, he could accuse me of stealing his property." I helped her carry the bag as the policeman returned to the militia station. "Ten years ago, I had no reason to associate with the police," Halia told me. "Their sphere of activity was separate from my sphere of activity. Now I know the name of the policeman, I need his protection."

Halia spotted a neighbor, another woman who apparently knew of her troubles. "Let him jump, hang, cut himself! Why does he threaten to kill everyone else and not kill himself?!" The conversation ended as we continued to walk to the tram station. Suddenly Halia stopped under a fluorescent streetlight. She was suddenly overcome with nervous tremors that had intensified in her arm and neck. We went to Sasha's apartment to drop the things off. Halia stayed there that night, as the doors to the hospital were already locked.

A few weeks later, Halia called me from Ivana's house. She said that the medications and treatments at the hospital were extremely invasive. She had gotten a computerized tomographic brain scan at the Pavlova. The scan showed cerebral scarring. She knew I was leaving Ukraine and wanted to say goodbye. She said she would return to the apartment to live with Anton: "Nothing will come of this, we are back to the same thing. Anton drank himself to nothing. I have no way out of this situation."

Where could she go except to the apartment cell that the couple jointly owned—the home they had waited years for, and that also sheltered Little Halia. "Nothing changed," as Halia was apt to tell me in several subsequent letters. When I spoke to Anton last, he told me that the neurologist had suddenly died of a heart attack. "They gave me lifetime," was the first thing Anton said.

Chapter 8
Conclusion

The Chernobyl aftermath is a prism reflecting, containing, and re-configuring the vexed political-economic, scientific, legal, and social circumstances that characterized this interim period. Lawmakers, radiation scientists, health professionals, and groups of sufferers all stood at different points along the continuum of knowledge production, power, moral sensibility, and self-disclosure. The efforts of scientists and clinicians to continually reformat the Chernobyl event and to localize radiation as a set of concrete and embodied effects, combined with efforts of citizens to gain state protection, effected a social mechanism that appeared to be, or was made to appear as, an impersonal and self-authorizing force. Many personal narratives spoke of its effects in terms of physical crippling. Patients cited it as the cause of their symptoms ("It's as if something is not letting that leg walk"); as the cause of their speechlessness ("It tugged at my voice"); or as the cause of their emotional distress ("I am not weeping. It weeps by itself"). Bureaucrats cited it in order to invest clinical and research structures with the authority to decipher illness claims ("We can't stop the illness, the whole state is integrated into it"). Health seemed an impossible goal—technically out of the question. Rather, there was a painful determinacy to the radiation illness. It found new niches in terms of the social relations, identities, and symptoms it produced, superimposed itself on, or assailed.

A surprising finding of this research was that this impersonal force was crafted at every step. The physical reality of the Chernobyl disaster and its sheer magnitude were initially refashioned and refracted through a series of informational omissions, technical strategies, errors, semiempirical

models, approximations, international cooperations, and limited interventions. Combined, these practices initially produced a picture of a
known, circumscribed, and manageable biological reality. Later, these
biological effects were seen as political products; technical unknowns
were reshaped in the subsequent Ukrainian period as part of a new biopolitical regime. Informal economies of knowledge, codified symptoms, dif-
ferential medical access, a continuum of diagnoses, and "Chernobyl ties"
were mobilized and began to function as institutions in parallel with the
state's official, legal social protection system. These new resources resembled credit advances, ensuring social protections in the uncertain future
for people whose temporal horizons were short. The clinical research
process facilitated the naturalization of illnesses in bodies as a matter of
"social health." The deep intrusion of illness into personal lives fostered
a type of violence that went beyond the line of what could be policed.
There was no place that provided natural immunity from these unnatural
and technical forces. Instead, there was a complete breakdown of immunities. This state of total unprotectedness constituted a baseline from
which people in this world were refashioning themselves (and their bodies) as persons to be protected by the biopolitical regime in which they
now lived.

How much that has been described here happens elsewhere in analogous situations, and how much is peculiar to this place and time, and
why? In one sense, this ethnography delineates some similarity between
Chernobyl and other large-scale technological disasters. As other anthropologists have shown, the social aftermaths of the Union Carbide chemical disaster in Bhopal and the nuclear attacks on Hiroshima and
Nagasaki are inflected by the socioeconomic and political contexts and
institutions whose policies have also legitimated or served to rebuild
states' internal bureaucratic mechanisms. Many persons who have survived these large-scale technological disasters have been caught in a long-
term and vicious bureaucratic cycle in which they carry the burden of
proof of their physical damage while experiencing the risk of being dele-
gitimated in legal, welfare, and medical institutional contexts (Das 1995,
Todeschini 1999). That suffering appears to be ongoing in these cases
reflects, to some degree, the logic of the legal and state structures through
which it is addressed.

One difference between Chernobyl and these other disasters involves
the number, physical variability, and duration of the kinds of harmful (in
this case radioactive) particles that were released. The disaster is marked
by a nonclosure of its biological effects. This means that the spread of
health effects is difficult to control and difficult to monitor, so that, along
with intermediating social complexities, it is not easy to conceptualize
what an end to aftermath may mean. Rather, what we have seen estab-

lished are a series of containments. Different states, political and economic interests, and sciences have taken up these containment processes in ways that have revealed variable ethical commitments and human tolls. This variability in itself suggests not only the intensely political nature of science, but the extent to which the very scientific and political construction of aftermath can affect its lived experiences. These processes, as I have shown, have produced their own spiraling effects, disrupting family lives, creating senses of injustice and insecurity, and shaping individual prospects and interpersonal and political transactions. Those effects become so deeply entrenched that they come to define the fabric of human health: the dimensions that protect or undermine it, and the ethical commitments informing its value and responsibilities.

Is there a way to separate the need for political legitimation following major disasters with just approaches to remediation? Do outside agencies have a legitimate role in influencing the nature of these processes, or will they continue to be shaped by the specific interests of international economic and scientific agencies? How are we to judge how future changes in social and economic contexts will affect the legitimacy of mechanisms of compensation and categories of suffering? And who is to say when such mechanisms and categories should be phased out, and on what basis? Finally, how should such questions be weighed against the reality of nonclosure of Chernobyl's biological effects? All of these are new ethical issues that bear on the fate of these populations; a sustained scientific and ethnographic engagement is required for their understanding.

The life of these affected populations is interwoven with and determined by the larger historical events of the Soviet Union's collapse and the harsh political-economic restructuring that followed. Their combined cumulative effects do not lend themselves to easy psychological labels. Nor can they be reduced to assessments of isolated individuals' perceptions and measures of social adaptation. By outlining the social, scientific, and political constructions of their experiences, I have illustrated the kinds of subject positions these affected populations have taken up over time in an effort to cope with their changing political, moral, and biomedical circumstances.

The dynamism of this process was made clear to me in my last visit to the clinical wards in 2000, right at the time when the Russian submarine, the *Kursk*, sank in the Barents Sea. The patients with whom I watched the disaster's television coverage noted the government's denial of any responsibility for the disaster and the delay of rescue and recovery efforts. To these particular viewers, the story of the *Kursk* read like a replay of the story of Chernobyl, but only to an extent. As I gathered the opinions of those interned in the neurological ward, I documented, as Martha Minow has done in the wake of South Africa's democratization, how present-day processes of recompense, of which these patients were a part, were entangled with new patterns of inequality that themselves presented the most immediate issues of social injustice (1998:157). The very framing of "injury" now entailed the social and health costs associated with state and market transformations and emerging inequalities.

The extent to which new health costs are created by social and political circumstances has been shown by a number of anthropologists. They were also being accounted for by these patients in terms of a troubling cost-benefit assessment. A middle-aged man working as an engineer at Chernobyl expected that, given international pressure for the plant's closure by the end of that year, his prospects of keeping his well-paid job were nil. It was time for him to stop hiding his thyroid problems and to register himself as a disabled person. A middle-aged woman wanted to keep working in the Zone in spite of her heart problems because the salary she earned there allowed her to pay her son's law school tuition. These examples illustrate the problematic interaction between compensation and market conditions inasmuch as those interactions produce incentive for further health deterioration and illness. Such incentives, however, do not represent an argument for the abolition of the compensation system as such. The social conditions that have limited other options only make these workers desire their one remaining option much more, and at a greater personal cost. Compensation no longer means a simple payment for past damages; it is an attempt to balance or neutralize opposing forces that give or take life.

The effects of the economy on health are changing the nature and terms of citizenship. The theme of citizenship is particularly important here not only because of its traditional role in framing individuals' life chances by increasing their welfare and health care access—benefits formerly guaranteed by permanent employment in socialist enterprises. The very idea of citizenship is now charged with the superadded burden of survival. This process represents a shift, perhaps even a reversal, in the underlying principles of a classical citizenship, inasmuch as those principles cannot guarantee the basic biological existence of populations that is a prerequisite for political life. Though this may seem like an obvious point, it is also a devastating one. The collective/individual survival strategy of biological citizenship represents a complex intersection of social institutions and the intense vulnerabilities of populations exposed to the determinations of the international political economy; it is also part of a larger story of democratization and new structures of governance in the postsocialist states. In these states, emergent democratic forms now coincide with distinct patterns of social inclusion and exclusion through which rights are sometimes realized, but only on a basis. Taken together, these dynamics alternately mask and exstark, if not overwhelming, tension that informs the specifics of this case but also represents trends in the governance and politics of life more generally.

As confirmed by statistical increases in preventable disease and illness, developing and postsocialist countries are experiencing the social and health costs of political collapse, economic restructuring, and new or ongoing poverty (Desjarlais et al. 1995). Along with this process, and as I have shown in this book, the biology of citizens is becoming part of a political process and a medium of government. There is much evidence to show that in areas where life expectancy increased and mortality decreased under the auspices of a "health transition," lives are in fact becoming shorter, hungrier, more diseased, and less protected (Chen et al. 1994). Interventions into already compromised lives increasingly take the form of human capital assessments and cost-benefit and health utility analyses. Critical awareness of this selective give-and-take is reflected in Africa, where a delay of efforts by international pharmaceutical companies to reduce treatment costs has indirectly contributed to growing AIDS mortality and is now leading to calls for compensation. A political economics of expendability was recently highlighted in the Czech Republic, where an American cigarette manufacturer, in an attempt to reduce cigarette taxes, argued that smokers save the state millions of health dollars by dying prematurely. The nuclear industry has recently implemented international standards that legitimate uneven protection among nuclear workers on the basis of what is "reasonably achievable," given variable socioeconomic environments.

These examples suggest that in the former Soviet Union, where democratic state building is evolving in tandem with market formations, existing forms of inequality are being naturalized and administered in new political and technical ways. Indeed, these inequalities are being inscribed in the lives of populations through policies, scientific standards and regulations, and selective social protection and access to health care—all the while broadening the meaning of the term "compensation." The naturalization and capitalization of socioeconomic difference, in parallel with processes of democratization, has been one of the most paradoxical and troubling phenomena for any ethnographer working in the former Soviet Union to watch. There are now many people in these areas grappling with the price they have to pay for living and, less so these days, laboring in their socioeconomic and political worlds. They belong to new experimental arenas in which science, state building, and market developments are intertwined, and where new social and institutional forms are testing the limits of citizenship and ethics. In such contexts, ethnography's role involves detailing the elements that unsettle and entangle people's lives, and maintaining a prospective sense of the contingencies of human existence, such that its forms find a place within the discipline of observation.

Notes

Chapter 1 Life Politics after Chernobyl

1. "The purpose of the experiment was to test the possibility of using the mechanical energy of the rotor in a turbo-generator cut off from steam supply to sustain the amounts of power requirements during a power failure" (IAEA, *Soviet State Committee on the Utilization of Atomic Energy* 1986:16).

2. See Sich 1996. With these and all other compounding factors, "estimates of the long-term health consequences of the Chernobyl accident are uncertain even as to the order of magnitude" (Von Hippel 1991:235).

3. By May 2, 1986, short reports were published in local newspapers.

4. Thirteen thousand children in affected regions absorbed a radiation dose to the thyroid of more than twice the maximum allowable dose for nuclear workers for an entire year. See Shcherbak 1996.

5. Iodine pills raise the amounts of iodide in the bloodstream so that the thyroid cannot absorb more. The radioactive iodine to which a person is exposed is excreted in the urine.

6. Estimates vary from 600,000 to 800,000. These workers were recruited from all over the Soviet Union. But the labor pool drew most heavily from Ukrainian and Russian populations.

7. The karbovanets (Krb) was Ukraine's legal tender from 1992 to 1996. Exchange rates per $1.00 US plunged between 1992 and 1993. In March 1992, the exchange rate was 640 Krb:$1. By March 1993, that rate had lowered to 12,610 Krb:$1. Subsequent rates were as follows: 1994—104,200:$1; 1995—179,900:$1; 1996—188,700:$1. The hryvna (HRN) replaced the karbovanets at HRN1:Krb100,000 in September of 1996. The exchange rates were as follows: 1997—1.84:$1; 1998—2.04:$1; 1999—4.13:$1; 2000—5.44:$1.

8. Such values are calculated on the basis of "rem-expenditures" workers accrue; their amounts are limited by international standards. Despite the existence of such standards, norms of worker exposures are being decided locally and within the constraints of local economies that "undervalue" workers' lives by exposing them to more risk for less pay.

9. Social suffering "results from what political, economic, and institutional power does to people, and, reciprocally, from how these forms of power themselves influence responses to social problems" (Kleinman, Das, and Lock 1996:i).

10. The Soviet period refers to the years 1986–1991. The post-Soviet period refers to 1991 and beyond.

11. Differences between sufferers and the disabled will be addressed in chapter 4.

12. Personal communication, Ministry of Emergencies (Chernobyl Section, Division of International Relations). In Russia, the number of people considered affected and compensatable has been kept to a minimum and remains fairly stable (about 350,000, including 300,000 Zone laborers and 50,000 persons now resettled in noncontaminated areas).

13. In fact, the Belarussian government has encouraged its own people, as well as Russians living outside the new borders of Russia (mainly in Central Asia and the Caucasus, where war is ongoing), to take up residence in contaminated areas, offering them housing, jobs, and resident status. See Ackerman 2000.

14. As of 1999, 50 percent of the population lives below the poverty line. The inflation rate is at 20 percent. The gross domestic product (GDP) has fallen by 60 percent since independence. This figure, however, overstates the fall in output, since the informal economy has been expanding (Country Brief, World Bank, 1999).

15. Yet even this view is contradicted within Belarus. The director of the Research and Clinical Institute of Radiation Medicine and Endocrinology in Minsk indicated that "perhaps the biggest surprise in the first few years after the explosion was that a spate of leukemia cases, predicted from Japanese atom bomb survivor studies, never materialized." See Stone 2001.

16. Here I draw on insights from Shapin and Schaffer 1985:15, "Solutions to the problem of knowledge are embedded within practical solutions to the problem of social order, and . . . different practical solutions to the problem of social order encapsulate contrasting solutions to the problem of knowledge."

17. As Frank Von Hippel (2000) notes, the main battleground for the debate over whether there is a threshold dose below which radiation is not harmful is the regulation of nuclear power.

18. For Foucault, the nuclear era represented biopower's culmination. "If nuclear energy is the modern capacity to expose populations to unprecedented kinds of risk and potential death, it is also the underside of the power to generate life through the biological administration of individuals and populations (1980a:137).

19. The United States Department of Energy initiated the Human Genome Project the same year that Chernobyl happened. See, for example, Cook-Deegan 1994.

20. "In the future, the new genetics will cease to be a biological metaphor for modern society and will become instead a circulation network of identity terms and restriction loci, around which and through which a truly new type of autoproduction will emerge, which I call 'biosociality' " (Rabinow 1996a:99).

21. Veena Das has illustrated the ways pain and suffering are rationalized within state mechanisms and affected societies. In the case of India's Bhopal chemical disaster, state health professionals and bureaucrats de-authenticated the suffering of victims by insisting that objective measures replace self-reports of victims as means of assessing the consequences of chemical exposure. Something similar happened in the Soviet administration of the Chernobyl disaster. As an effect, pain and suffering "may also be experiences which are actively created and distributed by the social order itself" (1995:138). See "Suffering, Legitimacy, and Healing: The Bhopal Case," in Das 1995.

22. The consequences of Chernobyl are an important example of what Ulrich Beck termed "manufactured uncertainties." See Beck 1999.

23. This is a pseudonym. I refer to it throughout the book interchangeably as the "Radiation Research Center" and the "center."

24. Literary critic George Steiner reminds us of the power of words in contexts of violence in which affect and perception are reduced to a code. During his purge in the late thirties, Steiner tells us, Russian writer Boris Pasternak was invited into an auditorium where he was scheduled to undergo a public interrogation in front of a large audience. Before his questioning began, the interrogator told him that he could say one word in his defense. Pasternak uttered the number twenty-five, when, in a most poignant act of defiance, the audience stood up and began to recite a Shakespearean sonnet, number twenty-five, one that Pasternak had translated into Russian. Lecture, Massachusetts Institute of Technology, Department of the Humanities, March 6, 1998.

25. The country's current population growth rate is −0.83 percent. The population numbers 49,153,027.

26. This figure is based on an estimation made by historian Robert Conquest in his important but contested contribution to the history of the famine. See Conquest 1986.

27. Historians might argue that Pavlo Skoropadsky's government was also at least semisovereign, as was Symon Petliura's.

28. Main ethnic groups as registered by the country's Ministry of Statistics include Ukrainians, Russians, Jews, and Armenians. Ukraine was the first country in the world to give up its nuclear arsenal. Rights of citizenship, religious expression, and speech were granted to all inhabitants, regardless of ethnic and religious affiliation. Police violence toward immigrant populations (particularly toward Africans and Muslims) in Kyiv was commonly reported in 1996.

29. Indeed, public social spending nearly doubled from 1990 to 1991, jumping from 25 percent to 44.1 percent of the gross domestic product.

30. According to Schnapper (1997), claims rights define the rights of citizens "to receive services from the state: the right to a job, material well-being, education, time off, etc." In contrast to liberty rights, "these rights imply state intervention to benefit the individual" (202). For an excellent review of Soviet

concepts of citizenship, see "Nationality in Soviet and Post-Soviet Ukraine," in Wanner 1998.

31. The First Five-Year Plan called for a total collectivization of individual peasant farms in Ukraine as well as in Kazakhstan and parts of Russia. All grain produced by peasants was collected and sold to finance industrialization. Those who resisted such collections by hiding grain met certain death, often by gunshot. As Wanner points out, "Famine conditions were produced more by the regime's inflated demands for grain and seed than by the size of the harvest in any particular year" (1998:43). See Krawchenko 1985 and Subtelny 1994 for a detailed description of events that led to the famine. The famine affected all citizens of Ukraine, urban and rural, ethnic Ukrainian, Russian, and Jewish.

32. There are over twenty political parties in Ukraine. They include the Communist, Socialist, and the Socialist Party–Peasant Party on the left, to the Hromada, the Greens, and the Democratic Party in the center, to the nationalistic Rukh and National Front, to the far right UNA. For an account of the short-lived alliance, see Torbakov 2000. For an account of the relatively short-lived relationship between environmental movements and independence politics, see Dawson 1996.

33. Throughout the book, I refer to the rem, the gray, and the mSv (milliSievert). The rem is a unit of equivalent dose for biological damage. Another such unit is the Sievert (Sv), where 1 Sv = 100 rem. The gray (Gy) is a unit of absorbed dose. A group of scientists working in the damaged reactor building over several years may have accumulated doses in the range of 0.5 to 13 grays (approximately 500 to 13,000 Sv, or 50 to 1,300 rem).

34. Anatolii Romanenko is widely known as having played a pivotal role in pathologizing his countrymen as "radiophobic" in a Soviet campaign to paper over the scale of the disaster. He presided over the May Day Parade that all were required to attend on May 1, when levels of radiation peaked in Kyiv. He did not issue health warnings that day.

35. The Cusan's free speculations opposed a late medieval emphasis on God's omnipotence and hence were considered antichurch and suspicious.

36. "For a theoretical attitude, imprecision could never be an ultimate characteristic of its objects, but only an intervening phase between the supposed precision of an imagined stellar 'simplicity' and a future, more complex precision of superimposed periodicities. . . . Imprecision is not the speculatively anticipated and necessary state of affairs but rather first of all a scandalous contingent fact" (Blumenberg 1983:504).

Chapter 2 Technical Error: Measures of Life and Risk

1. As a disabled person, Dmytro earned $150/mo. His wife was a civil servant and earned $40/mo. His pension would have been adequate had he not had to spend half of it for medicines. He wanted level two disability, by which he would be officially certified as having lost 80 percent or more of his work capacity. This upgrading would have doubled his pension to $300/mo.

224

2. During this information blackout "no technical details were given" of the emergency measures undertaken to control the accident situation. Medvedev defines emergency measures in terms of "the initial response to the accident in the first ten days when officials were acting under the protection of the news blackout. They also include the attempts to decontaminate the area, to construct a 'sarcophagus' around the reactor to isolate it from the environment, to establish hydrological isolation of the plant site and to set up effective dosimetric control of food" (1990:41).

3. In the absence of Soviet data on the plume's source, Sullivan and his team inferred its origin on the basis of weather charts provided by the United States Air Force.

4. This mapping occurred between April 28 and 29. Sullivan told me that separate teams affiliated with the Nuclear Regulatory Commission and the International Atomic Energy Agency were working on the same thing and cross-checking their data.

5. Ruthenium's melting point is 2,250 degrees Celsius. The presence of ruthenium in the plume's trace meant that a meltdown of the reactor core had taken place. Zirconium, used for cladding nuclear fuel, melts at 1,852 degrees.

6. According to Sullivan, "We suddenly realized that we needed an enormous amount of data. The quantity of data we were not at all set up to receive in terms of spatial size nor in terms of extent in time. For example, in a usual model calculation we were limited to five upper air stations and where there are fifteen or thirty or something like that surface stations. And now we are dealing with hundreds of upper air stations and thousands of surface stations."

7. After Chernobyl, Sullivan's team started to model such things as volcanic ash fires and the Kuwaiti oil fires in real time.

8. The Soviets had a large network of radiation-monitoring stations.

9. The initial Soviet report to the IAEA in August 1986 stated that "environmental monitoring devices, or individual radiation meters or badges, were of limited value at Chernobyl." *IAEA, Soviet State Committee on the Utilization of Atomic Energy* 1986. *The Accident at Chernobyl Nuclear Power Plant and Its Consequences.* Information compiled for the IAEA Experts' Meeting, August 25–29, 1986, Vienna. Working Document for the Post-Accident Review Meeting.

10. The lake evaporated, leaving behind dangerous doses of radioactive dust.

11. They had been exposed to radiation from weapons testing and other nuclear accidents, such as the one in the Urals in the 1950s.

12. She was noted for her efforts to combine radiobiology with clinical medicine. See Guskova 1997.

13. According to Medvedev, "There was no proper agreed scientific method in the Soviet Union for making these estimates. Different experts used different approaches" (1990:130).

14. Though primary medical attention focused on the group of workers under Guskova's care in Moscow, many Soviet biologists, cytogeneticists, and biologists associated with the Radiation Research Center in Kyiv were dispatched to the Zone in the first few days following the disaster. They collected blood from children and adults, and documented changes in blood indicators, chromosomes, and genetic constitution (HLA markers).

15. The distribution of toxic effects in nuclear accidents can be thought of as encompassing three bodily domains: skin, bone marrow, and other. The fact that each accident results in differing degrees of intensity of injury to each of the three domains means that "it is not possible to devise a specific medical plan for all accidents or to draw conclusion about the value of different medical interventions from a single accident" (Baranov et al. 1989:206).

16. He currently enjoys all the Ukrainian state benefits associated with his ARS diagnosis.

17. See *Chornobyl'ska Tragediia* 1996.

18. "All those things that we call the environment," according to one specialist trained in Soviet medical classification. Vegetovascular dystonia (VvD) is a term for disturbances of the autonomic nervous system. It approximates a class of diseases known in the United States as somatoform disorders, which include anxiety disorders with somatic manifestations. VvD is not a diagnosis, nor does it appear in the International Classification of Diseases. Nor does it refer to any specific pathology. VvD is a premorbid state; a person with VvD exhibits "tendencies" to subsequent developments of a pathological state. It is a description of an unspecified state, that is, of a state "between two functional states of the organism, one normal and the other pathological."

19. "About the Diagnostics of the Illnesses of Individuals Who Were Exposed to Ionizing Radiation," May 21, 1986 (*Chornobyl': Problemy Zdorov'ia Naselennia* 1995:144).

20. The Ukrainian health minister's informational bulletin made one request: "Until now, the Soviet Ministry of Health has not provided us with a list of diagnoses associated with the activity of ionizing radiation." "Information from the Ukrainian Ministry of Health to the Central Committee of the Ukrainian Communist Party about Difficulties in Designating Work Capacity of Workers in the Zone," December 29, 1986 (*Chornobyl': Problemy Zdorov'ia Naselennia* 1995:67).

21. Blood indicators went largely unmonitored. Radiation's effects, at least those traceable in the blood, were disappearing (largely as a function of natural physiological processes). Blood lymphocytes repopulate at high rates so that the very chromosomal damage containing original evidence of exposure had been lost over time. Their biological effects were being eliminated as nonevents.

22. The five-member team arrived on May 6, 1986. Dr. Gale headed the International Bone Marrow Transplant Registry and was admitted under the aegis of the industrialist and philanthropist Armand Hammer.

23. Gorbachev asserted in a speech on June 9, 1986, that "the Soviets are anxious to use the aegis of the IAEA to give respectability to their determination to carry on with their own nuclear energy programme." The general secretary wanted to "use the IAEA as a basis for increased international cooperation on safety and compensation matters, and in the design of a new generation reactor" (Economist Intelligence Unit 1986:13).

24. Financial assistance was provided by an array of American institutions, such as the National Cancer Institute (grant no. CA23175), the National Institute of Health, Sandoz Pharmaceuticals, Occidental Petroleum Corporation, Baxter Healthcare, SmithKline Beckman, and others.

25. Recombinant human granulocyte-macrophage colony-stimulating factors or (rhGM-CSF)

26. The testing of the molecule, according to the scientist, had the approval of the U.S. FDA.

27. Donahue et al. 1986; Monroy et al. 1986.

28. V. D. Lisovyi, member, Parliamentary Commission on Chernobyl, Kyiv, Ukraine, June 1993. According to the current standards developed by the International Commission on Radiological Protection, the maximum permissible annual dose for the general public is 0.5 rem (or 35 rem over an average seventy-year life span). The approximate annual dose from natural background radiation is 0.1 rem (or 7 rem over an average seventy-year life expectancy). Adapted from Medvedev 1990.

29. Such cost-benefit analyses of existing nuclear sites are becoming globalized as standard practice. They influence local responses and local tolerances for heightened nuclear risk and have played a key role in the negotiation for international funds for cleanup of nuclear sites such as the Chernobyl power plant.

30. See IAEA 1991a, 1991b.

31. Professor Kindzelskyi of the Radiation Oncology Institute in Kyiv explained how the 35-rem limit, for example, was deduced: based on North American studies, "0.5 rem is what a nuclear plant worker receives. This is the maximum safe dose. And then they multiplied 0.5 by seventy years (a possible life span) to get 35 rem." For further explication of the negotiation of the threshold, see Chernousenko 1991.

32. "If life is the production, transmission and reception of information, then clearly the history of life involves both conservation and innovation. How is evolution to be explained by genetics? The answer, of course, involves the mechanism of mutation. . . . To be sure, many mutations are monstrous—but from the standpoint of life as a whole, what does monstrous mean? Many of today's life forms are nothing other than normalized monsters. . . . Thus, if life has meaning, we must accept the possibility of a loss of that meaning, of distortion, of misconstruction. Life overcomes error through further trials (and by error I mean simply a dead end)" (Canguilhem 1994:318).

33. In citing what Anspaugh and colleagues have claimed, I am aware that the quoted zero percent figure, the bottom of the range, does not make sense here.

34. According to Pass et al., "Quantification of the biologically relevant dose is required for the establishment of cause-and-effect radiation detriment or burden and important biological outcomes" (1997:390).

35. The BEVALAC was considered the only suitable accelerator for comprehensive studies of heavy ions. The decommissioning of the BEVALAC in 1994 put significant constraints on animal studies, as well as on experimental radiation therapy for terminally ill cancer patients at LBL.

36. "There is no doubt that theoretical approaches are going to play a major role, not only in terms of unifying various experimental data in a systematic manner, but also in terms of providing additional knowledge that may not be accessible to experimental procedures" (Chatterjee and Holley 1994:222).

37. According to Paul Rabinow, "Although this gap is not a new one, to be

sure, the potential for its widening nonetheless poses a new range of social, ethical and cultural problems" (1996a:100).

38. FISH, which evolved over twenty years, is a useful tool in prenatal screening, tumor biology, and gene mapping, as well as biological monitoring for radiation induction.

39. It was also the tool available to some patients to calculate their dose burdens and risk status, although these calculations tended to be made on the basis of an examination of smaller numbers of metaphases, two hundred, for example.

40. Rad = Radiation absorbed dose. This unit indicates the amount of radiation dose absorbed in a unit of tissue or organ.

41. In the recent wave of current biotechnological ventures related to potential stem cell treatments, Gale has given up focusing on Chernobyl-related issues and directs research at a private biotechnology company specializing in stem cell research.

Chapter 3 Chernobyl in Historical Light

1. For further reading on contemporary accounts of Soviet terror, see Merridale 2000.

2. The city was a major border-controlling point at the time of the Bolshevik revolution; there the Extraordinary Commission to Combat Counterrevolution, the dreaded Cheka police, was given total authority to arrest and execute "counterrevolutionaries" and individuals who attempted to escape into northern Moldavia, Romania, or Poland. During the period of collectivization in the early thirties, the "kulaks" or the recalcitrant peasant "fists," who refused to give up their land to the state, were rounded up there, shot, or deported to forced labor camps. Later, in 1941, Hitler established the city as one center of his *Reichkommissariat* in Ukraine, controlling the movement of migrants and refugees hoping to escape to Western Europe or at least to Poland and northward. Continual violence was targeted at heterogenous ethnic and religious populations on this site over a thirty-year period.

3. As a result of the state's confiscating the foodstuffs of peasant populations, combined with drought, a famine ravaged Ukraine and the Volga region between 1921 and 1922. This famine, unlike the one in 1932–1933, was officially acknowledged.

4. It was unclear to me whether Mr. Pasichnyk had moved all of them himself. I asked and he answered, "Alone, I moved them, as if forever." Bila-Skala, Ukraine, July 1992.

5. This church was quickly restored as a Polish Catholic church with the financial help of the Catholic Church in Poland.

6. The Old City of Bila-Skala once contained over forty Orthodox, Catholic, and Protestant churches on a relatively small land area. For the past sixty years, this Old City has remained in a state of ruin. The Armenian church was bombed during the war, and, like the Dominican church, its crypts are filled with human skeletons. One remaining synagogue was converted into a restaurant. Remaining

Ukrainian Orthodox, Polish Catholic, and Ukrainian Greek Catholic groups were reclaiming ownership of religious property confiscated by the Soviet state under Stalin. Ukrainian Greek Catholicism was outlawed and operated as the "Church in Catacombs," while Ukrainian Orthodox and Polish Catholic believers had some freedom of expression. The Russian Orthodox Church was the official church and a branch of the Soviet government.

7. In his book *Camera Lucida*, Roland Barthes described a process of discovering himself being turned into an object in the moment of being photographed: "[W]hat I see is that I have become a Total Image, which is to say, Death in person; others—the Other—do not dispossess me of myself, they turn me, ferociously, into an object, they put me at their mercy, at their mercy, classified as a file" (Barthes 1981:14).

8. Interviews with the Strokat family were conducted July/August 1992, Bila-Skala, Ukraine.

9. As Barbara Heldt points out, "There [was], of course, a gaping dichotomy between the rhetoric of reverence for women [in the former Soviet Union] and the actual use of their bodies in truly dangerous work, whether outside the home or in domestic drudgery. The high abortion rate . . . is also part of this disregard; contraceptive devices are in *defitsit* or not used by men" (Heldt 1989:163).

10. According to Dr. Tereshchenko of the Institute of Endocrinology and Metabolism, incidences of thyroid cancer in Ukrainian children living in contaminated territories were the following: 1986—7; 1989—13; 1991—26; 1992—47; 1993—43; 1995—46. The sharp rise in incidence also reflects the fact that monitoring had become more widespread in regions contaminated as a result of the Chernobyl disaster.

11. Offices of the Parliamentary Commission on Chernobyl, Kyiv, August 10, 1994

12. The minister, much admired, died suddenly two years later.

13. Categories represent further subdividing of disability status. Category One refers to workers who were recruited to clean up the plant in the first days following the disaster.

14. He continued, "So dentists do the ultrasound monitoring for us." Cases of thyroid cancer are expected to peak between 2000 and 2005.

15. Sveta was diagnosed with a condition called hypothyroidism. She was born in the western Ukrainian region of Zakarpattia, an area known for endemic iodine deficiency. Her deficiency was most likely not related to Chernobyl.

Chapter 4 Illness as Work: Human Market Transition

1. Territories surpassing the threshold limit were designated as state protected. Resettlement for populations living in these territories was guaranteed. Under Ukrainian law, the size of contaminated territories and types of contamination considered dangerous were expanded. The Exclusion Zone fell under the protection of the national government. The other three zones were demarcated

according to the severity of radioactivity measured in those areas. For example, Zone Two contains radioactivity in the following amounts: cesium 15 ki/km^2, strontium 3ki/km^2, plutonium 0.1ki/km^2. Zone Three contains radioactivity on the order of cesium 5–15ki/km^2, strontium 0.15–3ki/km^2, plutonium 0.01–0.1ki/km^2. The following radioactivity is found in Zone Four: cesium 1–5ki/km^2, strontium 0.02–0.15ki/km^2, plutonium 0.005–0.01ki/km^2. As of 1996, benefits to inhabitants of Zone Four were eliminated.

2. The complete name of the law is "On the Social Protection of Citizens Who Have Suffered as a Result of the Chernobyl Disaster." I refer to its provisions here as social protection acts.

3. Research in Russia shows that social organizing in response to economic pressures also transcends class, educational, and employment categories. See Ahl 1999.

4. To enter the system, sufferers were required to show proof of dose. Acceptable forms included documentation of (1) residency in one of the four zones; (2) a dose of irradiation exceeding the allowable threshold norms; (3) a dose value deduced from work routes, meteorological measurements, or chromosomal aberration counts; (4) a period of work in the zones; (5) degree of loss of labor capacity based on medical records; or (6) a court appearance in the company of witnesses testifying to the claimant's presence in the zones.

5. These numbers do not include children. In return for gaining and keeping their status, sufferers are obligated to undergo mandatory annual medical examinations. Compensation for sufferers includes free access to medicine, dental work, specialized medical care, and annual treatments in sanatoria. If a person has changed to a lower-paid or lower-ranked occupation owing to illness, the difference in salary is paid by the state. Paid sick leave is guaranteed during periods of treatment in sanatoria or of occupational disability. Other compensatory items include a guaranteed apartment, a free car, "clean groceries" at special stores, free public transport, free telephone service, interest-free loans for starting one's own business, paid vacation, monthly apartment rental subsidy, annual fuel subsidies, interest-free loans with government repayment of 25–50 percent of the principle for purchase of residence, allowances for persons living in high radiation zones, construction loans for relocated families, the right to purchase food at 50–75 percent of its actual cost, food items or cash equivalents for families with children too ill to go to school, and exemptions from payment of all taxes and customs duties. One of the best state protection packages is offered to parents with children who were born on or after April 26, 1986, in the zones. These children are given complete state protection until they reach school age. Families with children who are "disabled" receive yearly payment in the form of three minimal salaries as compensation for the damage of each child. Thus the system doubles as a form of welfare. For a complete list of benefits, see World Bank 1993:213–216.

6. "Center for Informing the Population on Questions Regarding the Liquidation of the Consequences of The Accident," *Vidlunnia*, October 4, 1996, Zhytomyr, Ukraine.

7. Ibid.

8. I take this appropriation as one aspect of the way images of suffering become objectified, how these objectifications are enacted by sufferers in ways that mask the stakes of human pain in bureaucratic and policy arenas. See Kleinman and Kleinman 1997.

9. Volodymyr Shatylo, Chernobyl Ministry, Zhytomyr, Ukraine, November 1996.

10. This statement refers to persons who did not hold a job within the official economy and were suspected of living on "unearned income."

11. Correspondence, April 15, 1997.

12. These committees are related to the overall Medical-Labor Expert Commission (in Russian, *Vrachebno-Trudovaya Expertna Kommissiia*). I refer to them as the *Ekspertiza*. These committees were founded throughout the Soviet Union in 1932 and at the height of Stalinist collectivization and industrialization campaigns. Their function was to arbitrate occupational disability claims.

13. Since 1991, Ukraine's economy has been characterized by economic and labor market declines and increased poverty. Exchange rates per $1.00 US plunged between 1992 and 1993. Instead of decreasing or phasing out state benefits or targeting most vulnerable groups, the state opted to maintain the real value of cash benefits, increasing social benefits and cash allowances to pensioners, the disabled, and other vulnerable groups. In 1992, the country's spending on the social sector constituted 40 percent of the GDP, far more than that of any other country in the world (World Bank 1996:1–3).

14. This to some degree follows a Soviet tradition in which higher wages were paid to compensate for hard manual or risky labor in difficult climatic conditions, such as in Siberia or at remote nuclear installations.

15. This organization is called the Medsanchas (medical sanitation unit). It contracts with the center to provide partial salaries and patient referrals from the Zone, particularly for cases in which a worker should receive additional monitoring before going on disability.

16. *Po blatu* means "by protection," or "by patronage."

17. See *Chornobyl'ska Tragediia 1996*.

18. These requests were made from the Council of Ministers of the USSR to the Ministry of Finance of the USSR, from the Council of Ministries of the republic of Ukraine to the Central Committee of the Communist Party of Ukraine or to the Ministry of Energy of the Soviet Union (*Chornobyl'ska Tragediia 1996*).

19. *Mohyl'nyky* are scattered across the Zone; in them contaminated equipment was destroyed and radioactive debris was buried.

20. Under Soviet laws governing worker disability, professional trade unions (*profspilky*), not individual state enterprises, were financially responsible for compensating the disabilities and deaths of workers returning from work in the Zone. The cost of the health burden of the Chernobyl cleanup essentially fell on these unions. To eliminate the cost, the unions began to work very closely with the Ukrainian republican apparatus to draft the Chernobyl laws.

21. Volodymyr Yavorivskyi, chair of the Democratic Party, Kyiv, November 1996.

22. Thus "no one was responsible for them. If these things were really

contaminated, then the authorities should have registered these items with some actual value, so that in the case they are taken out of the Zone, some tariff on these goods could be extracted, so that some responsibility for these items could be guaranteed." Member, Ukrainian Parliamentary Commission on Chernobyl, September 1996.

23. See Kovalchuk, "Ukraine: A Ministry That Started with a Bang," 1995.

24. "The Ukrainian SSR mandates the juridical regime of the Exclusion Zone, establishes contracts regarding work within the Zone with state organs of the Soviet Union and its other republics, foreign countries, and international organizations." "State Declaration on the Legacy of the Chernobyl Disaster,"1991.

25. There are 77 regionally based facilities; 24 *oblast* children and adult facilities; 121 specialized dispensaries (*spetz dispensary*). For example, the Kyiv *oblast* hospital No. 2 has 240 beds. The Kyiv *spetz dispensar* for radiation protection has 140 beds. The Radiation Research Center has 250 beds. Since 1990, the number of sufferers increased thus: 1990—94,000; 1991—1,200,000; 1992—2,800,000; 1993—2,915,000; 1994—3, 193,000; 1995—3,200,000.

26. The name of this village has been changed.

27. Personal communication, Radiation Research Center, Kyiv.

28. Payments-in-kind such as these have increased and are a supplement to unpaid salaries.

29. In fact, compensation to victims of the atomic bombs in Hiroshima and Nagasaki were not paid out in onetime payments. As in the Chernobyl case, authorities required victims to undergo some form of clinical monitoring in order to be eligible for compensations. See *Hiroshima and Nagasaki* 1981. For a history of the role of American science in accounting for the medical effects of the atomic bombings, see Lindee 1994.

30. Current laws guarantee that additional pensions on the basis of a Chernobyl-related disability cannot be lower, per month, than:

182.82 *hryvni* ($90)—for level one disability
145.43 *hryvni* ($72)—for level two disability
108.03 *hryvni* ($54)—for level three disability

Approximately half of the Chernobyl disabled obtain 100–200 *hryvni* (or $50–100).

31. Benedicte Ingstad and Susan Reynolds Whyte (1995) have shown how disability is as much a product of social definitions and restrictions and opportunities of access as it is a physical or functional limitation or disease.

32. He transported contaminated building materials from the reactor to burial pits (*mohyl'nyky*) scattered throughout the Exclusion Zone.

33. From the perspective of one medical examiner I interviewed, Chernobyl deaths "look like any other deaths." Kyiv City Morgue, November 1996.

34. The incidence of alcoholism in Ukraine was second-highest among all republics in the former Soviet Union; it was 136.4 per 100,000 in 1990.

35. He also abolished state requirements imposed on enterprises to make contributions to the fund.

36. "President Governs by Decree," *Ukrainian Weekly*, July 6, 1998, 1.

Chapter 5 Biological Citizenship

1. The half-life is the time it takes for half of an original amount of radiation to decay. Following the first half-life period, one-half of the original quantity remains. After the subsequent half-life period, one-quarter of the original quantity remains, and so forth, until no radiation is left.

2. For an anthropological account of scientific measures as they figure costs, see Petryna 1998.

3. For a historical look at the importance of the role of complaint mechanisms and denunciation practices in Soviet society, see Fitzpatrick 1999.

4. Because "there is no specific illness for radiation," its clinical pathological course is considered highly "individual," according to the view of many scientists, including Roman Protas, Kyiv-Mohyla Academy, Kyiv.

5. See also Michel Foucault's reflections on Lysenkoism as a starting point for his reflections on power and knowledge in Western psychiatry, in the essay "Truth and Power" (in Foucault 1984).

6. 0.01 rem represents the allowable threshold dose, in this case, specifically for the nervous system.

7. To this day, Rita has no witnesses testifying to her even having been at the Chernobyl plant at the time of the explosion.

8. Their numbers are broken down according to age: to 1 year of age—6 persons; to 3 years—5 persons; to 7 years—12 persons; to 14 years—19 persons; to 20 years—18 persons; 21–30 years—110 persons; 31–40 years—115 persons; 41–50 years—110 persons; 51–60 years–24 persons; 60+ years—8 persons.

9. Among the cases studied, 118 were found to have no relevance to the questions; the majority of individuals were considered to be experiencing acute radiation effects and exhibiting symptoms associated with radiation-induced damage; 9 had contracted ARS. The first reported indications of ARS were nausea, vomiting, and weakness, followed by typical manifestations of ARS (changes in the blood—leukopenia, lymphopenia, thrombocytenia, hemorrhagic syndrome, hair loss, and an asthenic disposition).

10. Some of these 148 displayed high blood pressure and gastrointestinal pains; 11 had skin lesions. Health disorders lasted up to 21 days or less. Some experienced disorders for 17 days, and in some the disorders lasted no more than 6 days.

11. He retired from this position in 2000.

12. See also "Index of Illnesses through Which a Connection with Ionizing Radiation and Other Negative Factors Can Be Established in the Adult Population Which Suffered as a Result of the Chernobyl Nuclear Disaster," Ukrainian Ministry of Health, 1996.

13. "The diagnosis of [these] disorders is to be registered by the neuropathologist after a detailed review of the state of health, the results of the electroencephalogram, rheoencephalogram, echocardiogram, computerized tomographic scan, roentgenography, consultation with the opthalmalogist and the psychologist" (*Chornobyl'ska Katastrofa* 1995:459).

14. A. P. Kartish, a neuropathologist, reorganized the work and nosographic

criteria by which the new Chernobyl medical-labor committees operated in the context of a keynote address at the eighth congress of neuropathologists, psychiatrists, and narcologists in Kharkiv in 1991. See also Bobileva 1994b.

15. In fact, she complained of leg pains, which she said the doctors would not treat.

16. Lev continued with his litany, reiterating familiar themes: "We didn't know anything. The first of May, everyone went to the streets for the demonstrations, there was an international bike race. In general it was kept quiet. Nobody said anything to anyone. They said everything was fine. The minister of health was on TV, Romanenko. He said there was no trouble, nothing terrible happened, not to worry. But the officials got their children out on the 26th of April, over the border. And you people, you die here. The Communist Party had that tendency, just for itself and the people are of no concern." Psychoneurological Hospital, March 1996, Kyiv.

17. Patient hunger strikes continued to occur, particularly in clinics in the Kharkiv area, where many coal miners had been recruited for Chernobyl work.

18. There were a great many of these meat items available on the streets, and people were stumped by the fact that these "tasteless" processed foods were in fact cheaper and becoming more abundant than domestically raised meats—more signs of national economic stagnation.

19. In Kyiv, some grave diggers reportedly began to charge more than five hundred dollars to bury a corpse, a fee considered astronomical by Ukrainian standards. Where autopsies had once been routine, they were now carried out only in extreme situations (for example, to ascertain cause of a wrongful death, such as homicide). Even the reporting of death was bureaucratically backlogged. While I was examining these statistics, the head statistician at the Ministry of Statistics asked me, rhetorically, "What's normal, anyway?"

20. State statistics provide a profile of the transition's human toll. Source: *Demohrafichnyi Istochnyk Naselennia Ukrainy* 1994.

	Birth Rate	Mortality Rate	Growth/Decline
1989	690,981	600,590	+90,391
1990	657,202	629,602	+27,600
1991	630,813	669,960	−39,147
1992	596,785	697,110	−100,325
1993	557,467	741,662	−184,195
1994	521,545	764,669	−243,124

21. See Ukrainskyi Blahodiinyi Soyuz Spilok Sotsial'noho Zakhystu Invalidiv Chornobylia 1994.

22. He headed a local facility for bone marrow transplantation and blood transfusion at the time of the disaster and was appointed deputy director of the center in 1986. Dr. Mudrak, the center's manager, also attended the meeting. His main function at the meeting was to remind Lehkyi of the center's needs. Mudrak added, "They are cutting off the food supply to forty of our leukemia patients, we need to pay our gas bill."

Chapter 6 Local Science and Organic Processes

1. This is of special interest in the current internationalization of human subjects research, where economic pressures can result in inadequate subject protection. My concern is with how a normative ethics of human subjects protection assumes variability across political-economic spheres; and with how ethics can be used to reify social and biological differences rather than to even the starting conditions in which research is done. See Petryna 2002.

2. For an illuminating treatment of tragic modes of emplotment, see White 1973:9.

3. Many workers at the Chernobyl plant were to be laid off owing to the plant's closure in December 2000.

4. Her characterization harmonizes with Kharkhordin's description of Soviet society as being governed by "mutual horizontal surveillance," which ensured the dominance of the collective and the suppression of individual public disloyalty. "Through reinforcing images of a monolithic society a typical Soviet citizen persuaded himself that an individual deviant had no chances of survival" (1999:278).

5. To live in this social arrangement involved ambivalence. The Ukrainian word for ambivalence is *dvoyeridnist'*, literally translated as "two natures." Ambivalence will be an important thematic undercurrent throughout this chapter. Sigmund Freud used the term to account for the emotional state of neurotics in clinical settings, a state characterized by simultaneous affirmation and negation of will (Laplanche and Pontalis 1973:214).

6. Thanks to Joseph Dumit for this phrasing.

7. Ceanu's collaborators in the center's experimental radiobiological division conducted analyses of rodent brains to show that large doses (up to 2 gray) did not influence the electrophysiology of brain cuts.

8. According to these researchers, contact with radiation leads to immediate injury that was "masked" and unregistered for five to six years after the disaster. A "pseudorecovery" and subsequent "decompensation" set in by 1991, when lesions and scars started to be registered in various exposed populations (Romodanov et al. 1994:78).

9. Ceanu's researchers used control populations from state-designated "clean" territories within Ukraine, as well as from Kyiv.

10. He described it as an "extraordinary complex" that was very hard to resolve. Persons suffering from radiophobia, he argued, "do not believe anyone or anything." They "connect the most trivial ailments with the effect of radioactive substances." As a result, common illnesses become something more complicated and the person "does himself a terrible service" (Marples 1988:49).

11. Some Ukrainian state officials have used this view as an argument to stop costly resettlements of people living in state-designated contaminated zones.

12. Most research into long-term mental health effects has typically been based on self-reports and subjective scaling. Researchers use state-specified zone boundaries to demarcate experimental populations and rely on healthy

populations living in "distant clean territories" as their control (Rumyantseva et al. 1996:529).

13. As we have seen in the case of Kyryl in chapter 5, such approaches also invited certain forms of political abuse.

14. According to Borovsky, controversy over the neuropsychiatric effects of ionizing radiation has lasted for the past 100 years. "Some authors object to the basic fact of the existence of the problem and say these effects do not exist below 20–60 gray. That debate isn't yet decided: some researchers think there are effects below 1 gray, others think they start somewhere at 2–4 gray. The disagreement occurs not so much in the acknowledgment of the actual psycho-neurological symptoms, but in the attribution of the role of ionizing radiation to their origin."

15. Borovsky also coordinates internationally sponsored research on radiation-related schizophrenia and schizophrenic spectrum disorders. He is developing a classification of mental disorders linked with Chernobyl and to be incorporated (and updated every two years) in the state administration of Chernobyl patients. A person subject to radiation, according to Borovsky, can experience a specific psychoneurological course, from neurosis-like and psychopathic-like disorders (cerebrasthenia), to psychosomatic disorders and encephalopathy, to organic personality development and endogenous-like organic processes.

16. Talal Asad critiques an anthropological thesis that ascribes the agency and creativity of non-European people to their being "local" in relation to a "world system" of cultural domination. "In a literal sense, of course, all people most of the time are 'local' in the sense of being locatable." Saudi theologians "who invoke the authority of medieval Islamic texts are taken as local; Western writers who invoke the authority of modern secular literature claim they are universal [and] located in universes that have rules of inclusion and exclusion." The difference is power and what Asad calls "the discursive definitions of authorized space" (1993:8).

17. Their circumstances, akin to what Allan Young notes in the context of PTSD research, permit them "to buy time for their findings—the time to work with them, time to mature them into facts through connecting them (via research technologies) to fact-rich sciences" (Young 1995:272).

18. Ukrainians were referred to as "little Russians" (*malorossy*) in the Russian czarist empire.

19. He switched to police work. I tried to contact him three times, and three times he hung up on me, leading me to believe that he had left the ward on bad terms.

20. A *soroksotok* is a typical parcel of land, forty meters in width and a hundred meters in length.

21. I checked his medical records afterward. They indicated that Pylypko "drove people out of the Zone during the disaster at Chernobyl." He "complained of pains in the heart," he "neither drank nor smoked," and his "dose is unknown."

22. This practice contrasts with the more well-known abuses aimed at political dissidents, who were often subjected to experimental drug treatments and tranquilization. See Reich 1999.

23. For a rich discussion of Pavlov's laboratory culture, see Todes 1997.

24. Tolkach continued to reflect upon Freud's absence from Soviet psychiatric texts. "Freud writes about spiritual activity. But a Communist denies the very existence of the soul, there's no god and there is no soul. The Communist has a materialistic outlook on the human. He is born, dies, and is buried, and doesn't have an afterlife. For this reason, the theories of Pavlov had long-lasting interest."

25. Topographical mapping of short and long SSEP (somato-sensory evoked potentials) allows a characterization of the processes of perception and the workings of somato-sensory afferentation in all directions from the periphery to the brain stem. The machine measuring the electrical activity of the brain was used monopolarly, with referent electrodes placed on the lobes of the ear. Scalp electrodes were used according to the international scheme "10–20." See Maurer and Dierks 1991:104. Also see Zenkov and Roikin 1991:640. See Dumit 1995 for an ethnographic analysis of the science of neuroimaging and reclassifications of psychiatric disorders.

26. See Flor-Henry 1979:189–193. This case analysis is based, in part, on Petryna and Biehl 1999.

27. The observation of this case took place in June 1996, Radiation Research Center, Kyiv.

28. Oleg had two children from a previous marriage.

29. This measure was applied over a seventy-year average life span (see chapter 2).

30. For details on this area of uranium ore extraction and public health effects, see Garb 1994.

31. Children are defined as persons below the age of fourteen. Statistics for the years 1986, 1987, 1996, and 1997 are not available.

32. *Oblast* is a territorial administrative unit analogous to a county in the United States.

33. The category of adults includes teenagers who are fourteen or older.

34. According to the United Nations Scientific Committee on the Effects of Radiation (1969), defects in the internal organs, spine, cranium, and brain stem appear on the fortieth day of the life of the forming fetus, and serious head defects begin to appear on the fiftieth day (Guskova and Baysogolov 1971:245–246).

35. This analysis draws in part on Claude Lévi-Strauss's analysis of the effectiveness of symbols in healing to illuminate how individual histories and family dramas fuse with a clinical research program to induce illness. In the essay, a Cuna woman loses one of her spirit doubles (*purba*), a spirit whose role is to provide necessary vital strength for childbirth. Assisted by tutelary spirits, the shaman undertakes a journey to the supernatural world, constructing a "mythical anatomy" that "lights the healer's way" to the malevolent spirit (the abusive "Muu"). He succeeds in snatching the double, the power responsible for the formation of the fetus, from the Muu. By restoring it to its owner, he achieves the cure (1963:188). In applying some of the lessons of this scene, I consider what scientific research restores to the mother, and what the mother's narrative restores to science.

36. These recommendations are part of the ongoing "Brain Damage *In Utero*" research program in the affected parts of Belarus, Ukraine, and Russia.

37. "Exposed adults, particularly women, had elevated somatization, anxiety, depressive, and post-traumatic stress symptoms during the first decade after the accident" (Bromet et al. 2000:564).

38. The tests were borrowed from the book *Controlled Projection for Children*, by J. C. Raven (London: H. K. Lewis, 1951); and *Children's Drawings as Measures of Intellectual Maturity*, by D. B. Harris (New York: Harcourt, Brace, and World, 1963).

Bibliography

Ackerman, Galia. 2000. "Belarus: Facing the Disaster Alone." *UNESCO Courier*, October, 14–20.

Agamben, Giorgio. 1998. *Homo Sacer: Sovereign Power and Bare Life*. Translated by D. Heller-Roazen. Stanford: Stanford University Press.

Ahl, Richard. 1999. "Society and Transition in Post-Soviet Russia." *Communist and Post-Communist Studies* 32, no. 2:175–182.

Anspaugh, L. R., et al. 1988. "The Global Impact of the Chernobyl Reactor Accident." *Science* 242:1513–1519.

Arendt, Hannah. 1989. *The Human Condition*. Chicago: University of Chicago Press.

Aronowitz, Robert. 1998. *Making Sense of Illness: Science, Society, and Disease*. Cambridge: Cambridge University Press.

Asad, Talal. 1993. *Genealogies of Religion: Discipline and Reasons of Power in Christianity and Islam*. Baltimore: Johns Hopkins University Press.

———. 1994. "Ethnographic Representation, Statistics, and Modern Power." *Social Research* 61, no. 1:55–89.

Ashwin, Sarah. 1999. "Redefining the Collective: Russian Mineworkers in Transition." In *Uncertain Transition: Ethnographies of Change in the Postsocialist World*, edited by Michael Burawoy and Katherine Verdery, 245–273. Lanham, MD: Rowman & Littlefield.

Baranov, A., et al. 1989. "Bone Marrow Transplantation after the Chernobyl Nuclear Accident." *New England Journal of Medicine* 321, no. 4:205–212.

Barthes, Roland. 1981. *Camera Lucida: Reflections on Photography*. Translated by R. Howard. New York: Hill and Wang.

Beck, Ulrich. 1987. "The Anthropological Shock: Chernobyl and the Contours of the Risk Society." *Berkeley Journal of Sociology* 32:153–165.

Beck, Ulrich. 1992. *Risk Society: Towards a New Modernity*. London: Sage.

———. 1999. *World Risk Society*. Cambridge: Polity Press; Malden, MA: Blackwell.

Bergson, Henri. 1991. *Matter and Memory*. Translated by N. M. Paul and W. S. Palmer. New York: Zone Books.

Berkovitz, Don. 1989. "Price-Anderson Act: Model Compensation Legislation?—The Sixty-Three Million Dollar Question." *Harvard Environmental Law Review* 13, no. 11:1–49.

Biehl, João. 1999."Other Life: AIDS, Biopolitics, and Subjectivity in Brazil's Zones of Social Abandonment." Ph.D. diss., University of California, Berkeley.

———. 2001. "Technology and Affect: HIV/AIDS Testing in Brazil." *Culture, Medicine, and Psychiatry* 25:87–129.

Blumenberg, Hans. 1983. *The Legitimacy of the Modern Age*. Translated by R. Wallace. Cambridge: MIT Press.

Bobileva, Natalia. 1994a. *Issues of Radiation Psychiatry*. Kyiv: Institute of Forensic Psychiatry and the Ministry of Chernobyl of Ukraine.

———. 1994b. *Methodological Recommendations of the Ministry of Health and NAMS of 'Express-Evaluation' of Psychiatric Status*. Kyiv: Ministry of Health of Ukraine.

Bohatiuk, Yurii. 1986. "The Chornobyl Disaster." *Ukrainian Quarterly* 42, no. 1–2:5–21.

Bol'shaia Meditsinskaia Entsiklopediia. 1956. Edited by A. N. Bakulev. Moscow: Gosudarstvennyi Izdatel'stvo Meditsinskoi Literaturi.

Bondar, A. Y., et al. 1996. "Spectrum of Chromosomal Aberrations in Peripheral Lymphocytes of Workers of the Zone of Exclusion." Draft manuscript, Scientific Center of Radiation Medicine.

Borneman, John. 1997. *Settling Accounts: Violence, Justice, and Accountability in Post-Socialist Europe*. Princeton: Princeton University Press.

Brandt, Allan. 1997. "Behavior, Disease, and Health in the Twentieth-Century United States: The Moral Valence of Individual Risk." In *Morality and Health*, edited by A. Brandt and P. Rozin, 53–78. New York: Routledge.

Bromet, Evelyn, et al. 2000. "Children's Well-being Eleven Years after the Chornobyl Catastrophe." *Archives of General Psychiatry* 57:563–571.

Brown, Lesley, ed. 1993. *The New Shorter Oxford English Dictionary on Historical Principles*. 2 vols. Oxford: Clarendon Press.

Brown, Wendy. 1995. *States of Injury: Power and Freedom in Late Modernity*. Princeton: Princeton University Press.

Bullard, Robert. 2000. *Dumping in Dixie: Race, Class, and Environmental Quality*. Boulder, CO: Westview Press.

Burawoy, Michael, and Katherine Verdery, eds. 1999. *Uncertain Transition: Ethnographies of Change in the Postsocialist World*. Lanham, MD: Rowman & Littlefield.

Burchell, Graham, Colin Gordon, and Peter Miller, eds. 1991. *The Foucault Effect: Studies in Governmentality*. Chicago: University of Chicago Press.

Cabinet of Ministers of Ukraine. 1996. "Results of the Liquidation of the Consequences of the Chornobyl' Catastrophe after Ten Years." Address. *Dzerkalo Nedeli*, April 27–May 6, 1.

Callahan, Daniel. 1999. "The Social Sciences and the Task of Bioethics." *Daedalus* 128, no. 4:275–294.

Calloway, Paul. 1991. *Russian/Soviet and Western Psychiatry: A Contemporary Comparative Study*. New York: Wiley.

Canguilhem, Georges. 1989. "A New Concept of Pathology: Error." In *The Normal and the Pathological*, 275–288. New York: Urzone.

———. 1994. *A Vital Rationalist: Selected Writings of Georges Canguilhem*. Edited by F. Delaporte. New York: Urzone.

Chatterjee, A., and W. Holley. 1994. "Computer Simulation of Initial Events in the Biochemical Mechanisms of DNA Damage." In *Advances in Radiation Biology*, vol. 1, edited by J. Lett and W. Sinclair, 181–225. Washington, DC: Academic Press.

Chen, Lincoln, Arthur Kleinman,and Norma Ware, eds. 1994. *Health and Social Change in International Perspective*. Cambridge: Harvard University Press.

"Chernobyl's Legacy to Science." 1996. *Nature* 380:653.

Chernousenko, Vladimir. 1991. *Chernobyl: Insight from the Inside*. Berlin, New York: Springer-Verlag.

Chornobyl': Problemy Zdorov'ia Naselennia. Vol. 1. 1995. Kyiv: Academy of Science of Ukraine and the Institute of History.

Chornobyl': The Ten Year Battle. 1996. Kyiv: Ministry of Chernobyl of Ukraine.

Chornobyl'ska Katastrofa. 1995. Kyiv: Naukova Dumka.

Chornobyl'ska Tragediia: Dokumenty I Materialy. 1996. Kyiv: Naukova Dumka.

Churchill, Larry. 1999. "Are We Professionals? A Critical Look at the Social Role of Bioethicists." *Daedalus* 128, no. 4:253–274.

Cirlot, J. E. 1971. *A Dictionary of Symbols*. Translated by J. Sage. New York: Philosophical Library.

Cohen, Lawrence. 1999. "Where It Hurts: Indian Material for an Ethics of Organ Transplantation." *Daedalus* 128, no. 4:135–166.

Conquest, Robert. 1986. *The Harvest of Sorrow: Soviet Collectivization and the Terror-Famine*. New York: Oxford University Press.

Cook, Linda. 1996. *The Soviet Social Contract and Why It Failed*. Cambridge: Harvard University Press.

Crossette, Barbara. 1995. "Chernobyl Trust Fund Depleted as Problems of Victims Grow." *New York Times*, November 29, A11.

Das, Veena. 1995. *Critical Events: An Anthropological Perspective on Contemporary India*. Delhi and New York: Oxford University Press.

———. 1998. "Wittgenstein and Anthropology." *Annual Review of Anthropology* 27:171–195.

Dawson, Jane. 1996. *Eco-Nationalism: Anti-Nuclear Activism and National Identity in Russia, Lithuania, and Ukraine*. Durham, NC: Duke University Press.

Demohraphichnyi Istochnyk Naselennia Ukrainy. 1994. Kyiv: Ministry of Statistics of Ukraine.

Department of Energy. 1993. *DNA Damage by Radon Particles and Molecular Mechanisms of Its Repair in Human Cells*. Washington, DC.

Desjarlais R., et al. 1995. *World Mental Health: Problems, and Priorities in Low-Income Countries*. New York: Oxford University Press.

241

Dobbs, Michael. 1992. "Chernobyl's 'Shameless Lies.'" *Washington Post*, April 27, A12.

Donahue, R. E., et al. 1986. "Stimulation of Haematopoiesis in Primates by Continuous Infusion of Recombinant Human GM-CSF." *Nature* 321:872–875.

Drottz-Sjoberg, B. M. 1995. "Risk Perception Research and Disaster." In *Mental Health Consequences of the Chernobyl Disaster: Current State and Future Prospects*, edited by K. Loganovsky and K. Yuriev, 25. Kyiv: Physicians of Chernobyl.

Dubrova, Y. E., et al. 1996. "Human Mini-Satellite Mutation Rate after the Chernobyl Accident." *Nature* 380:683–686.

Dumit, Joseph. 1995. "Mindful Images: PET Scans and Personhood in Biomedical America." Ph.D. diss., University of California, Santa Cruz.

———. 2000. "When Explanations Rest: 'Good Enough' Brain Science and the New Biomental Disorders." In *Living and Working with the New Medical Technologies: Intersections of Inquiry*, edited by Margaret Lock, Alan Young, and Alberto Cambrosio, 209–232. Cambridge: Cambridge University Press.

Dunham, Vera. 1976. *In Stalin's Time: Middle-Class Values in Soviet Fiction*. Cambridge: Cambridge University Press.

Estroff, Sue. 1993. "Identity, Disability, and Schizophrenia: The Problem of Chronicity." In *Knowledge, Power, and Practice: The Anthropology of Medicine and Everyday Life*, edited by S. Lindenbaum and M. Lock, 247–286. Berkeley and Los Angeles: University of California Press.

Estroff, Sue, et al. 1997. "'No Other Way to Go': Pathways to Disability Income Application among Persons with Severe Persistent Mental Illness." In *Mental Disorder, Work Disability, and the Law*, edited by R. Bonnie and J. Monahan, 55–104. Chicago: University of Chicago Press.

Farmer, Paul. 1999. *Infections and Inequalities: The Modern Plagues*. Berkeley and Los Angeles: University of California Press.

Favor, J. 1989. "Risk Estimation Based on Germ-Cell Mutations in Animals." *Genome* 31:844–849.

Feshbach, Murray, and Alfred Friendly. 1989. *Ecocide in the USSR: Health and Nature under Siege*. New York: Basic Books.

Field, Mark. 1957. *Doctor and Patient in Soviet Russia*. Cambridge: Harvard University Press.

———. 1967. *Soviet Socialized Medicine: An Introduction*. New York: Free Press.

Fitzpatrick, Sheila. 1999. *Everyday Stalinism: Ordinary Life in Extraordinary Times: Soviet Russia in the 1930s*. New York: Oxford University Press.

Flor-Henry, Pierre. 1979. "Neurophysiological Studies of Schizophrenia, Mania, and Depression." In *Hemisphere Asymmetries of Function in Psychopathology*, edited by J. Gruzelier and P. Flor-Henry. Amsterdam and New York: Elsevier/North Holland Biomedical Press.

Foucault, Michel. 1973. *Birth of the Clinic: An Archaeology of Medical Perception*. London: Sheridan.

———. 1980a. *The History of Sexuality*. Vol. 1. New York: Vintage.

———. 1980b. *Power/Knowledge: Selected Interviews and Other Writings, 1972–1977*. Edited by Colin Gordon. Brighton, Sussex: Harvester.

242

——. 1984. *The Foucault Reader*. Edited by P. Rabinow. New York: Pantheon Books.

Freud, Sigmund. 1950. *Totem and Taboo*. Translated by J. Strachey. New York: W. W. Norton.

Garb, Paula. 1994. "Sociocultural Responses to Radiation Contamination in Russia and Some Comparisons with the United States." Paper presented at the annual meeting of the American Anthropological Association. Washington, DC.

Geertz, Clifford. 1983. *Local Knowledge: Further Essays in Interpretive Anthropology*. New York: Basic Books.

Gerovitch, Slava. 1999. "Speaking Cybernetically: The Soviet Remaking of an American Science." Ph.D. diss., Massachusetts Institute of Technology.

Gledhill, John. 2000. *Power and Its Disguises: Anthropological Perspectives on Politics*. 2d ed. London: Pluto Press.

Gofman, John. 1981. *Radiation and Human Health*. San Francisco: Sierra Club Books.

Gordon, Colin. 1991. "Government Rationality: An Introduction." In *The Foucault Effect: Studies in Governmentality*, edited by G. Burchell, C. Gordon, and P. Miller, 1–52. Chicago: University of Chicago Press.

Gould, Jay. 1993. "Chernobyl—The Hidden Tragedy." *Nation*. March 15, 31–34.

Graham, Loren. 1987. *Science, Philosophy, and Human Behavior in the Soviet Union*. New York: Columbia University Press.

——. 1993. *Science in Russia and the Soviet Union: A Short History*. Cambridge: Cambridge University Press.

——. 1998. *What Have We Learned about Science and Technology from the Russian Experience?* Stanford: Stanford University Press.

Grant, Bruce. 1995. *In the Soviet House of Culture: A Century of Perestroikas*. Princeton: Princeton University Press.

Green, Peter. 2001. "Czechs Debate Benefits of Smokers' Dying Prematurely." *New York Times*, July 21, B2.

Greenberg, Daniel. 2000. "Slow Progress towards Protecting People in US Clinical Trials." *Lancet* 355, no. 9214:1527.

Groys, Boris. 1992. *The Total Art of Stalinism: Avant-Garde, Aesthetic Dictatorship, and Beyond*. Translated by C. Rougle. Princeton: Princeton University Press.

Guskova, Angelina. 1995. "Radiation and the Brain." In *Mental Health Consequences of the Chernobyl Disaster: Current State and Future Prospects*, edited by K. Loganovsky and K. Yuriev, 22. Kyiv: Physicians of Chernobyl.

——. 1997. "Current Issues in Clinical Radiobiology and Ways of Resolving Them Experimentally." *Radiatsionnaia Biologiia, Radioecologiia* 37, no. 4:604–612.

Guskova, A., and G. Baysogolov. 1971. *Radiation Sickness in Man: Outlines*. Moscow: Meditsina.

Hacking, Ian. 1990. *Taming of Chance*. Cambridge: Cambridge University Press.

——. 1991. "How Should We Do a History of Statistics?" In *The Foucault Effect: Studies in Governmentality*, edited by G. Burchell, C. Gordon, and P. Miller, 181–197. Chicago: University of Chicago Press.

243

Hamilton, James, and Kip Viscusi. 1997. "The Benefits and Costs of Regulatory Reforms for Superfund." *Stanford Environmental Law Journal* 16, no. 159:159–197.

Havenaar, J. M., et al. 1996. "Psychological Consequences of the Chernobyl Disaster." In *The Radiological Consequences of the Chernobyl Accident*, 435–453. Brussels: European Commission.

Heldt, Barbara. 1989. "Gynoglasnost: Writing the Feminine." In *Perestroika and Soviet Women*, edited by M. Buckley, 160–175. Cambridge: Cambridge University Press.

Hiroshima and Nagasaki: The Physical, Medical, and Social Effects of the Atomic Bombings. 1981. Translated by Eisei Ishikawa and David L. Swain. New York: Basic Books.

Humphrey, Caroline. 1999. "Traders, Disorder, and Citizenship Regimes in Provincial Russia." In *Uncertain Transition: Ethnographies of Change in the Postsocialist World*, edited by Michael Burawoy and Katherine Verdery, 19–52. Lanham, MD: Rowman & Littlefield.

Hunt, W. A. 1987. "Effects of Ionizing Radiation in Behavior." In *Military Radiobiology*, edited by J. J. Conklin and E. I. Walker, 321–330. San Diego: Academic Press.

IAEA (International Atomic Energy Agency). 1986. *Soviet State Committee on the Utilization of Atomic Energy, Report to the IAEA*. Vienna.

———. 1991a. *The International Chernobyl Project: Assessment of Radiological Consequences and Evaluation of Protective Measures*. Report by an International Advisory Committee. Vienna.

———. 1991b. *The International Chernobyl Project: Proceedings of an International Conference Held in Vienna*.

Index of Illnesses through Which a Connection with Ionizing Radiation and Other Negative Factors Can Be Established in the Adult Population Which Suffered as a Result of the Chernobyl Nuclear Disaster. 1996. Kyiv: Ministry of Health of Ukraine.

Indicators of Health and Assistance among Sufferers of the Chornobyl Nuclear Power Plant Disaster. 1998. Kyiv: Ministry of Health of Ukraine.

Indicators of Health among Sufferers of the Chornobyl Nuclear Power Plant Disaster (1987–1995). 1995. Kyiv: Ministry of Chernobyl and Ministry of Health of Ukraine.

Ingstad, Benedicte, and Susan Reynolds Whyte, eds. 1995. *Disability and Culture*. Berkeley and Los Angeles: University of California Press.

Inkeles, Alex, and Raymond Bauer. 1959. *The Soviet Citizen: Daily Life in a Totalitarian Society*. Cambridge: Harvard University Press.

International Classification of Diseases, 9th revision. Washington, DC: U.S. Department of Health and Human Services, 1991.

International Nuclear Safety Advisory Group. 1986. *Summary Report on the Post-Accident Review Meeting on the Chernobyl Accident*.

Ionizing Radiation: Sources and Biological Effects: Report to the General Assembly. 1982. United Nations, New York.

IPHECA Pilot Project. 1991. *Brain Damage In-Utero*. Geneva: World Health Organization.

Jacob, François. 1988. *The Statue Within*. New York: Basic Books.

Jasanoff, Sheila. 1997. "NGO's and the Environment: From Knowledge to Action." *Third World Quarterly* 18, no. 3:579–594.

Jensen, R., et al. 1994. "Molecular Cytogenetic Approaches to the Development of Biomarkers." In *Biomarkers for Worker Health Monitoring*, 100–120. Washington, DC: Department of Energy.

———. 1995. "Elevated Frequency of Glycophorin A Mutations in Erythrocytes from Chernobyl Accident Victims." *Radiation Research* 141, no. 2:129–135.

Keller, Evelyn Fox. 1989. *Secrets of Life, Secrets of Death*. New York: Routledge.

Khaliavka, Irina. 1996. *State of Health of Individuals with Acute Radiation Sickness during the Chernobyl Catastrophe and Avenues toward Treatment*. Kyiv: Academy of Medical Sciences of Ukraine.

Kharkhordin, Oleg. 1999. *The Collective and the Individual in Russia: A Study of Practices*. Berkeley and Los Angeles: University of California Press.

Khomaziuk, Inna. 1994. *Functional Changes in the Circulatory System Have Psychogenic Etiologies in Sufferers of the Chernobyl Catastrophe: Conceptions, Disputed Issues, and Errors in Diagnostics*. Kyiv: Ministry of Health of Ukraine.

Kimeldorf, D. J., and E. L. Hunt. 1965. *Ionizing Radiation: Neural Function and Behavior*. New York: Academic Press.

Kleinman, Arthur. 1986. *Social Origins of Distress and Disease*. New Haven: Yale University Press.

———. 1988. *The Illness Narratives: Suffering, Healing, and the Human Condition*. New York: Basic Books.

———. 1999. "Moral Experience and Ethical Reflection: Can Ethnography Reconcile Them? A Quandary for 'The New Bioethics.'" *Daedalus* 128, no. 4:69–99.

Kleinman, Arthur, Veena Das, and Margaret Lock. 1996. "Introduction." *Daedalus* 125, no. 1:xi–xx.

Kleinman, Arthur, and Joan Kleinman. 1997. "The Appeal of Experience, the Dismay of Images: Cultural Appropriations of Suffering in Our Times." *Daedalus* 135, no. 1:1–24.

Kleinman, Arthur, and Adriana Petryna. 2001. "Health: Anthropological Perspectives." In *International Encyclopedia of the Social and Behavioral Sciences*. London: Elsevier Science.

Kohler, Robert. 2001. "The Particularity of Biology in the Field." Manuscript, Princeton Workshop in the History of Science. "Model Systems, Cases, and Exemplary Narratives." Princeton University.

Kommunist. 1996. 36, no. 129:4.

Kornai, Janos. 1992. *The Socialist System: The Political Economy of Socialism*. Princeton: Princeton University Press.

Kostenko, Lina. 1996. "Dahlias along the Chernobyl Path." *Zhyva Voda*, April, 5.

Kovalchuk, Vasyl. 1995. "Ukraine: A Ministry That Started with a Bang." *DHA News* (Department of Humanitarian Affairs, United Nations), no. 16 (September/October): 4.

Krawchenko, Bohdan. 1985. *Social Change and National Consciousness in Twentith-Century Ukraine*. Basingstoke, Hampshire: Macmillan.

245

Kristeva, Julia. 1989. *Black Sun: Depression and Melancholia*. Translated by L. S. Roudiez. New York: Columbia University Press.

Kuzmin, Y. S. 1963. "On the Content of Soviet Psychology." *Voprosi Psikhologii* 9, no. 1:142–145.

Lacan, Jacques. 1977. *Ecrits: A Selection*. Translated by A. Sheridan. New York: Norton.

———. 1978, "Tuche and Automaton." In *The Four Fundamental Concepts of Psycho-Analysis*, edited by J.-A. Miller, translated by A. Sheridan, 53–67. New York: W. W. Norton.

Laplanche, J. and J. B. Pontalis. 1973. *The Language of Psychoanalysis*. Translated by D. Nicholson-Smith. New York: Norton.

Latour, Bruno, and Steve Woolgar. 1986. *Laboratory Life: The Construction of Scientific Facts*. Princeton: Princeton University Press.

Lazjuk, G. I., D. I. Nikolaev, and R. D. Khmel. 2000. "Epidemiology of Congenital Malformations in Belarus and the Chernobyl Accident." *American Journal of Human Genetics* 67, no. 4:214.

Ledeneva, Alena. 1998. *Russia's Economy of Favours: Blat, Networking, and Informal Exchange*. Cambridge: Cambridge University Press.

Lévi-Strauss, Claude. 1963. "The Effectiveness of Symbols." In *Structural Anthropology*, 186–205. New York: Basic Books.

Lewontin, Richard. 1992. *Biology as Ideology: The Doctrine of DNA*. New York: HarperPerennial.

Lifton, Robert. 1967. *Death in Life: Survivors in Hiroshima*. New York: Random House.

Lindee, Susan. 1994. *Suffering Made Real: American Science and the Survivors at Hiroshima*. Chicago: University of Chicago Press.

Lock, Margaret. 1993. *Encounters with Aging: Mythologies of Menopause in Japan and North America*. Berkeley and Los Angeles: University of California Press.

Loganovsky, K. and K. Yuriev, eds. 1995. *Mental Health Consequences of the Chernobyl Disaster: Current State and Future Prospects*. Kyiv: Physicians of Chernobyl.

Long-Term Health Consequences of the Chernobyl Disaster. 1998. Proceedings of the second International Conference, June 1–6. Kyiv: Chernobylinterinform.

Managing the Legacy of Chernobyl. 1994. Washington, DC: World Bank.

Marples, David. 1988. *The Social Impact of the Chernobyl Disaster*. New York: St. Martin's Press.

———. 1989. *Ukraine under Perestroika: Ecology, Economics, and the Worker's Revolt*. New York: St. Martin's Press.

Martin, Emily. 1994. *Flexible Bodies: Tracking Immunity in American Culture from the Days of Polio to the Age of AIDS*. Boston: Beacon Press.

Maurer, K., and T. Dierks. 1991. *Atlas of Brain Mapping: Topographic Mapping of EEG and Evoked Potentials*. Berlin: Springer-Verlag.

Mauss, Marcel. 1985. "A Category of the Human Mind: The Notion of Person; the Notion of Self." In *The Category of the Person*, edited by M. Carrithers, S. Collins, and S. Lukes, translated by W. D. Halls. Cambridge: Cambridge University Press.

————. 1990. *The Gift: The Form and Reason for Exchange in Archaic Societies.* New York: Norton.

Medvedev, Zhores. 1990. *The Legacy of Chernobyl.* New York: W. W. Norton.

Merridale, Catherine. 2000. *Night of Stone: Death and Memory in Russia.* London: Granta.

Minow, Martha. 1998. *Between Vengeance and Forgiveness: Facing History after Genocide and Mass Violence.* Boston: Beacon Press.

Monroy R. L., et al. 1986. "The Effect of Recombinant GM-CSF on the Recovery of Monkeys Transplanted with Autologous Bone Marrow." *Blood* 70, no. 5:1696–1699.

Nyagu, Angelina, et al. 1995a. "Psychoneurological Characteristics of Persons with Acute Radiation Sickness." In *Mental Health Consequences of the Chernobyl Disaster: Current State and Future Prospects*, edited by K. Lohanovsky and K. Yuriev, 115. Kyiv: Physicians of Chernobyl.

————. 1995b. "Remote Psychoneurological Consequences of Chernobyl NPP: Results and Priority Directions." In *Mental Health Consequences of the Chernobyl Disaster: Current State and Future Prospects*, edited by K. Lohanovsky and K. Yuriev, 31. Kyiv: Physicians of Chernobyl.

Nyagu, A., et al. 1996. "Mental Health of Prenatally Irradiated Children: A Psychophysiological Study." *Social and Clinical Psychiatry* (in Russian) 6, no. 1:23–36.

Nyagu, A., and Loganovsky, K. 1998. *Neuropsychiatric Effects of Ionizing Radiation.* Kyiv: Physicians of Chernobyl.

Nyagu, A., K. N. Loganovsky, and T. K. Loganovskaja. 1998. "Psychophysiological Aftereffects of Prenatal Irradiation." *International Journal of Psychophysiology* 30, no. 3:303–311.

————. 2000. "Intelligence and Brain Damage Following Prenatal Irradiation." Draft manuscript. Scientific Center of Radiation Medicine, Kyiv, Ukraine.

One Decade after Chernobyl: Summing Up the Consequences of the Accident, Proceedings of an International Conference. 1996. Vienna: International Atomic Energy Agency.

Palsson, Gisli, and Paul Rabinow. 1999. "Iceland: The Case of a National Human Genome Project." *Anthropology Today* 15, no. 5:14–18.

Parsons, Talcott. 1991. *The Social System.* London: Routledge.

Pass, B., et al. 1997. "Collective Dosimetry as a Dosimetric Gold-Standard: A Study of Three Radiation Accidents." *Health Physics* 72, no. 3:390–396.

Pearce, Fred. 2000. "Chernobyl: The Political Fall-out Continues." *UNESCO Courier*, October, 10.

Petryna, Adriana. 1998. "A Technical Error: Measures of Life after Chernobyl." *Social Identities* 4, no. 1:73–92.

————. 1999. "Chernobyl Effects: Social Identity and the Politics of Life in Post-Socialist Ukraine." Ph.D. diss., University of California, Berkeley.

————. 2002. "The Human Subjects Research Industry." Manuscript. W.H.R. Rivers Workshop. "Global Pharmaceuticals: Ethics, Markets, Practice." Harvard University.

Petryna, Adriana, and João Biehl. 1999. "O Estado Clinico: A Constituicao de uma Crianca Invalida." *Revista da Associação Psicanalitica de Porto Alegre* (Porto Alegre, Brazil) 7, no. 13.

Petryna, Adriana, and Kleinman, Arthur. 2001. "La Mondialisation des catégories: la Dépression à l'épreuve de l'universel." *L'Autre Cliniques, Cultures et Sociétés* 2, no. 3:467–480.

Pierce, D. A., et al. 1996. "Studies of the Mortality of Atomic Bomb Survivors." Report 23, Part 1. Cancer: 1950–1990. *Radiation Research* 146:1–27.

Pilinskaya, M. A. 1999. "Cytogenetic Effects in Somatic Cells of Chernobyl Accident Survivors as Bio-Marker of Low Radiation Doses Exposure." *International Journal of Radiation Medicine* 2, no. 2:83–95.

Pilinskaya, M. A., and C. C. Dibskyi. 2000. "The Frequency of Chromosome Exchanges in Critical Groups of Chernobyl Accident Victims." *International Journal of Radiation Medicine* 1, no. 5:83–95.

"President Governs by Decree." 1998. *Ukrainian Weekly*, July 6, 1.

Proctor, Robert. 1988. *Racial Hygiene: Medicine under the Nazis.* Cambridge: Harvard University Press, 1988.

———. 1995. *Cancer Wars: How Politics Shapes What We Know and Don't Know about Cancer.* New York: Basic Books.

Prysyazhnyuk, A. Y., et al. 1999. "Epidemiological Study of Cancer in Population Affected After the Chernobyl Accident, Results, Problems, Perspectives." *International Journal of Radiation Medicine* 2, no. 2:42–50.

Rabinow, Paul. 1996a. *Essays on the Anthropology of Reason.* Princeton: Princeton University Press.

———. 1996b. *Making PCR: A Story of Biotechnology.* Chicago: University of Chicago Press.

———. 1999. *French DNA: Trouble in Purgatory.* Chicago: University of Chicago Press.

Rapp, Rayna. 1999. *Testing Women, Testing the Fetus: The Social Impact of Amniocentesis in America.* New York: Routledge.

Raven, J. C. 1951. *Controlled Projection for Children.* London: H. K. Lewis.

Reich, W. 1999. "Psychiatric Diagnosis as an Ethical Problem." In *Psychiatric Ethics*, 3d ed., edited by S. Bloch, P. Chodoff, and S. A. Green, 81–104. Oxford: Oxford University Press.

Rheinberger, Hans-Jorg. 1995. "From Experimental Systems to Cultures of Experimentation." In *Concepts, Theories, and Rationality in the Biological Sciences: The Second Pittsburgh-Konstanz Colloquium in the Philosophy of Science*, edited by G. Wolters, J. Lennox, and P. McLaughlin, 107–122. Pittsburgh: University of Pittsburgh Press.

Ries, Nancy. 1997. *Russian Talk: Culture and Conversation during Perestroika.* Ithaca: Cornell University Press.

Romodanov, A. P., et al. 1994. *Post-Radiation Encephalopathy: Experimental Research and Clinical Observations.* Kyiv: Nauka.

Rumiantseva, G. M., et al. 1996. "Dynamics of Social-Psychological Consequences Ten Years after Chernobyl." In *The Radiological Consequences of the Chernobyl Accident*, 529–535. Brussels: European Commission.

Samborski, Zoltan. 1996. "Tax Privileges Are Eating Away at the Budget Planners' Salaries." *Halytski Kontrakty* 46, no. 96:12.

Sassen, Saskia. 1998. *Globalization and Its Discontents: Essays on the New Mobility of People and Money*. New York: New Press.

Scheper-Hughes, Nancy. 1979. *Saints, Scholars, and Schizophrenics: Mental Illness in Rural Ireland*. Berkeley and Los Angeles: University of California Press.

———. 1992. *Death without Weeping: The Violence of Everyday Life in Brazil*. Berkeley and Los Angeles: University of California Press.

———. 1993. "The Primacy of the Ethical." *Current Anthropology* 36, no. 3:409–420.

Schnapper, Dominique. 1997. "The European Debate on Citizenship." *Daedalus* 126, no. 3:199–223.

Schroeder, P. 1986. "Rights against Risks." *Columbia Law Review* 86, no. 495.

Schweitzer, Glenn. 1989. *Techno-diplomacy: US-Soviet Confrontations in Science and Technology*. New York: Plenum Press.

Sergeev, G. V. 1988. "Mediko-Sanitarnye Meropriiatiia po Likvidatsii Posledstvii Avarii na Chernobyl'skoi Atomnoi Elektrostantsii." In *Meditsinskii Aspekti Avarii na Chernobyl'skoi AES*, 15–26. Kyiv: Zdorov'ia.

Shapin, Steven. 1994. *A Social History of Truth: Civility and Science in Seventeenth-Century England*. Chicago: University of Chicago Press.

Shapin, Steven, and Simon Schaffer. 1985. *Leviathan and the Air-Pump: Hobbes, Boyle, and the Experimental Life*. Princeton: Princeton University Press.

Shcherbak, Yuri. 1992. "Strategy for Survival: Problems of Legislative and Executive Power in the Field of Environmental Protection in the Ukraine." *Boston College Environmental Law Review* 19, no. 3:505–509.

———. 1996. "Ten Years of the Chernobyl Era." *Scientific American*, April, 45–49.

Sich, Alexander. 1993. "The Chernobyl Accident Revisited: Source Term Analysis and Reconstruction of Events during the Active Phase." Ph.D. diss., Massachusetts Institute of Technology.

———. 1996. "The Denial Syndrome." *Bulletin of Atomic Scientists* 52, no. 3:38–40.

Slezkine, Yuri. 1994. "The USSR as a Communal Apartment, or How a Socialist State Promoted Ethnic Particularism." *Slavic Review* 53, no. 2:414–452.

Slobin, Dan, ed. 1966. *Soviet Psychology and Psychiatry* 4, nos. 3–4.

Solchanyk, Roman. 1992. Introduction to *Ukraine: From Chernobyl to Sovereignty*, edited by R. Solchanyk, i–xiii. New York: St. Martin's Press.

"Some Material for a Campaign in Support of Radiation Sciences." 1996. *Radiation Research* 145, nos. 1–2:1.

Steele, Jenny. 1995. "Remedies and Remediation: Foundational Issues in Environmental Liability." *Modern Law Review* 58, no. 5:615–636.

Stone, Richard. 2001. "Living in the Shadow of Chernobyl." *Science* 292, no. 5376:420–424.

Strathern, Marilyn. 1993. "Environments Within: An Ethnographic Commentary on Scale." In *The Linacre Lectures*:1–23. Linacre College, Oxford.

Straume, T., et al. 1993. "Validation Studies for Monitoring of Workers Using Molecular Cytogenetics." In *Biomarkers and Occupational Health: Progress and Perspectives*, edited by M. Mendelsohn, J. Peeter, and M. Normandy, 174–193. Washington DC: Academic Press.

249

Subtelny, Orest. 1988. *Ukraine: A History*. Toronto: University of Toronto Press.

———. 1994. *Russocentrism, Regionalism, and the Political Culture of Ukraine*. Washington, DC, and College Park, MD: University of Maryland at College Park.

Taussig, Michael. 1987. *Shamanism, Colonialism, and the Wild Man: A Study in Terror and Healing*. Chicago: University of Chicago Press.

———. 1993. "The Public Secret." Lecture, February. University of California at Berkeley.

———. 1999. *Defacement: Public Secrecy and the Labor of the Negative*. Stanford: Stanford University Press.

Teague, Elizabeth. 1988. *Solidarity and the Soviet Worker*. London: Croom Helm.

Todes, Daniel. 1997. "From the Machine to the Ghost Within: Pavlov's Transition from Digestive Physiology to Conditional Reflexes." *American Psychologist* 52, no. 9:947–955.

Todeschini, Maya. 1999. "Illegitimate Sufferers: A-Bomb Victims, Medical Science, and the Government." *Daedalus* 128, no. 2:67–101.

Torbakov, Igor. 2001. "Ukraine: Vagaries of the Post-Soviet Transition," *Demokratizatsiya* 8, no. 4:461–470.

Trosko, J. 1993. "Biomarkers for Low-Level Exposure Causing Epigenetic Responses in Stem Cells." *Stem Cells* 13:231–239.

Turner, Bryan. 1987. *Medical Power and Social Knowledge*. London: Sage.

Ukraine Human Development Report. 1995. Kyiv: Blitz-Inform Press.

Ukrainskyi Blahodiinyi Soyuz Spilok Sotstiial'noho Zakhystu Invalidiv Chornobylia. 1994. "Analiz, Sotsiial'no-Ekonomichnykh Ta Pravovykh Aspektiv Stanovyshcha Invalidiv—Likvidatoriv Chornobyl'skoi Katastrofy." Draft manuscript, Kyiv.

UNESCO. 1996. *Living in a Contaminated Area*. Geneva: Chernobyl Programme.

UNSCEAR (United Nations Scientific Committee on the Effects of Atomic Radiation). 2000. UNSCEAR 2000 Report to the General Assembly with Scientific Annexes. New York.

USSR State Committee on the Utilization of Atomic Energy. 1986. *The Accident at Chernobyl Nuclear Power Plant and Its Consequences*. Information compiled for the IAEA Experts' Meeting, August 25–29, 1986, Vienna. Working Document for the Post-Accident Review Meeting.

Verdery, Katherine. 1996. *What Was Socialism, and What Comes Next?* Princeton: Princeton University Press.

Volkov, Vadim. 2000. "The Concept of Kul'turnost': Notes on the Stalinist Civilizing Process." In *Stalinism: New Directions*, edited by Sheila Fitzpatrick, 210–230. London: Routledge.

Von Hippel, Frank. 1991. *Citizen Scientist*. New York: American Institute of Physics.

———. 2000. "'Radiation Risk and Ethics': Health Hazards, Prevention Costs, and Radiophobia." *Physics Today*, April, 11.

Vynnychenko, Volodymyr. 1920. *Vidrodzhennia Natsii*, 1:258. Vienna.

Wagemaker, E., et al. 1996. "Clinically Observed Effects." *IAEA Bulletin* 3:29–33.

Wanner, Catherine. 1998. *Burden of Dreams: History and Identity in Post-Soviet Ukraine*. Pennsylvania State University Press.

Ware, Norma. 1998. "Sociosomatics and Illness Course in Chronic Fatigue Syndrome." *Psychosomatic Medicine* 60:394–402.

Weber, Max. 1946. "Science as a Vocation." In *From Max Weber: Essays in Sociology*, translated, edited, and with an introduction by H. H. Gerth and C. Wright Mills, 129–156. New York: Oxford University Press.

Wells, Harry. 1960. *Sigmund Freud: A Pavlovian Critique*. New York: International Publishers.

White, Hayden. 1973. *Metahistory: The Historical Imagination in Nineteenth-Century Europe*. Baltimore: Johns Hopkins University Press.

Whitehead, Alfred North. 1926. *Science and the Modern World*. New York: Pelican.

WHO (World Health Organization). 1996. *Health Consequences of the Chernobyl Accident*. Results of the IPHECA Pilot Projects and Related National Programmes. Geneva.

World Bank. 1993. *Ukraine: The Social Sectors in Transition*. Washington, DC.

———. 1996. *Poverty in Ukraine*. Report No. 15602-UA, Kyiv.

Yalow, R. 1993. "Concern with Low-Level Ionizing Radiation." *Mayo Clinic Proceedings* 69:436–440.

Yamazaki, James N., and William J. Schull. 1990. "Perinatal Loss and Neurological Abnormalities among Children of the Atomic Bomb: Nagasaki and Hiroshima Revisited, 1949 to 1989." *Journal of the American Medical Association* 264, no. 5:605–610.

Young, Allan. 1995. *The Harmony of Illusions: Inventing Post-Traumatic Stress Disorder*. Princeton: Princeton University Press.

Zenkov, L. P., and M. A. Roikin. 1991. *Funktsional'naia Diagnostika Nervnikh Boleznei*. Moscow: Meditsina.